Race and Nation: A Reader

TAURIS HISTORY READERS

British Imperial History, 1773-1960
   edited by *Douglas M. Speers*   Hardback 1 86064 159 8
                                   Paperback 1 86064 160 1

British Women's History
   edited by *Gerry Holloway*   Hardback 1 86064 161 X
                                   Paperback 1 86064 162 8

Race and Nation
   Clive Christie   Hardback 1 86064 195 4
                                   Paperback 1 86064 194 6

Twentieth Century International History
   Stephen Chan & Jarrod Weiner   Hardback 1 86064 301 9
                                   Paperback 1 86064 302 7

Race and Nation:
A Reader

Clive Christie

I.B. Tauris Publishers

London • New York

Published in 1998 by
I.B. Tauris & Co Ltd
Victoria House
Bloomsbury Square
London
WC1B 4DZ

In the United States of America
and Canada, distributed by
St Martin's Press
175 Fifth Avenue
New York
NY 10010

A full CIP record of this book is available from
the British Library and the US Library of Congress.

ISBN   Hardback   1 86064 195 4
        Paperback   1 86064 194 6

Designed and typeset by Dexter Haven, London
Printed in Great Britain by Hillman Printers (Frome) Ltd, Somerset

Contents

Preface and Acknowledgments   viii

Part I   **Nationalism and the Nation**   1

     Chapter 1   Unity and Diversity in the European and
Mediterranean Tradition   3

     Chapter 2   Eighteenth- and Nineteenth-Century
Concepts of the Nation   32

     Chapter 3   National Consciousness and Self-
Determination   54

Part II   **Case Studies in National Self-Determination**   73

     Chapter 4   The First World War and National Self-
Determination in Europe   75

     Chapter 5   Problems of National Consciousness and
Self-Determination: the Case of Ireland   98

Part III   **Race and Nation: the Phenomenon of Antisemitism**   119

     Chapter 6   Antisemitism in Nineteenth-Century Europe   121

     Chapter 7   Antisemitism and the Origins of Genocide
in Twentieth-Century Europe   139

Part IV   **Race, Nation and Colonialism**   163

     Chapter 8   Zionism   165

     Chapter 9   Colonialism and Arab Nationalism   195

     Chapter 10   Conclusion – Race and Nation: Unity and
Diversity in the Modern World   218

Select Bibliography   239

Index   256

Preface and Acknowledgments

'Race and Nation', as topics for theoretical discussion, invite speculation that is almost hopelessly vague, broad and indiscriminate. As political phenomena, however, they have had an immediate and brutal impact on events. The primary objective of this reader has been to strike a balance between the intellectual and the historical approaches to the subject: to focus on the historical context of the development of the national idea, to compare historical examples of dilemmas of national identity, and to trace the relationship between 'race' and 'nation' – both as ideas and as political forces – within actual historical events.

It is not possible, in a single volume, to cover all aspects or all examples of the interaction between the ideas of race and nation. Choices have had to be made. One of the major challenges in writing this volume and in selecting themes, specific topics and documents has, therefore, been to maintain a reasonable balance between general thematic coherence on the one hand, and concrete examples of issues of national identity, race and nation on the other.

Part I of the text provides a very broad historical introduction to the ideology of nationalism, treated as a phenomenon with specifically European origins. These origins have been placed in the context of a background examination of the relationship between ideas of 'unity' and 'diversity' in the European and Mediterranean tradition. Within this overall framework, the Reader uses, in Part II, the First World War, the events leading to it, and its immediate and long-term aftermath, as the historical focus that will – it is hoped – help to tie together the specific examples of the dilemmas of national identity that are dealt with in Parts III and IV.

My particular thanks go to the staff of the National Library of Wales in Aberystwyth; to Theo Hoppen in the History Department, Lester Grabbe of the Theology Department, and Alan Hindley of the French Department – all from Hull University. The latter have no responsibility, of course, for the approach that I have – for better or worse – adopted in this book.

As always, my especial thanks go to my wife, Jan Christie, who – despite her own publishing commitments – has provided invaluable help throughout, and particularly in the last hectic stage of producing this book.

I am grateful to the following publishers for granting me permission to reprint extracts for this reader.

The extract from Dante's *Monarchy*, translated by Donald Nicholl and Colin Hardie, is reprinted by kind permission of the publishers, Weidenfeld and Nicolson.

The extract from Johann Gottfried von Herder's *Reflections on the Philosophy of the History of Mankind*, abridged by Frank E. Manuel, is reprinted by kind permission of the publishers, The University of Chicago Press.

The extract from Elie Kedourie's *Nationalism* is reprinted by kind permission of the publishers, Hutchinson Books Ltd.

The extract from *Imagined Communities: Reflections on the Origin and Spread of Nationalism* by Benedict Anderson is reprinted by kind permission of the publishers, Verso.

The extract from *Hitler: A Study in Tyranny* by Alan Bullock is reprinted by kind permission of the publishers, Penguin Books.

The extract from *The Zionist Idea*, edited by Arthur Hertzberg, is reprinted by kind permission of the Jewish Publication Society, Philadelphia.

The extract from the article entitled 'Palestine and Israel' by Albert Hourani in *The Observer* newspaper is reprinted by kind permission of Guardian News Service Limited.

Part I

Nationalism and the Nation

Chapter 1

Unity and Diversity in the European and Mediterranean Tradition

> ... Romulus shall call
> that people 'Romans', after his own name.
> I set no limits to their fortunes and
> no time: I give them empire without end.
>
> Jupiter foretells the founding of the Roman Empire, in
> Virgil's *Aeneid*, translation by Allen Mandelbaum
> (Bantam Books, New York, 1972), pp 10-11

Introduction

At the heart of any discussion of the nation and nationalism lies the issue of identity. And, if we go beyond the purely personal level, questions of identity divide the world between 'we/us' and 'they/them'. By defining who we are, we naturally exclude all those who cannot be fitted into the definition.

Forms of identity exist in any human society, radiating out from the immediate family, the extended family group to the tribe or clan, and beyond that to the organised state. It will, therefore, be evident that in any complex society there will be layers of identity, including social groupings, religious affiliations, gender and class loyalties, and countless others. Some of these identities will – as it were – have been imposed upon us by the accident of birth; others will be the consequence of the exercise of our will. The relative importance of these identities will largely depend on an interplay between personal choice and the force of circumstances; between the primary identities that we choose for ourselves, and the identities that are imposed on us by others. A German of Jewish origin born at the beginning of the twentieth century may, for example, have identified himself primarily as a German; to the Nazi, however, he would have been a Jew.

It is a fundamental contention of this book that the concept of 'nation' or 'nationalism' emerged as a conscious definition of identity in a specific historical era and in a specific region: namely in late eighteenth- to twentieth-century Europe. Nationalism as a political ideology evolved out of the general revolution in political ideas from the late eighteenth century onwards. Likewise, the interest in the concept of 'race' and the attempt to define racial categories formed part of the scientific revolution of roughly the same period. Concepts of race and the phenomenon of 'racism' subsequently infiltrated the realm of political ideas, particularly those connected with the nation and nationalism; this book will be considering race in this restricted political sphere, rather than in its wider scientific ramifications. Associated revolutions in philology – the study of the origins and the categories of language – and in history, both of which can generally be linked to the late eighteenth and the nineteenth centuries, also played a decisive role in entrenching the concept of the nation in European history.

Nationalism as an idea and a political force took shape in an era that we can, broadly, date from the French Revolution of 1789. It is important to realise, however, that the issue of identity in general – that fundamental us/them dichotomy – has always played a fundamental role in the history of humanity and in the general history of ideas. The concept of the nation, therefore, forms but a small part of the history of the conflicts of identity in human societies and – in particular – the history of the tension between ideas and forms of political and religious organisation that have emphasised the unity of humanity and those that have emphasised its diversity.

The impact of ideas of unity and diversity in the European and Mediterranean tradition: a brief survey

Any history of identity must also be a history of concepts of 'morality', since morality is fundamentally a commonly accepted code of behaviour that binds together a group of people, normally in some kind of organised religion (probably the Latin word 'religio' originally meant 'binding together'). The evidence of anthropologists suggests that in small-scale pre-literate societies, the group (whether it be defined as tribe, clan, or in other more technical terms), the religious structure and the code of morality went hand-in-hand.

Codes of behaviour, reinforced by divine sanctions specific to the group, would apply to that group only, but not beyond it. In such societies the us/them dichotomy would, therefore, have been absolute; communities would have lived in a self-contained moral universe, with their own identity, religion and rules of behaviour.

The us-them dichotomy is a central theme in Homer's two epics, the *Iliad* and the *Odyssey*, which collectively form the undisputed 'bible' of ancient Greek civilisation.[1] In the *Odyssey*, the treatment of the 'outsider' or 'guest' ('xeinos', hence 'xenophobia') is an issue that runs through the entire epic. In the various stories of the *Odyssey*, treatment of outsiders ranges from the brutally simple – Polyphemos the one-eyed monster ate his guests – to the highly subtle and complex, as in the story of Odysseus's visit to Phaiakia.[2] In the *Iliad*, which relates episodes of the tenth year of the war between the Greeks and the Trojans after the abduction of Helen from Greece to Troy, the treatment of identity is ambiguous. On the one hand, the Greeks and the Trojans clearly share the same moral universe – the same gods, the same code of heroic behaviour. On the other hand, the Trojan War is more than just a feud between neighbouring statelets: there is the underlying sense of a more fundamental confrontation between one identity, the Greek-Hellenic world, and another, the alien world of Troy.[3] This is an embryonic version of the notion of a crucial 'Europe-Asia' divide that will become a consistent theme in the history of European identity.

The philosophy of Plato (429-347BC) and Aristotle (385-322BC) forms one of the principle cornerstones of Western thought. Of the two, Aristotle's ideas are of more consequence in pursuing the theme of identity than those of Plato. It is interesting to note that, despite the enormous contribution that Aristotle made to the intellectual foundations of Europe, he accepted the basic 'mores' of his time, particularly the justification for slavery. In the *Politics*, Aristotle argued that certain peoples were 'naturally' inferior, and therefore should not be treated on the same moral basis as fully-developed human beings.[4] This notion of the inherent inferiority of certain categories of humanity not only justified slavery, but also reinforced what would now be called racist political concepts.

Aristotle made another crucial contribution to the history of identity in his emphasis on the diversity of human societies and states. It was he above all who popularised the notion that differences in climate and terrain produce different human traits and different characteristics in societies, and that these different characteristics would naturally be reflected in different types of states and political organisations. This emphasis on the natural diversity of human types, societies and states is a theme that will constantly recur in the history of European ideas.

One of the most striking early expressions of unity in Europe was embodied not so much in a set of ideas as in a political and historical phenomenon: the Roman Empire. Other large states had emerged in the Mediterranean world; what was significant about Rome was its size, its endurance, and its explicit, self-conscious sense of destiny and mission. Nowhere is this sense of mission more clearly stated than in the Roman imperial epic, the *Aeneid*, written by the poet Virgil (70-19BC) during the principate of Augustus, the founder of the Roman imperial system. In the *Aeneid*, Rome's destiny to global ('sine fine' or 'without limits') imperial power is seen as willed by the Gods. Rome's genius was for good government, and its mission, therefore, was to bring peace and civilisation to all the peoples under its rule.[5] This confrontation, between Roman order and unity on one side, and the malignant forces of chaotic disorder and barbarism on the other, is vividly illustrated on the shield of Aeneas, the mythical founder of Rome, which depicts the future battle of Actium (31BC) and the triumph of Roman Augustus over the conspirator Mark Anthony and his motley Asiatic allies, including Cleopatra.[6]

In sharp contrast, the Roman historian Tacitus, born around 54AD, saw imperial Rome not as a model of unity, harmony and good government, but rather as a huge moral cess-pit, where absolute power and the expansion of a hotch-potch empire had corrupted the original ideals of the state. His study of the German tribes to the north of the empire, the *Germania*, was an early example of an ethnographic survey; but it also served indirectly to illustrate the simple virtues that he felt the Roman people had lost. Some of the main characteristics of the Germans outlined by Tacitus included: the maintenance of racial purity; an emphasis on warrior virtues and honour; the hardiness and chastity of the women-folk; and simple forms of government under tribal elders and chieftains. It will be immediately obvious why the *Germania* became a central text in the history of identity and racial ideology. It is a tacit hymn of praise to those qualities of 'indigenousness' and untainted cultural and racial purity that were to become a vital feature of nineteenth-century nationalism (see document 3 at the end of this chapter).

Religion, the state and unity

Thus far, religion had not played a separate, autonomous role in the history of identity. In the pre-Christian communities of Europe, religion was in general no more than the expression of the identity of a community. Religion was essentially a community cult providing supernatural sanction for the enforcement of community codes of conduct. Till the establishment of Christianity as the state religion of the Roman Empire (324AD), the religion of Rome was little more than a confused conglomeration of local and borrowed cults. It is through the history and religion of the Jewish people that we see the gradual extension in Europe and the Mediterranean of the idea of a universal religion transcending state and community identities.

What is significant, indeed revolutionary, about the Torah (Law) and the Jewish Bible as a whole is that unlike other creation myths, it clearly places the Jewish people in a context of the wider history of the origins of humanity. The God of the Torah is not just a god of the Jews, but of the universe and of humanity, of which the Jews – whose lineage is minutely described – form a part. In the Torah, God singles out the Jews to play a special role, privileged and sacrificial at the same time, as a symbol of God's relationship with humanity. While other peoples had their land and their local cults, the nomadic Jews were directly bound by a 'covenant' to God, which was in effect an agreement to live as a community under God's law. In return, the Jews were granted the conditional right to the holy land of Israel. Throughout the Jewish Bible, the fate of the Jewish people, and the whole pattern of exile from and return to Israel, is determined by the maintenance or abandonment by the Jews of this special and symbolic relationship with God.[7]

The mission of Jesus Christ, as described in the Gospels of the New Testament, had its foundations in these religious ideas. The organised Christian religion that emerged after Christ's death, however, based itself on a 'new covenant' between God – embodied in Christ – and all humanity, and superseded the 'old covenant' of the Jews. From the point of view of the history of identity, the important point to note is that Christianity announced the spiritual equality of all humanity under God, and constituted a religious organisation with a universal mission.

From the outset, the universal Christian church that set itself up within the Roman Empire detached itself from the world of politics. The break between the world of religion and that of politics was a revolutionary innovation. Christ's famous injunction, 'Render unto Caesar the things which are Caesar's, and unto God the things that are God's', and his reply to Pontius

Pilate that Christ's kingdom was not 'of this world', are the clearest possible signs of the fundamental division between the spiritual and political realms.[8] However, this notion that one could in effect split one's loyalty and identity between a spiritual affiliation to the Christian Church and a political loyalty to Rome violated one of the central concepts of the pre-Christian era: that political and religious loyalty went hand-in-hand. The refusal of the early Christians to accept the state cults of the Roman Empire was seen, therefore, not just as religious impiety, but as political treason. This fundamental dispute over differing concepts of loyalty was resolved, of course, when the emperor Constantine I declared Christianity to be the state religion of the Roman Empire in 324AD. This laid the foundation for a 'church-state' partnership where 'Christendom' and the Roman Empire were to a degree coterminous, and both the secular and the religious ideals of universal empire could be comprehended in the single Greek word 'oikoumene', or 'the civilised world', the boundaries of empire.[9]

With the gradual division and disintegration of the Roman Empire, however, the question of the relationship between these two fundamental identities of Church and State remained a source of continual tension. St Augustine of Hippo argued in his *City of God* (completed around 426AD) that there was an absolute divide between the Christian Church, which catered for the community of believers during their 'pilgrimage' on earth, and the state – even the Roman Empire – which was merely a human creation that catered for the earthly needs of both 'the just and the unjust'. St Augustine, therefore, uncoupled the Church from any special relationship with the Roman Empire. Augustine argued that all states were, for Christians, mere habitations during a period of exile from the heavenly city. This was not, however, an invitation to political disloyalty on the part of Christians: rather it was simply a denial of the divinely-ordained status of any terrestrial empire.[10]

In the centuries after the sacking of Rome by the Visigoths in 410AD, an event of huge symbolic importance in Europe, the principal binding organisation in the western, Latin-speaking section of the Roman Empire was the Christian Church under the authority of the Pope in Rome. The political unity of the empire had, however, already been given a death-blow by the emergence of a separate empire in the East, the Byzantine, after 395AD. This was more than just a political divide: it was a divide between two distinct cultures, the Latin-speaking West and the Greek-speaking East. This cultural divide was complemented by a religious divide between separate eastern and western churches. When the eastern ('Orthodox') portion of the

Church within the Byzantine Empire definitively separated itself from the ('Catholic') Papacy in 1054AD, the former Roman world, or oikoumene, was thenceforth divided by a profound religious, cultural and political chasm that affects Europe to this day.[11]

In 800AD, Charles the Great (Charlemagne) tried to revive the Roman ideal by reinstating, with the support of the Papacy, the empire in the West. In subsequent centuries, however, this reconstituted Holy Roman Empire proved to be unable to sustain its unifying role. It became embroiled in damaging 'demarcation' disputes with the Papacy over issues of sovereignty, and it could not stem the process of fragmentation in Western Europe. By the time of the birth of Dante Alighieri in Florence in 1265, the process of political and even religious fragmentation appeared to be unstoppable, particularly in Italy itself.

It was despair over this political anarchy and spiritual degradation that impelled Dante to write his *Monarchy*, which constitutes one of the most comprehensive and forceful arguments for global political unity. Dante looked back beyond the Europe of his day, beyond the Papacy and the fragmented Holy Roman Empire, to the original Roman Empire founded by Augustus, and based his argument for the need to resuscitate that global Roman Empire on philosophical and religious foundations. Following Aristotle, he argued that, if the organised state was a necessary guarantee for the fulfilment of man's nature and potential – not least because it provided a basis for peace and stability – then it followed that a universal state and universal peace was the best guarantee for the fulfilment of the potential of humanity as a whole. He also argued that Rome's destiny had been guided by divine providence through all the vicissitudes of its expansion and survival; and that this divine sanction for Rome was finally and fully confirmed by the birth of Christ, within the empire, and at the very height of the realisation of the Roman imperial ideal.

Though Dante did not deny the crucial spiritual role of the Papacy, he fundamentally differed with the view (held by St Augustine before him) that the Roman Empire was, like any other state, a mere temporary convenience. 'Unity' for him was a divinely-ordained principle, both in the spiritual sphere of Christendom, and in the political sphere of Rome. The one could not survive without the other (see document 1 at the end of this chapter).

The kind of spiritual and political unity of which Dante dreamed had been achieved for a while in the southern and eastern Mediterranean by the prophet Muhammad (571-631AD) and his Islamic state, and the Islamic empire of his successors, the Caliphs. Muhammad followed Judaism in making the one-ness of God the key tenet of his belief; his break with Judaism centred on his claim that he was a messenger of God in succession to the prophets of the Jewish tradition, that his prophetic mission was for all mankind, and that he was the last ('the seal') of the divinely-inspired prophets. In the religion of Islam (or 'submission to God') that Muhammad established, the concept of 'tauhid', or unity, is fundamental. For example, in the Islamic religious community ('umma') that Muhammad founded, the realms of politics, law and custom were entirely subordinated to the unalterable divine precepts conveyed to Muhammad in the Qur'an. There is in Islam, therefore, no sense that the spiritual world and the political world are separate, as in Christianity.

The fundamental unity of the Islamic state under the 'divine constitution' of the Qur'an was matched by its global mission to enlarge the Islamic world ('Daru'l-Islam') and convert the portion of humanity outside the Islamic world ('Daru'l-Harb'). Although the single Islamic Empire founded by Muhammad soon broke up into separate states, the concept and ideal of a united community of believers, and the absolute primacy of the religious precepts of the Qur'an over all aspects of life, remains a powerful aspiration in the Islamic world.

It can easily be seen, therefore, that Islam has great difficulties with modern ideas of nationalism. Nationalism offends the spirit of Islam on two major counts: it exalts a merely human creation, the nation, at the expense of a divine creation, the united Islamic community or umma; and it divides human beings by emphasising their differences rather than, in the case of Islam, uniting them by highlighting their common allegiance to God.

Identity in the secular era

In the period roughly between the sixteenth and eighteenth centuries, Western Europe witnessed increased political and religious fragmentation. The Holy Roman Empire gradually transformed into just one of the dynastic states that dominated Europe, and the unity of European Catholic Christendom under the Papacy was broken up by the impact of the Protestant Reformation. In general terms, the most significant political development of the time was the increasing power of regional dynasties and the entrenching of the states that they had created. In fact, the most settled of these dynastic states, such as Spain, France and England, were acquiring characteristics that could be described as 'national' in the modern sense. Just as significant for the future, however, was the fact that the notion of separate German, Italian, French, Spanish and English identities or 'characteristics', exemplified by the development of distinct languages, was becoming part of the common currency of political debate and statecraft.[12] In other words, distinct national identities were taking shape, even in areas (such as Italy) where no central, dominant state gave expression to that identity.

It was during this period of transition, too, that a fundamental revolution in humanity's perception of the world was very gradually taking shape in Europe. The basis of this 'Enlightenment' revolution was the notion that the principles underlying the structure of all forms of existence could be grasped by humanity through the exercise of reason. From this standpoint, it became possible to assert that the 'world-view' and the institutions of humanity could be changed so as to accord with the general rational principles underpinning the natural world and humanity. The Enlightenment revolution therefore implied a challenge to the existing and inherited world-view in the areas of religion, science and the workings of society, and a challenge to existing sources of authority in the political and religious spheres. This intellectual transformation was to have profound consequences. For example, a challenge to the authority of the Church – the 'Reformation' – gradually opened the door to a wider challenge to the actual precepts of Christianity itself and the growth of a secular (non-religious) world-view. In the political realm, hitherto unquestioned political systems and sources of authority were subjected to rational scrutiny, and the fundamental question of 'political legitimacy' was posed: 'By what right do governments govern?'

This question led in radical circles to a search for the general principles that should underpin political systems. Out of this search came the following general propositions: that human beings had certain innate, God-given or 'natural' characteristics, and 'natural rights' that stemmed from these characteristics; that governments should be formed the better to protect and promote these rights on the basis of a 'contract' between a community and its government; and that governments only had legitimacy so long as they operated on the basis of such a contract. These new principles, which could be summed up as the notion that government only had a right to exist so long as it was sanctioned by its community of 'citizens' – the only basis of a true 'republic' – clearly posed a fundamental challenge to existing systems of government based on dynastic inheritance sanctioned by 'divine right'. With the American Revolution's challenge to the right of George III to govern the American colonies in 1776, and the French Revolution of 1789, the notion that government should be based on natural human rights transformed the political landscape.

From the point of view of the history of the interplay between notions of unity and of diversity, it is important to note that this new 'republican' principle of natural rights was seen as a universal principle. In the Declaration of the Rights of Man and of Citizens issued by the French National Assembly in 1789 at the beginning of the French Revolution, the rights outlined were applicable in the first instance to the French nation. But these rights were based on principles that had universal applicability; and the truly global – or at least pan-European – implication of the French Revolution lay in the notion that any government that was not based on these universal principles was a mere illegitimate 'usurpation' (see document 2 at the end of the chapter).

There was, inevitably, a strong reaction to the ideas that stimulated the French Revolution, and to the whole Enlightenment ethos that lay behind it. Two key figures in this ideological resistance were Edmund Burke (1730-1797) and Joseph de Maistre (1753-1821).[13] The fundamental objection of de Maistre was to the assertion by Enlightenment theorists of the omnipotence of human reason, and of the ability of humanity to understand and control its own destiny. Rather, de Maistre asserted that the fate of humanity was determined by a divine providence that lay beyond the grasp of human reason. It therefore followed that attempts to transform society on the basis of assumed fundamental rational principles were not only doomed to fail, but often achieved the exact opposite of the ends intended. The other pillar of resistance to the values of the French Revolution was the insistence – by Edmund Burke in particular – on the ultimate diversity, not uniformity, of human societies and states. Communities and states that had evolved through history were not to be seen as mere shallow social mechanisms that could overturn their systems of government, their laws and their traditions on the basis of a purely abstract concept of the 'rights of man' that was in fact merely the expression of the transient political values of one particular generation. Communities and states were organic entities with deep roots binding generation to generation, where culture, society, religion and government were linked by a unique historical experience.

If the American and French Revolutions asserted what might be called a liberal view of the nation, where the 'legitimacy' of a nation is ultimately based on the wishes of its inhabitants, de Maistre and Burke can be seen as the fathers of the conservative concept of the nation. For the latter, the nation was a community that had developed organically through time. Its traditions and systems of government were not disposable items, but an intrinsic part of its evolving identity.

Though he cannot be seen as a conservative thinker in the same sense as Burke or de Maistre, the German philosopher Johan Gottlieb von Herder (1744-1803) played a similarly important role in emphasising the importance of diversity and variety in our understanding of human society and organisations. Herder could indeed be described as the philosopher of diversity; and, like Tacitus, a champion of 'indigenousness'. He concentrated, however, not so much on governments and political systems, as on the extent to which language, culture, everyday behaviour and music were expressions of the innermost and unique 'soul' of a particular people. Not only did he emphasise the importance of these differences among humanity, but he passionately asserted the right of even the most 'primitive' societies to live undisturbed within their own world, and denied the right of the 'superior' cultures of Europe to impose their ideas and their power over the rest of the world, or to dispossess supposedly inferior peoples (see document 4 at the end of the chapter).

Concluding comments

In this all-too-brief survey of the ideas of unity and diversity in European and Mediterranean history up to the time of the French Revolution, it can be seen that certain key themes persist. The ideal of unity – essentially a yearning for stability and peace – can be seen in Virgil's justification for the Roman Empire. This vision of unity was given a specifically religious shape in the concept of universal Christendom, and a secular shape in the later assertion of a universally-valid 'rights of man'. Christianity, however – with the exception of Dante in particular – made a distinction between the aspiration for spiritual unity and the reality of political diversity. The ideal of complete spiritual, political and social unity is, however, expressed in the religion of Islam, both in the precepts of the Qur'an and the religious empire that the prophet Muhammad created.

Ideas that highlight diversity are sometimes simply based on a pessimistic recognition of reality – the fact that the 'us-them' divide between identities is an inescapable element of human existence – but sometimes suggest the value of diversity. We see hints of this in Tacitus's comments on the 'racial purity' of the German tribes. More significant, however, is Aristotle's view that different terrains and climates create markedly different characteristics among communities, that are inevitably expressed in different habits, cultures and systems of government. It is from this intellectual tradition that we can trace the concept of 'roots', an idea that is strongly emphasised in the writings of de Maistre and Burke; and of Herder, who, while he recognised the common characteristics of humanity at the fundamental level, celebrated (to use the modern idiom) the diversity of the human species, and regarded such diversity as an essential part of human development.

Documents

(Nb: in all the following extracts, editorial comments at the beginning of texts, or amendments and explanations in the texts themselves, will be placed in square brackets. Headings and subdivisions will be put in italics.)

SECTION A: UNITY
1 – Dante Alighieri and the idea of the universal state

[Dante Alighieri (1265-1321), author of the famous epic poem, *The Divine Comedy*, provides in his *Monarchy* (c1312-1318) one of the most complete arguments for humanity's need for a universal monarchy. In the outline of his argument, Dante relies on the classic sources of authority of his time: the Greek philosophers, particularly Aristotle; Roman poets and historians, particularly Virgil; and the New and the Old Testaments.]

Statement of the key issues to be addressed

... We must first consider the meaning of 'temporal monarchy', what its essence is and what its end. The temporal monarchy that is called the Empire is [as opposed to the eternal kingdom of God] a single Command ('unicus principatus') exercised over all persons in time, or at least in those matters which are subject to time. Doubts about temporal monarchy give rise to three principal questions. The first is the question whether it is necessary for the well-being of the world. The second is whether it was by right that the Roman people took upon itself the office of the Monarch. And, thirdly, there is the question whether the Monarch's authority is derived directly from God or from some vicar or minister of God.

Whether a single empire is necessary for the well-being of the world

... Since the individual man becomes perfect in wisdom and prudence through sitting in quietude, so it is in the quietude or tranquillity of peace that mankind finds the best conditions for fulfilling its proper task... Hence it is clear that universal peace is the most excellent means of securing our happiness. That is why the message from on high to the shepherds announced neither wealth, nor pleasure, nor honour, nor long life, nor health, nor strength, nor beauty, but peace. The heavenly host, indeed, proclaims: 'Glory to God on high, and on earth peace to men of good will' (Luke ii 14). 'Peace be with you' was also the salutation given by the Saviour of men, because it was fitting that the supreme Saviour should utter the supreme salutation – a custom which, as everyone knows, his disciples and Paul sought to preserve in their own greetings.

This argument shows us what is the better, indeed the very best means available to mankind for fulfilling its proper role; and also what is the most direct means of reaching that goal to which all our doings are directed – universal peace.

... If we consider a home, the purpose of which is to train its members to live well, we see that there has to be one member who directs and rules, either the 'pater familias' or the person occupying his position, for, as the Philosopher [Aristotle] says, 'every home is ruled by the eldest'. And his function... is to rule the others and lay down laws for them; hence the proverbial curse, 'May you have an equal in your home'. If we consider a village, whose purpose is mutual help in questions of persons and goods, it is essential for one person to be supreme over all others, whether he is appointed from outside or raised to office by the consent of the others; otherwise, not only would the community fail to provide mutual sustenance, but in some cases the community itself would be utterly destroyed through some members' scheming to take control. Similarly if we examine a city, whose purpose is to be sufficient unto itself in everything needed for the good life, we see that there must be one governing authority... Lastly, every kingdom (and the end of a kingdom is the same as that of a city but with a stronger bond of peace) needs to have a king to rule over and govern it; otherwise its inhabitants will not only fail to achieve their end as citizens but the kingdom itself will crumble, as it is affirmed by the infallible Word: 'Every kingdom divided against itself shall be laid waste' (Matt xii 25).

If this is true of all communities and individuals who have a goal towards which they are directed, then our previous supposition is also valid. For, if it is agreed that mankind as a whole has a goal (and this we have shown to be so), then it needs one person to govern or rule over it, and the title appropriate to this person is Monarch, or Emperor.

Thus it has been demonstrated that a Monarch or Emperor is necessary for the well-being of the world.

The harmony between mankind and the universe

... Mankind is in one sense a whole (that is, in relation to its component parts), but in another sense it is itself a part. It is a whole in relation to particular kingdoms and peoples ('gentes'), as we have previously shown; but in relation to the whole universe it is, of course, a part. Therefore just as its component parts are brought to harmony in mankind, so mankind itself has to be brought into the harmony of the appropriate whole. The component parts of mankind are brought into harmony by a single principle (as may easily be gathered by the preceding argument); and mankind itself is similarly related to the whole universe, or to its principle (that is, God, the Monarch); this harmony is achieved by one principle only, the one Prince.

It follows that Monarchy is necessary for the well-being of the world

... The human race is at its best and most perfect when, so far as its capacity allows, it is most like to God. But mankind is most like to God when it enjoys the highest degree of unity, since He alone is the true ground of unity – hence it is written: 'Hear, O Israel, the Lord thy God is one' (Deut vi 4). But mankind is most one when the whole human race is drawn together into complete unity, which can only happen when it is subordinate to one Prince, as is self-evident.

Therefore when mankind is subject to one Prince, it is most like to God and this implies conformity to the divine intention, which is the condition of perfection...

God and the Emperor

Again, a son's condition is most perfect when the son, as far as his nature allows, reproduces the perfection of the father. Mankind is the son of the heavens, which is perfect in all its works... Therefore mankind's condition is most perfect when it reproduces the perfection of the heavens, so far as human nature allows. And just as the heavens are governed and directed in every movement by a single mover, which is God... so, if our argument has been correct, mankind is at its best when all its movements and intentions are governed by one Prince as its sole mover and with one law for its direction.

Hence it is obvious that the world's well-being demands a Monarch or single government known as the Empire.

But, realistically speaking, the single Emperor will rule over a diversity of subordinate states

Of course, when we say 'mankind can be governed by one supreme Prince' we do not mean to say that minute decisions concerning every township can proceed directly from him... For nations, kingdoms and cities have different characteristics which demand different laws for their government, law being intended as a concrete rule of life. The Scythians [from north-eastern Europe], for instance, live outside the seventh circle, experience extreme inequalities of day and night and endure an almost intolerably piercing frost; they require a different rule from the Garamantes [from Africa] who live in the equinoctial zone, where the days and nights are of equal duration and where the excessive heat makes it unbearable to wear clothes. But our meaning is that mankind should be ruled by one supreme Prince and directed towards peace by a common law issuing from him and applied to those characteristics which are common to all men.

    ... It is not only possible for one movement to issue from a single source, it is necessary for it to do so in order to eliminate confusion about universal principles. Indeed this was precisely what Moses says he did in writing the Law: having called together the chiefs of the tribes of Israel he left minor judgements to them whilst reserving to himself the major decisions that affected everyone; these were then applied by the chiefs of the tribes according to the particular needs of each tribe.

Summing-up, and the evidence for divine sanction for the Roman Empire

... We can now develop the argument for the proposition we wish to maintain: all concord depends upon the unity of wills; mankind is at its best in a state of concord; for as a man is at his best in body and soul when he is in a state of concord, the same is true of a house, a city and a kingdom, and of mankind as a whole. Therefore mankind at its best depends upon unity in the wills of its members. But this is impossible unless there is one will which dominates all others and holds them in unity, for the wills of mortals, influenced by their adolescent and seductive delights, are in need of a director... Nor can there be such a single will unless there is a Prince over all, whose will guides and rules those of all others. Now if the preceding conclusions are all true – as they are – then Monarchy is necessary for the perfect order of mankind in this world. Consequently a Monarch is essential to the well-being of the world.

The preceding arguments are confirmed by a noteworthy historical fact, that is, by the state of humanity which the Son of God either awaited or himself brought about when He was to become man for the salvation of men. For if we survey the ages and condition of men since the fall of our first parents (the false step from which all our errors have proceeded) at no time do we see universal peace throughout the world except during the perfect monarchy of the immortal Augustus. The fact that mankind at that time was resting happily in universal peace is attested by all the historians and the illustrious poets. Even the recorder of Christ's gentleness has deigned to bear witness to it (Luke ii 1). Finally Paul, also, described that blissful state as 'the fullness of time' (Gal. iv 4). The times were indeed full, and temporal desires fulfilled because nothing that ministers to our happiness was without its minister. [That is, Christ ministered to humanity's spiritual needs; Augustus ministered to their earthly need for peace and good government.]

Unity the true end of humanity

O humanity, in how many storms must you be tossed, how many shipwrecks must you endure, so long as you turn yourself into a many-headed beast lusting after a multiplicity of things! You are ailing in both your intellectual powers, as well as in heart: you pay no heed to the unshakeable principles of your higher intellect, nor illumine your lower intellect with experience, nor tune your heart to the sweetness of divine counsel when it is breathed into you through the trumpet of the Holy Spirit: 'Behold how good and pleasant it is for brethren to dwell together in unity' (Psalms cxxxiii 1).

[extracts from Dante's *Monarchy*, translated by Donald Nicholl (London, Weidenfeld and Nicolson, 1954), pp 4, 8-13, 23-27

Dante's assertion of the Divine destiny of Imperial Rome also appears in poetic form in lines 1-96 in Canto VI of the 'Paradiso' section of his *Divine Comedy*, of which there are many translations.]

2 – Declaration of the Rights of Man and of the Citizen, decreed by the French National Assembly in August 1789

[The following declaration of rights was considered to have a universal applicability, and was also seen as the basis of all legitimate government. The declaration, therefore, both affirmed the idea of the nation – a government, that is, based on the principle of the 'Rights of Man' – and asserted the existence of universally valid principles of government. In this sense, the Declaration can be seen as a classic statement of 'liberal nationalism', the notion that while humanity is divided into separate political states and nations, it is unified by common political values.

The National Assembly announced the following to be the basic rights of 'man and of the citizen' ('de l'homme et du citoyen')]:

1   Men are born, and always continue, free, and equal in respect of their rights. Civil distinctions, therefore, can be founded only on public utility.
2   The end of all political associations is the preservation of the natural and imprescriptable rights of man; and these rights are liberty, property, security, and resistance of oppression.
3   The nation is essentially the source of all sovereignty; nor can any individual, or any body of men, be entitled to any authority which is not expressly derived from it.
4   Political liberty consists in the power of doing whatever does not injure another. The exercise of the natural rights of every man has no other limits than those which are necessary to secure to every other man the free exercise of the same rights; and these limits are determinable only by the law.
5   The law ought to prohibit only actions hurtful to society. What is not prohibited by the law should not be hindered; nor should any one be compelled to that which the law does not require.
6   The law is the expression of the will of the community. All citizens have a right to concur, either personally, or by their representatives, in its formation. It should be the same to all, whether it protects or punishes; and all being equal in its sight, are equally eligible to all honours, places, and employments, according to their different abilities, without any other distinction than that created by their virtues and talents.
7   No man should be accused, arrested, or held in confinement, except in cases determined by the law, and according to the forms which it has

prescribed. All who promote, solicit, execute, or cause to be executed, arbitrary orders ought to be punished; and every citizen called upon or apprehended by virtue of the law ought immediately to obey, and renders himself culpable by resistance.

8 The law ought to impose no other penalties but such as are absolutely and evidently necessary; and no-one ought to be punished, but in virtue of a law promulgated before the offence, and legally applied.

9 Every man being presumed innocent till he has been convicted, whenever his detention becomes indispensable, all rigour to him, more than is necessary to secure his person, ought to be provided against by the law.

10 No man ought to be molested on account of his opinions, not even on account of his religious opinions, provided his avowal of them does not disturb the public order established by the law.

11 The unrestrained communication of thoughts and opinions being one of the most precious rights of man, every citizen may speak, write, and publish freely, provided he is responsible for the abuse of this liberty in cases determined by law.

12 A public force being necessary to give security to the rights of men and of citizens, that force is instituted for the benefit of the community, and not for the particular benefit of the persons with whom it is entrusted.

13 A common contribution being necessary for the support of the public force, and for defraying the other expenses of government, it ought to be divided equally among the members of the community, according to their abilities.

14 Every citizen has a right, either by himself or his representative, to a free vote in determining the necessity of public contributions, the appropriation of them, and their amount, mode of assessment and duration.

15 Every community has a right to demand of all its agents, an account of their conduct.

16 Every community ('toute société') in which a separation of powers and a security of rights is not provided for, wants a constitution [ie, needs a constitution, which is the basis for legitimate government].

17 The right to property being inviolable and sacred, no-one ought to be deprived of it, except in cases of evident public necessity, legally ascertained, and on condition of a previous just indemnity.

[Translation by Thomas Paine from his *Rights of Man*, first published in 1791/2. See Thomas Paine, *Rights of Man: Being an answer to Mr Burke's attack on the French Revolution* (London, J.M. Dent and Sons, 1921), pp 94-97]

SECTION B: DIVERSITY
3 – Cornelius Tacitus's description of the German people

[Tacitus (around 56-120AD) was one of the most famous Roman historians, whose main historical works cover the early period of the Roman Empire from the time of the death of the Emperor Augustus in 14AD. His short study of the German people, the *Germania*, was probably written in 98AD. At face value, it is a straightforward description of a remote and primitive people living outside the civilised boundaries of the Roman Empire. It was also, however, with its description of the simple virtues of the German tribes, an indirect criticism of the luxury, corruption and tyranny of the Roman Empire. Its outline of the fundamental 'racial' characteristics of the German people – particularly patriarchal authority, the emphasis on military honour, and the 'leadership principle' – made it a 'bible' of German nationalism in the nineteenth and twentieth centuries. At a wider level, it suggests the intrinsic value of racial purity and 'indigenousness'.

The Latin terms used by Tacitus expressing different forms of identity are included in brackets. The word 'gens' (hence 'gentile', 'genealogy', 'generation' etc) is the Latin equivalent of the Greek 'ethnos/ethné'. These terms have acquired a great resonance in the vocabulary of modern nationalism.]

Geography

The rivers Rhine and Danube separate Germany as a whole from the Gauls, Rhaetians and Pannonians; mutual fear, as well as mountain ranges, likewise divides the Germans from the Sarmatians and Dacians. The Ocean surrounds the rest [of Germany], as well as its wide gulfs and its large islands. It is only as a result of recent wars that the very existence of some German tribes ('gentes') and kingdoms have come to our knowledge.

I believe that the Germans are the indigenous people ('indigenae'), very little intermixed with immigrants and foreigners. In the old days, those who sought to travel did so, not by land, but by sea, and the vast, hostile northern ocean was rarely visited by ships from our part of the world. For, over and above the dangers of a threatening and unknown sea, who would leave Asia, Africa or Italy to visit Germany – with its harsh terrain, its bitter weather, its lack of civilisation or pleasing scenery – unless it was his own homeland ('patria')?

Racial purity and characteristics

I agree with those who hold that the German people have not been tainted ('infectos') by intermarriage with other peoples ('nationes') and that they stand out as a genuinely pure and unique race ('gens'). Hence the fact that, although their population is very large, there is among them a remarkable similarity of bodily appearance. Their fierce eyes are blue, their hair is red, and they have huge bodies suited for lives of violent exertion, not for steady routine work. Though they cannot endure thirst and heat, they can cope with the extreme cold and famine conditions caused by their weather and poor soil.

Whether through an act of mercy or of anger, the gods have denied them silver and gold. It is impossible to say for sure, however, that there are no deposits of silver or gold, for no surveys have been made. Generally, Germans are not at all interested in the possession or use of either metal. There are silver vessels, which have normally been given as presents to their ambassadors or chieftains ('principes'), but they are held in as low regard as earthenware. However, those Germans who live nearest to us, through the impact of constant trade, value gold and silver more highly, and they understand and recognise the different values of our coinage. The tribes of the interior of Germany – sticking to the plain old ways ('simplicius et antiquus') – use barter.

System of government, law and customs

They choose their kings ('reges') by virtue of their noble birth, and the military leaders ('duces') for their valour. The kings do not have unlimited or unrestricted power, and military leaders exert authority more by example than by inherent right of command. If they are swift to action, conspicuous in their courage, and lead from the front, then general admiration will ensure their status. However, they are not allowed to sentence anyone to death, nor put them in chains or beat them, unless the priests give express permission. Such punishments are not seen as sanctioned by military authority, but as the judgement of their god of war, who, they believe, is always present in battle.

They bring with them into battle sacred effigies and images taken from their forest groves. But the greatest mainstay of their courage is not a reliance on fate, nor on the size of their military formations, but the presence during battle of their families and kinsfolk, the shouts of their women and the crying out of their children. These are the most treasured witnesses of their military deeds, these are the people whose praise the warriors seek. They show their wounds to their mothers and wives; and the latter do not flinch from examining and treating them. While the battle is raging, the women give their warriors food and encouragement.

It is recorded that the womenfolk have saved many a battle line trembling on the brink of collapse by imploring the men to hold firm. By exposing their breasts to their menfolk, they give a warning of their impending slavery, something the warriors fear far more than their own fate...

While the tribal chieftains take decisions on routine matters, everyone takes part in discussing vital matters; but the chieftains do have the right to discuss these issues beforehand.

[The spontaneous nature of these general meetings] has the disadvantage that they do not assemble all at once, as would be the case if they were summoned, but two or even three days are wasted getting everyone together. When it is generally felt that a quorum has gathered, the assembled mass sit down with their arms in their hands. Then the priests, who have overall authority on these occasions, call for silence. Then kings or chiefs, according to their age, their noble birth, their glory in war, or their eloquence, are heard in turn. The authority of their words depends more on their power of persuasion than their status. If an opinion displeases the crowd, they roar out their disapproval; if they agree, they clash their spears. This clashing of arms is the most honoured form of applause.

Honour and warfare

When the Germans go into battle, it is a disgrace for the chieftain to show less valour than his followers, or for followers to show less valour than their chieftains. It is a lifelong shame and ignominy for a follower to retreat from a field of battle where his chieftain has been killed. It is the sacred duty of honour of soldiers to defend their chieftain, to guard him, and even to attribute their own deeds of glory to him. The chieftain fights for victory; the soldiers fight for their chieftain. If their native state should be sunk in a torpid condition of peace, young warriors will seek out other tribes ('nationes') where war is raging. Peace is regarded with contempt by the German race ('gens'); without war, warriors cannot gain either a reputation or a military following.

What followers demand of their leaders is a horse fit for combat, and a spear blood-stained by victory. Generous – if uncouth – victory feasts, provided for by the spoils of war, are substitutes for regular pay. Germans find it far more congenial to challenge their enemies to battle and seek war wounds, than to plough the land and wait for each season's harvest. It is considered weak and cowardly to produce by sweat what one could seize at the risk of bloodshed...

Moral purity safeguards racial purity

The most praiseworthy aspect of the Germans is their strict view of marriage. Almost alone among barbarians ('barbari') they are content with one wife – with the exception of a few people who, because of their high status rather than their lust, have a number of wives.

[Unlike the case in Rome] the wife does not give a dowry to her husband, but the husband to his wife. Parents and relatives inspect these gifts, which are not ornaments designed to please a wife or adorn a young bride, but rather oxen and a horse with bridle, or a shield with spear and sword. These are the gifts which will lure a wife, and she in return will bring some weapon for her husband. These gifts are in themselves the lasting bond, the sacred mysteries and the presiding gods of marriage. In order that the wife should value courage in the chances of war, the marriage ceremonies pledge her to share and endure with her husband the same labours and perils, both in peace and in war. This is symbolised by the yoked oxen, the harnessed horse and the gift of weapons. Thus she must live and die. This is a pledge she must hand over, inviolate, to her children, to her daughters-in-law, and to her grandchildren.

The Germans also guard their chastity, uncorrupted and unmoved by voluptuous public shows and banquets. Secret love-letters are equally unknown to both men and women. Among all the German people adultery is extremely rare. Punishment is such cases is immediate, and is carried out by the husband. The husband expels the adulteress from his home, naked and with her hair cut off, and beats her through the whole village. In fact, no indulgence whatever is given to such shameless behaviour; despite beauty, youth or wealth, the adulteress will not be able to find a husband. No-one in Germany treats such a vice lightly, nor is it considered 'fashionable' to corrupt or be corrupted...

The children are allowed to grow up naked and dirty, and naturally develop those attributes of strength and size that so astonish us. Each mother suckles her own children; she does not leave this task to female slaves or nurses. There is no refinement in the upbringing of either master or slave.

They live among the same cattle, and share the same hard earth, until the time comes for the freeborn to be separated from the slave, and to live the life of honour that is demanded of him. They do not indulge in sexual activity till they are mature, and thus conserve their virility. Neither are the young women rushed into marriage and, when they do marry, their age and size equals that of their menfolk. Since they are fully mature at marriage, the children inherit the strength of their parents...

No usury, and a simple life

Money-lending with interest or usury ('usurae') is unknown – a far better defence against its evils than any number of laws. Land is cultivated by whole villages according to the numbers involved, and is divided up according to their relative status. The wide extent of land makes this apportionment easy. They plough new fields yearly, and even then there is land to spare. They do not exert themselves to enhance the fertility of the soil or extend their holdings so that they could plant orchards, create meadows, or irrigate vegetable gardens; all that they demand from the soil is grain...

There is no public display at funerals. The only ceremony that is strictly observed is that the bodies of famous heroes are cremated with a special kind of wood. They do not pile clothes or incense on the funeral mound of a warrior; only his arms and his horse are added to the flames. A heap of earth suffices for the funeral mound. They reject huge and ornate mausoleums which would, they feel, lie too heavily on the dead. They quickly abandon outward shows of grief, but store their sorrow in their hearts. It is regarded as fitting that women should lament the dead, and that the menfolk should preserve their memory.

[Translated by C.J. Christie from the *Germania* of Tacitus, edited by Alfred J. Church and W.J. Brodribb (London, MacMillan, 1917]

4 – Herder and the celebration of diversity

[The density and subtlety of the ideas of Johann Gottfried von Herder (1744-1803) cannot easily be compressed into a few passages. But the following, drawn from his *Reflections on the Philosophy of the History of Mankind* (1784-1791), will serve to illustrate his view that the different nations and peoples of the earth are like families, with their own traditions and ways of life that are attuned to their local conditions, which make their own separate contribution to the well-being and development of humanity as a whole. It therefore follows that Herder particularly disliked all attempts on the part of one culture or civilisation to impose its ideas and systems on alien societies.

It is interesting to note Herder's view that music in particular is the most fundamental and intrinsic expression of the identity of a people, since it is also the most communicable aspect of a national identity. Whereas literature has to be translated, and culture in general has to be interpreted, music is instantly accessible, and therefore can easily be used to 'represent' – even if at a very superficial level – the character of a nation.]

Herder, drawing his information from books of travel, illustrates the huge diversity of human societies, where the local customs are determined by differences of climate and geography

In this manner I might go on, and exhibit climatic pictures of several nations, inhabiting the most different regions, from Kamtscatka to Tierra del Fuego... In India, the grand resort of commercial nations, the Arab and the Chinese, the Turk and the Persian, the Christian and the Jew, the Negro and the Malay, the Japanese and the Gentoo (Hindu), are clearly distinguishable: thus every one bears the characters of his country and way of life on the most distant shores. The ancient allegorical tradition says that Adam was formed out of the dust of all the four quarters of the Globe, and animated by the powers and spirits of the whole earth. Wherever his children have bent their course, and fixed their abode, in the lapse of ages, there they have taken root as trees, and produced leaves and fruit adapted to the climate. Hence let us deduce a few consequences, which seem to explain to us many things, that might otherwise be deemed striking singularities in the history of man.

... It is obvious why all sensual people, fashioned in their country, are so much attached to the soil, and so inseparable from it. The constitution of their body, their way of life, the pleasures and occupations to which they have been accustomed from their infancy and the whole circle of their ideas are climatic. Deprive them of their country, you deprive them of everything...

Slavery and colonialism are violations of this principle

No words can express the sorrow and despair of a bought or stolen Negro slave when he leaves his native shore, never more to behold it while he has breath... How many deplorable instances have been known of these poor stolen wretches destroying themselves in despair! Sparmann informs us, from the mouth of a slavedealer, that at night they are seized with a kind of frenzy, which prompts them to commit murder, either on themselves or others: 'for the painful recollection of the irreparable loss of their country and their freedom commonly awakes by night, when the bustle of the day ceases to engage their attention'. And what right have you, monsters! even to approach the country of these unfortunates, much less to tear them from it by stealth, fraud, and cruelty? For ages this quarter of the Globe has been theirs, and they belong to it: their forefathers purchased it at a dear rate, at the price of the Negro form and complexion. In fashioning them the African sun has adopted them as its children, and impressed on them its own seal: wherever you convey them, this brands you as robbers, as stealers of men.

Hence... the lasting hatred of the natives of America toward Europeans, even when these behave to them with tenderness: they cannot suppress the feeling: 'This land is ours; you have no business here'. Hence the treachery of all savages, as they are called, even when they appear altogether satisfied with the courtesy of European visitors. The moment their hereditary national feelings awake, the flame they have long with difficulty smothered breaks out, rages with violence, and frequently is not appeased, till the flesh of the stranger has been torn by the teeth of the native. To us this seems horrible; and it is so, no doubt; yet the Europeans first urged them to this misdeed: for why did they visit their country? Why did they enter it as despots, arbitrarily practising violence and extortion? For ages it had been to its inhabitants the universe: they have inherited it from their fathers...

... Does not nature revenge every insult offered her? Where are the conquests, the factories, the invasions of former times, when distant foreign lands were visited by a different race, for the sake of devastation or plunder! The still breath of climate has dissipated or consumed them, and it was not difficult for the natives to give the finishing stroke to the rootless tree...

The innately different characteristics of nations are revealed in all areas, including music, myths and dreams

… Nature has conferred another beneficent gift on our species, in leaving to such of its members as are least stored with ideas the first germ of superior sense, exhilarating music. Before the child can speak, he is capable of song, or at least of being affected by musical tones; and among the most uncultivated nations music is the first of the fine arts, by which the mind is moved… Music, however rude and simple, speaks to every human heart; and this, with the dance, constitutes Nature's general festival throughout the Earth. Pity it is, that most travellers, from too refined a taste, conceal from us these infantile tones of foreign nations. Useless as they may be to the musician, they are instructive to the investigator of man: for the music of a nation, in its most imperfect form, and favourite tunes, displays the internal character of a people, that is to say, the proper tone of their sensations, much more truly and profoundly, than the most copious description of external contingencies.

… The songs of a people are the best testimonies of their peculiar feelings, propensities, and modes of viewing things; they form a faithful commentary on their way of thinking and feeling, expressed with openness of heart. Even their customs, proverbs, and maxims, express not so much as these: but still more should we learn from the characteristic dreams of a nation, if we had examples of them, or rather if travellers would note them. In dreaming… man exhibits himself just as he really is.

… Compare the Greenland mythology with the Indian, the Laplandic with the Japanese, the Peruvian with that of Negroland; a complete geography of the inventing mind. If the *Voluspa* of the Icelander were read and expounded to a Brahmin, he would scarcely be able to form a single idea from it; and to the Icelander the Vedam [Hindu sacred books] would be equally unintelligible. Their own mode of representing things is the more deeply imprinted on every nation, because it is adapted to themselves, is suitable to their own earth and sky, springs from their mode of living, and has been handed down to them from father to son… Whence is this? Have all tribes of men invented their own mythology, and thus become attached to it as their own property? By no means. They have not invented, but inherited it.

… Most national fictions spring from verbal communications, and are instilled into the ear. The ignorant child listens with curiosity to the tales, which flow into his mind like his mother's milk, like choice wine of his father, and form its nutriment. They seem to him to explain what he has seen: to the youth they account for the way of life of his tribe, and stamp the renown of his ancestors; (to) the man they introduce the employment suited to his nation and climate, and thus they become inseparable from his whole life.

Against the uniformity imposed by the spread of European power and culture

I will not pursue the history of the dispersion of mankind any farther: with their division into different houses and families, the foundations of new societies, laws, manners, and even languages were laid. What do we learn from these different, these unavoidable dialects, which occur upon our Earth in such infinite numbers, and frequently at such little distance from each other? We learn that the object of our diffusive parent was not to crowd her children together, but to let them spread freely. As far as it may be, no tree is permitted to deprive another of air, so as to render it a stunted dwarf, or force it to become a crooked cripple, that it may breathe with more freedom. Each has its place allotted to it, that it may ascend from its root by its own impulse, and raise its flourishing head.

[Providence] has wonderfully separated nations, not only by woods and mountains, seas and deserts, rivers and climates, but more particularly by languages, inclinations, and characters; that the work of subjugating despotism might be rendered more difficult... Ye men of all the quarters of the Globe, who have perished in the lapse of ages, ye have not lived and enriched the Earth with your ashes, that at the end of time your posterity should be made happy by European civilisation: is not a proud thought of this kind treason against the majesty of Nature?

... Every man has the standard of happiness within himself: he bears about him the form, to which he is fashioned and in the pure sphere of which he alone can be happy. For this purpose has Nature exhausted all the varieties of human form on Earth, that she might find for each in its time and place an enjoyment, to amuse mortals through life.

[Johann Gottfried von Herder, *Reflections on the Philosophy of the History of Mankind*, edited by Frank E. Manuel (Chicago, University of Chicago Press, 1968), pp 10-12, 32-33, 40, 68, 77-78]

NOTES ON CHAPTER 1

1   The dates for Homer are very imprecise, possibly c800-900BC.

2   See Homer's *Odyssey*, especially books 6-9.

3   See Homer's *Iliad*. There are many translations of the *Iliad* and the *Odyssey*, but those of Robert Fitzgerald and Richmond Lattimore are particularly recommended.

4   See Aristotle's *Politics*, translated by Benjamin Jowett (Oxford, Clarendon Press, 1905), Book I, pp 31-37.

5   See Virgil's *Aeneid*, Book VI, lines 852-854.

6   See Virgil's *Aeneid*, Book VIII, lines 675-713.

7   There are innumerable references to these ideas in the Jewish Bible (the Christian Old Testament), for example: 1 Chronicles xxix 15; 2 Chronicles vii 19-22; Psalms cxviii 22.

8   See New Testament, Matthew xxii 21.

9   See New Testament, Luke ii 1.

10   See St Augustine's *City of God*, Chapter 19 verses 24, 26. St Augustine pointed out that the prophet Jeremiah had urged the Jews exiled in Babylon to pray for Babylon, 'because in her peace is your peace'. This encapsulates St Augustine's view on the relationship between Christians and the state.

11   If we exclude the exceptional cases of Greece and Greek Cyprus, the European Union will, after Poland, Hungary, the Czech Republic, Slovenia and Estonia are included, contain within its border almost the whole of western Christendom, and exclude the whole of the Orthodox world of Eastern Europe.

12   See Marc Fumaroli, 'A Scottish Voltaire', in *The Times Literary Supplement*, 19 January 1996, pp 16-17.

13   Edmund Burke, *Reflections on the Revolution in France*, edited with an introduction by Conor Cruise O'Brien (London, Penguin Books, 1986); Joseph de Maistre, *Works*, edited and translated by Jack Lively (London, Allen and Unwin, 1965).

Chapter 2

Eighteenth- and Nineteenth-Century Concepts of the Nation

> We hold these truths to be self-evident, that all men are created equal, that they are endowed by their Creator with certain inalienable rights, that among these are life, liberty and the pursuit of happiness. That to secure these rights, governments are instituted among men, deriving their just power from the consent of the governed.
>
> Declaration of Independence of the Thirteen United States of America, 4 July 1776

The birth of the 'dynastic' nation

Nationalism as an ideology and the nation as a concept could be said to emerge from the confluence of three processes: that of the modernisation and centralisation of the dynastic state; the emergence and dominance – in one form or another – of the concept of 'popular sovereignty' or democracy; and the growing interest – via the scientific revolution – in the laws of historical development as they affected the natural world and humanity, and in the origins of languages, races and cultures.

One observable process of the sixteenth to eighteenth centuries is the transformation of weak states, held together by a complex network of feudal obligations binding a monarch to powerful regional nobilities, into central-ised dynastic states. Marxist historians – who have tried to interpret historical change in terms of class conflict – have explained this development as a *de facto* alliance between monarchies and the growing power of a new 'bourgeois' or merchant class of the towns, directed against the regionally-based feudal nobility. This interpretation may at least partially explain the fact that the main dynasties of Europe were able over time to centralise wealth and therefore power, to impose a greater degree of administrative control and uniformity, and thereby weaken regional sources of authority. In certain parts of Europe, therefore – particularly those areas where dynasties controlled a territorially coherent area and not vast, sprawling empires – state sovereignty was being gradually consolidated in this era.

This process of state centralisation was very much a process imposed from above, consolidating the state in the image of the ruling dynasty. But, as has been suggested above, the centralisation of power was in the end the consequence of an alliance of interest between a dynasty and sections of the population who, in one way or another, stood to benefit from a more powerful, centralised state. It was, therefore, necessary for the dynasty to ensure loyalty from below, from the new political classes. In order to build a strong base for state loyalty, therefore, state languages (like English or French) were developed and encouraged at the expense both of the traditional languages of government, such as Latin, and regional dialects. This process of centralisation was taken a step further in England with the creation in the sixteenth century of a state religion controlled directly by the monarchy. The translation of the Bible and prayer-books into the state language, moreover, helped further to bind together the state, the monarchy and the educated – and therefore politically consequential – subjects of that state. No doubt this process of administrative, linguistic and – in some cases – religious centralisation was primarily designed to concentrate the power of the state, and bind the subjects to the state. Clearly, however, this process was also creating a common identity. 'States', in other words, were being transformed into 'nations', with a growing sense of a common identity and cohesion binding together the subjects of the state (see document 1 at the end of this chapter).

Democracy and the nation

The emergence and eventual dominance of the concept of popular sovereignty or democracy is another vital pillar in the formation of the idea of nationalism. As has already been mentioned in the first chapter, the Enlightenment phenomenon of the sixteenth to eighteenth centuries – what

might be called the rationalist and scientific revolution – attempted to eluci-
date the first principles of human society and the natural world. In the realm
of government and society, this rationalist endeavour started with an examination of the innate characteristics of human beings, and the relationship
between these innate characteristics – which form the foundation for the natural rights of humanity – and the origins and purposes of government. Out
of this emerged – as we have already seen – the radical view that humans had
certain innate rights; that governments had originally been formed to protect
these innate rights; and therefore that governments were only 'legitimate' if
they were fulfilling this role for which they had originally been created. From
this perspective it was inevitable that monarchic dynasties, which originally
imposed themselves by force, would be seen as illegitimate 'usurpations'.

From these original premises was built an edifice that was eventually to
evolve into modern democracy. Ultimate political authority ('sovereignty'), it
was argued, lay in the hands of those for whom and by whom governments
had been formed in the first place, the citizens of a community. A legitimate
government was one where the equal 'citizens' of a republic replaced the
'subjects' of a monarchy, and where assemblies, parliaments or senates would
represent the interests of these citizens, and ultimately appoint and control
governments through elections.

It should be noted, however, that the concept of the citizen was confined
– certainly in the late eighteenth century – to those who were deemed to be
able to exercise the faculty of reason fully; among the criteria normally
applied in this respect were membership of the male sex and the possession
of property and an education.[1] In addition, a distinction was often drawn
between a 'republican' system of government, where a constitution would
maintain a careful balance of power designed to preserve the rights of all
citizens, not just a majority; and a 'democratic' system, which could rapidly
descend into the tyranny of an uneducated majority.[2] This has led left-wing
historians to argue that the reality behind the rhetoric of the 'rights of man'
was that the bourgeois-mercantile class, having helped the monarchy create
an effective, centralised state, was now pushing aside the monarchy and
taking over the state for itself. It is certainly true that there was in many
modern democracies a long transition from a very restricted conception of
'the sovereignty of the citizen' to 'popular sovereignty' or democracy as we
define it today.

The interrelationship between this emerging definition of democracy on
one side, and the concept of the nation on the other, is vitally important, but
by no means straightforward. Generally speaking, the French revolutionaries

of the 1789 era defined the nation, not in terms of identity ('who are we?'), but in terms of the general principles of government ('how should we be ruled?'). The term 'la nation' was used to distinguish between the legitimate Republic created by the French Revolution on the basis of the sovereignty of the citizen, and the 'illegitimate' dynastic state dominated by the 'usurping' French monarchy. In other words, the terms republic and nation were virtually synonymous; the foundation of both was a state based on the sovereignty of the citizen.

The principle of citizens' sovereignty – leading eventually to democracy – does, however, inevitably merge with the issue of identity; and it is from this merger that the ideology of modern nationalism – nationalism from below, as it were – originates. If it is conceded that the people of a state have a right to determine their form of government, it must also follow that groups of people within that state should have the right to decide whether they wish to remain within that state or form their own state. If the people of France may legitimately decide that they wish to be governed by a republic, how can the province of Brittany, say, be denied its right to break away from France and create its own state if the citizens of Brittany should wish it? In his general discussion of democracy and its basic principles, John Stuart Mill put the matter in a nutshell:

> One hardly knows what any division of the human race should be free to do, if not to determine with which of the various bodies of human beings they choose to associate themselves.[3] (See document 3 at the end of the chapter.)

In other words, just as existing dynasties had no inherent God-given right to rule, so existing states had no inherent God-given right to remain territorially inviolate if a clearly-identifiable community among its citizens no longer wished to remain in the state. (The problem, of course, lies in trying to define a 'clearly-identifiable community'!)

It is the confluence of these two concepts of political rights – of citizens to choose their own type of government, and to choose the state within which they wish to be governed – that makes the United States Declaration of Independence such a fascinating document. The declaration begins with a statement of the universal and 'inalienable' rights of man on which all legitimate governments should be based; as such, it attacks not so much the fact of British authority, but the type of authority that is exercised. But the core of the document is of course a rejection of British authority as such, and a statement of the national – not merely republican – agenda of the delegates

in Philadelphia. But the principles legitimising the separation from Britain
are not based on issues of identity – the declaration does not, that is, say 'We
are a different people' – but on the system of government (see document 2 at
the end of this chapter). In this sense, as we shall see, the American
Declaration of Independence differed significantly from the documents of
later nationalist movements demanding independence.

The influence on the concept of the nation of race, culture and language

Along with the revolution in political ideas we have examined above, it is
now necessary to consider the 'revolution of identity' that occurred at roughly
the same time. In the eighteenth and nineteenth centuries, a new class –
which we can broadly describe as the educated urban middle class – was
beginning to participate in politics in Europe and North America. Along
with the growing political consciousness that inevitably accompanied this
development, however, went a growing consciousness of identity. As a
consequence, the issue of identity was now drawn into the political arena.

In part, this process was stimulated by political events. French
Revolutionary and Napoleonic incursions into Italy, for example, helped to
boost the sense of an Italian identity that transcended the myriad states of the
peninsula, and the aspiration to try to create a united Italy free of foreign
intrusions and local despots. French domination in Germany during the
same period generated a reactive assertion of a German identity that led to
the feeling that Germany could only overcome its weaknesses and humiliations
if a united German state were created.

In addition, however, this new consciousness of identity – the recognition
of an us/them divide – was given a rational shape and justification by the
scientific revolution of the time. As part of this revolution, the attempt to
understand and categorise the natural world was extended to the human
species itself, its origins and its historical development.

In these scientific investigations, one obvious area was that of race and
racial differences. Archaeology, history, linguistics, anatomy, skin colour and
skull shapes were examined in order to understand the common characteristics
of humanity and its differences. For some, this was a purely scientific exercise; for others, however, this search for racial difference had political
objectives, particularly for those who were trying to assert the existence,
say, of a 'German', 'Italian' or 'Hungarian' identity based on 'innate' racial
characteristics.

Scientific racial investigation, however, was never entirely satisfactory for these latter nationalist propagandists. The whole massive historical process of migration and intermarriage meant that 'innate' and clearly-defined racial differences were virtually impossible to define except in categories that were so broad – 'Mongolians' or 'Indo-Europeans' for example – and so riddled with punctilious caveats that they were virtually useless for the purposes of 'race'-based nationalism, at least as far as Europe was concerned.

Charles Darwin's definitive works, *The Origin of Species* and *The Descent of Man*, were scarcely any more useful. The central theme in *The Origin of Species* was that of the 'evolution' of the natural world through a process of 'natural selection' and – to put it at its simplest – 'the survival of the fittest', the ability of certain species to adapt to an ever-changing environment. While this could be adapted to a broad concept of human history as an endless 'struggle' between racial groups, Darwin's arguments in *The Descent of Man* were disappointing for those with an interest in emphasising the value of racial difference. Darwin argued that, in the struggle of human groups for domination over their environment – embodied during his own time by European colonial expansion throughout the world – 'hybrid vigour', not racial purity, was the key to success. Darwin argued that it was precisely those societies that remained racially isolated that were unable to adapt to a changing environment.[4]

The search for the roots of identity, which is the main starting-point for the ideology of nationalism, was, therefore, generally drawn to areas other than that of scientific racial study. The most fruitful areas were those of language, culture and history. The late eighteenth and the nineteenth centuries saw a revolution in the study of philology: that is, the study of the origins of languages and the categorisation of different language families. Along with this went a conscious attempt to revive local languages and literatures that had been 'lost', or were in the process of 'dying' through the combined impact of dominant state languages, and the all-pervading impact on European education of 'classical' Graeco-Roman literature and culture.[5]

The link here between language, culture and history needs to be stressed. In the first place, the retrieval of lost or dying languages and literatures necessarily involved the retrieval of the lost history of the communities that spoke those languages. Moreover, history was important in the broader search for the 'roots' of identity. Clearly, language in itself is an acquired attribute, not – like the colour of one's skin or the shape of one's skull – an innate aspect of identity. But the potent link between language, history and culture – which could be described as the collective behaviour and communication of a people through generations – would justify the notion of language as the expression of the innate characteristics of a people, whatever the mixture of their racial origins. These differences between communities in Europe were more comfortably described as an ethnic rather than as a racial difference. 'Ethnic' comes from the Greek word 'ethnos/ethné', which was used to describe any collectivity from a swarm of bees (Homer) to a distinctive 'people'. It should be noted, however, that the terms 'race' and 'ethnicity', 'racial' and 'ethnic', are normally used indiscriminately. Indeed, the very confusion in the use of these terms reflects the fact that they are in any case very imprecise and flexible definitions.

It will easily be understood that this search for the roots of identity was stimulated by, and helped stimulate, what might be called the 'politics of difference'. The different identities that were discovered by this process described themselves – following the parlance of the time – as nations.[6] This struggle for 'national consciousness' coincided with the concept of popular sovereignty to create a concrete political agenda: 'self-determination', or the demand that these self-defined nations should have their own sovereign states, 'nation-states'. This process will be examined in the next chapter.

Documents

(Nb: in all the following extracts, editorial comments at the beginning of texts, or amendments and explanations in the texts themselves, will be placed in square brackets. Headings and subdivisions will be put in italics.)

1 – Ernest Renan's 'What is a Nation?'

[Joseph Ernest Renan (1823-1892), a French philosopher and theologian, produced in his 1882 lecture given at the Sorbonne, 'What is a Nation?', the classic definition of the nation.]

I propose to ask you to join with me in analysing an idea which, though it appears simple, yet lends itself to the most dangerous misunderstandings. Human society assumes the most varied forms: great masses of human beings, such as we see in China, in Egypt and in the older Babylonia; the tribe as exemplified by the Hebrews and Arabs; the city, as in Athens and Sparta; the unions of various countries, as in the Achaemenian, Roman and Carlovingian Empires; communities having no mother country but held together by the bond of religion, as the Israelites and the Parsees; nations such as France, England and most modern European autonomous States; confederations, as in Switzerland and America; relationships, such as those set up by race, or rather by language, between the different branches of Germans or Slavs; all these various groupings exist, or have existed, and to ignore the differences between them is to create a serious confusion. At the time of the French Revolution it was believed that the institutions of small independent towns, such as Sparta and Rome, could be applied to our great nations comprising 30 or 40 million inhabitants. Nowadays, we observe a graver error. The terms 'race' and 'nation' are confused, and we see attributed to ethnographic, or rather linguistic, groups a sovereignty analogous to that of actually existing peoples. Let us try to arrive at some degree of exactness with regard to these difficult questions in which the least confusion at the outset of the argument as to the meaning of words may lead in the end to the most fatal errors. Our task is a delicate one; it amounts almost to vivisection; and we are going to treat the living as usually we treat the dead. We shall proceed coldly and with the most complete impartiality...

[Historical origins: the empires and city-states of the pre-Roman Empire are nothing like nations in the modern sense of the word. The Roman Empire itself did develop a self-conscious, corporate sense of identity – particularly among its educated classes – but it was still manifestly a state superimposed on a wide variety of identities, peoples and religions. As such it did not resemble a modern nation-state.

As the Roman Empire disintegrated, Germanic tribes swept into the areas that are now France, Spain, Italy and central Europe. On the whole, these invasions involved military conquest by a military caste, rather than settlement by a whole community. As such, these military groups of broadly Germanic origin (Franks, Burgundians, Goths, Lombards or Normans) formed a small ruling layer over the wider, Latin-speaking, Christian society that they had conquered. Gradually, this Germanic ruling caste – although it retained its aristocratic status – married into the wider society, adopted the Latin language, and converted to Christianity.

It is on this basis – the intermixture of an originally Germanic military élite and a Latin-Christian culture – that the most powerful dynasties managed, largely through brute conquest and expansion, to establish themselves. The most enduring and powerful of these dynasties formed the bases for states that subsequently transformed into modern nations, like those of France and Spain.]

The dynastic origins of some nations

We are told by certain political theorists that a nation is, above all, a dynasty representing a former conquest that has been at first accepted, and then forgotten, by the mass of the people... It is quite true that most modern nations have been made by a family of feudal origin, which has married into the country and provided some form of centralising nucleus. The boundaries of France in 1789 were in no way natural or necessary. The large area that the House of Capet [the then French royal house] had added to the narrow strip accorded by the Treaty of Verdun [843AD] was indeed the personal acquisition of that family. At the time when the annexations were made no-one thought about natural limits, the right of nations or the wishes of provinces. Similarly, the union of England, Ireland and Scotland was a dynastic performance. The only reason why Italy took so long to become a nation was that, until the present century, none of her numerous reigning families became a centre of union... Holland, self-created by an act of heroic resolution, has nonetheless entered into a close bond of marriage with the House of Orange, and would run serious risks should this union ever be endangered.

Is, however, such a law absolute? Doubtless, it is not. Switzerland and the United States, which have been formed, like conglomerates, by successive additions, are based on no dynasty. I will not discuss the question in so far as it concerns France. One would have to be able to read the future in order to do so. Let us merely observe that this great French line of kings had become so thoroughly identified with the national life that, on the morrow of its downfall, the nation was able to subsist without it. Furthermore, the eighteenth century had entirely changed the situation. After centuries of humiliation, man had recovered his ancient spirit, his self-respect and the idea of his rights. The words 'mother country' and 'citizen' had regained their meaning. Thus it was possible to carry out the boldest operation [the French Revolution] ever performed in history – an operation that may be compared to what, in physiology, would be an attempt to bring back to its former life a body from which brain and heart had been removed.

It must, therefore, be admitted that a nation can exist without any dynastic principle, and even that nations formed by dynasties can be separated from them without thereby ceasing to exist. The old principle, which takes into account only the right of princes, can no longer be maintained: and besides dynastic rights, there exists also national right. On what criterion is this national right to be based? By what sign is it to be known? And from what tangible fact is it properly to be derived?

Race and national identity

Many will boldly reply, from race. The artificial divisions, they say, the results of feudalism, royal marriages and diplomatic congresses, have broken down. Race is what remains stable and fixed; and this it is that constitutes a right and a lawful title. The Germanic race, for example, according to this theory, has the right to retake the scattered members of the Germanic family, even when these members do not ask for reunion. The right of the Germanic family over such-and-such a province is better than the right of its inhabitants over themselves. A sort of primordial right is thus created analogous to the divine right of kings; and the principle of ethnography is substituted for that of nations. This is a very grave error, and if it should prevail, it would spell the ruin of European civilisation. The principle of the primordial right of

race is as narrow and as fraught with danger for true progress as the principle
of nations is just and legitimate.

We admit that, among the tribes and cities of the ancient world, the fact
of race was of capital importance. The ancient tribe and city were but an
extension of the family. In Sparta and Athens all citizens were related more
or less closely to each other. It was the same among the Beni-Israel [children
of Israel]; and it is still so among the Arab tribes. But let us leave Athens,
Sparta and the Jewish tribe and turn to the Roman Empire. Here we have
quite a different state of affairs. This great agglomeration of completely
diverse towns and provinces, formed in the first place by violence and then
held together by common interests, cuts at the very root of the racial idea.
Christianity, characteristically universal and absolute, works even more effectively in the same direction. It contracts a close alliance with the Roman
Empire and, under the influence of these two incomparable unifying agents,
the ethnographic argument is for centuries dismissed from the government
of human affairs.

In spite of appearances, the barbarian invasions were a step further on this
road. The barbarian [Germanic] kingdoms which were then cut out have
nothing ethnographic about them; they were decided by the forces or whims
of the conquerors, who were completely indifferent with regard to the race of
the peoples whom they subjugated... The authors of the Treaty of Verdun
[843AD, dividing the empire of Charlemagne], calmly drawing their two
long lines from north to south, did not pay the slightest attention to the race
of the peoples to right or left of them. The frontier changes which took place
in the later Middle Ages were also devoid of all ethnographic tendencies...

Ethnographic considerations have, therefore, played no part in the
formation of modern nations. France is Celtic, Iberic and Germanic.
Germany is Germanic, Celtic and Slav. Italy is the country in which ethnography finds its greatest difficulties. Here Gauls, Etruscans, Pelasgians and
Greeks are crossed in an unintelligible medley. The British Isles, taken as a
whole, exhibit a mixture of Celtic and Germanic blood, the proportions of
which are particularly difficult to define.

The truth is that no race is pure, and that to base politics on ethnographic
analysis is tantamount to basing it on a chimera. The noblest countries,
England, France and Italy, are those where breeds are most mixed. Is
Germany an exception in this respect? Is she purely a Germanic country?
What a delusion to suppose it! All the south was Gallic; and all the East,
starting from the Elbe, is Slav. And as for those areas which are said to be
really pure from the racial point of view, are they in fact so? Here we touch

on one of those problems concerning which it is most important to have clear ideas and to prevent misunderstandings.

... What the sciences of philology and history call the Germanic race is assuredly a quite distinct family among human kind. But is it a family in the anthropological sense? Certainly not. The distinctive German character appears in history only a very few centuries before Jesus Christ. Obviously the Germans did not emerge from the earth at that period. Before that time, when mingled with the Slavs in the great shadowy mass of Scythians, they possessed no distinctive character. An Englishman is certainly a type in the whole sum of human kind. Now the type of what is very incorrectly termed the 'Anglo-Saxon' race is neither the Briton of the time of Caesar, nor the Anglo-Saxon of Hengist, nor the Dane of Canute, nor the Norman of William the Conqueror: it is the sum total of all these. The Frenchman is neither a Gaul, nor a Frank, nor a Burgundian. He is that which has emerged from the great cauldron in which, under the eye of the king of France, the most diverse elements have been simmering... Race, then, as we historians understand it, is something that is made and unmade. The study of race is of prime importance for the man of learning engaged on the history of human kind. It is not applicable to politics. The instinctive consciousness which has presided over the drawing of the map of Europe has held race to be of no account, and the leading nations of Europe are those of essentially mixed breed.

The fact of race, therefore, while vitally important at the outset, tends always to become less so. There is an essential difference between human history and zoology. Here race is not everything, as it is with the rodents and the cats; and one has no right to go about feeling people's heads, and then taking them by the throat and saying 'You are related to us; you belong to us'. Apart from anthropological characteristics, there are such things as reason, justice, truth and beauty which are the same for all. For another thing, this ethnographic policy is not safe. Today you may exploit it against others; and then you see it turned against yourself. Is it certain that the Germans, who have so boldly hoisted the banner of ethnography, will not see the Slavs arrive and, in their turn, analyse village names in Saxony and... say that they have come to settle accounts arising out of the massacres and wholesale enslavements inflicted upon their ancestors by the Ottos [German kings]? It is an excellent thing for us all to know how to forget.

I like ethnography very much, and find it a peculiarly interesting science. But as I wish it to be free, I do not wish it to be applied to politics. In ethnography, as in all branches of learning, systems change. It is the law of progress. Should nations then also change together with the systems? The boundaries of states would follow the fluctuations of the science; and patriotism would depend on a more or less paradoxical thesis. The patriot would be told: 'You were mistaken: you shed your blood in such-and-such a cause; you thought you were a Celt; no, you are a German'. And then, ten years later, they will come and tell you that you are a Slav. Lest we put too great a strain upon Science, let us excuse the lady from giving an opinion on problems in which so many interests are involved. For you may be sure that, if you make her the handmaid of diplomacy, you will often catch her in the very act of granting other favours. She has better things to do: so let us ask her just to tell the truth.

Language and national identity

What we have said about race applies also to language. Language invites union without, however, compelling it. The United States and England, as also Spanish America and Spain, speak the same language without forming a single nation. Switzerland, on the contrary, whose foundations are solid because they are based on the assent of the various parties, contains three or four languages. There exists in man a something which is above language, and that is his will. The will of Switzerland to be united, in spite of the variety of these forms of speech, is a much more important fact than a similarity of language, often attained by vexatious measures.

It is to the honour of France that she has never tried to attain unity of language by the use of coercion. Is it impossible to cherish the same feelings and thoughts and to love the same things in different languages? We were talking just now of the objections to making international politics dependent on ethnography. It would be no less objectionable to make them depend on comparative philology. Let us allow full liberty of discussion to these interesting branches of learning, and not mix them up with what would disturb their serenity. The political importance ascribed to languages comes from regarding them as tokens of race. Nothing could be more unsound. In Prussia, where nothing but German is now spoken, Russian was spoken a few centuries ago... Even in the beginning of things, similarity of language did not imply that of race... Languages are historical formations which afford little clue to the descent of those who speak them and which, in any case, cannot be permitted to fetter human liberty, when it is a question of deciding with what family one is to be linked for life and death.

This exclusive importance attributed to language has, like the exaggerated attention paid to race, its dangers and its objections. If you overdo it, you shut yourself up within a prescribed culture which you regard as the national culture. You are confined and immured, having left the open air of the great world outside to shut yourself up in a conventicle together with your compatriots. Nothing could be worse for the mind; and nothing could be more untoward for civilisation. Let us not lose sight of this fundamental principle that man, apart from being penned up within the bounds of one language or another, apart from being a member of one race or another, or the follower of one culture or another, is above all a reasonable moral being. Above French, German or Italian culture, there stands human culture. Consider the great men of the Renaissance. They were neither French, nor Italian, nor German. By their intercourse with the ancient world, they had rediscovered the secret of the true education of the human mind, and to that they devoted themselves body and soul. How well they did!

Religion and national identity

Nor can religion provide a satisfactory basis for a modern nationality. In its origin, religion was connected with the very existence of the social group, which itself was an extension of the family. The rites of religion were family rites. The religion of Athens was the cult of Athens itself, of its mythical founders, its laws and customs. This religion, which did not involve any dogmatic theology, was, in the full sense of the words, a state religion. Those who refused to practise it were not Athenians. At bottom it was the cult of the personified Acropolis; and to swear on the altar of Aglauros [an Athenian heroine] amounted to an oath to die for one's country. This religion was the equivalent of our drawing lots for military service or of our cult of the national flag. To refuse to participate in such a cult would have been tantamount to a refusal nowadays to serve in the army, and to a declaration that one was not an Athenian. On the other hand, it is clear that such a cult as this meant nothing for those who were not Athenians; so there was no proselytising to compel foreigners to accept it, and the slaves of Athens did not practise it...

Nowadays [in the secular era] the situation is perfectly clear. Everyone believes and practises religion in his own way according to his capacities and wishes. State religion has ceased to exist; and a man can be a Frenchman, an Englishman or a German, and at the same time a Catholic, a Protestant or a Jew, or practise no form of worship at all. Religion has become a matter to be decided by the individual according to his conscience, and nations are no longer divided into Catholic and Protestant. Religion... is now barely to be reckoned among the reasons that determine national frontiers.

Economic interest and national identity

Community of interest is certainly a powerful bond between men. But do interests suffice to make a nation? I do not believe it. Community of interest brings about commercial treaties. Nationality, which is body and soul both together, has its sentimental side: and a Customs Union is not a country.

Geography and national identity

Geography, and what we call natural frontiers, certainly plays a considerable part in the division of nations. Geography is one of the essential factors of history. Rivers have guided races: mountains have impeded them. The former have favoured, while the latter have restricted, historic movements. But can one say, as some people believe, that a nation's boundaries are to be found written on the map, and that it has the right to award itself as much as is necessary to round off certain outlines, or to reach such-and-such a mountain or river, which are regarded as in some way dispensing the frontier *a priori?* I know of no doctrine more arbitrary or fatal than this, which can be used to justify all kinds of violence... No: it is not the soil any more than the race which makes a nation. The soil provides the substratum, the field for struggle and labour: man provides the soul. Man is everything in the formation of this sacred thing that we call a people. Nothing that is material suffices here. A nation is a spiritual principle, the result of the intricate workings of history; a spiritual family and not a group determined by the configuration of the earth.

What is the key to national identity?

A nation is a soul, a spiritual principle. Two things, which are really only one, go to make up this soul or spiritual principle. One of these things lies in the past, the other in the present. The one is the possession in common of a rich heritage of memories; and the other is actual agreement, the desire to live together, and the will to continue to make the most of the joint inheritance. Man cannot be improvised. The nation, like the individual, is the fruit of a long past spent in toil, sacrifice and devotion. Ancestor-worship is of all forms of religion the most justifiable, since our ancestors have made us what we are. A heroic past, great men and glory – I mean real glory – these should be the capital of our company when we come to found a national idea. To share the glories of the past, and a common will in the present; to have done great deeds together, and to desire to do more – these are the essential conditions of a people's being. Love is in proportion to the sacrifices one has made and the evils one has borne. We love the house that we have built and that we hand down to our successors...

In the past, a heritage of glory and of grief to be shared; in the future, one common plan to be realised; to have suffered, rejoiced and hoped together; these are things of greater value than identity of customs-houses and frontiers in accordance with strategic notions. These are things which are understood, in spite of differences in race and language. I said just now 'to have suffered together', for indeed common suffering unites more strongly than common rejoicing. Among national memories, sorrows have greater value than victories; for they impose duties and demand common effort.

Thus we see that a nation is a great solid unit, formed by the realisation of sacrifices in the past, as well as of those one is prepared to make in the future. A nation implies a past; while, as regards the present, it is all contained in one tangible fact, viz. the agreement and clearly expressed desire to continue a life in common. The existence of a nation is (if you will forgive me the metaphor) a daily plebiscite, just as that of the individual is a continual affirmation of life... According to the notions that I am expounding, a nation has no more right than a king to say to a province: 'You belong to me; so I will take you'. A province means to us its inhabitants; and if anyone has a right to be consulted in the matter, it is the inhabitant. It is never to the true interest of a nation to annex or keep a country against its will. The people's wish is after all the only justifiable criterion, to which we must always come back...

And now, let me sum it all up. Man is the slave neither of his race, nor his language, nor his religion, nor of the winding of his rivers and mountain ranges. That moral consciousness which we call a nation is created by a great assemblage of men with warm hearts and healthy minds: and as long as this moral consciousness can prove its strength by the sacrifices demanded from the individual for the benefit of the community, it is justifiable and has the right to exist...

[Extract from Alfred Zimmern (ed.), *Modern Political Doctrines* (London, Oxford University Press, 1939), pp 187-205]

2 – The United States' Declaration of Independence, 4 July 1776

[This document can be read in two ways. It can be seen as primarily an assertion of political rights that had been violated by the British monarchy and government of the time. This perspective is supported by the fact that both American and British society were divided over the issue of the American Revolution. In the colonies, a large number of 'loyalists' – whose role and importance has been to a large extent written out of the history books – supported the British cause; in Britain, on the other hand, a significant section of British political opinion supported the rebel colonists. That the American Revolution was not seen at the time as a 'national' issue as we would understand it today is suggested by the fact that those British who opposed their own government most vehemently on the issue of American rights – like John Wilkes – described themselves as 'Patriots'.

The second interpretation of the document is, however, entirely different. It would suggest that the declaration was the recognition of a fundamental chasm between a British and an American identity that had already emerged. The formulators of the declaration, however, expressed this national difference, not in the language of nationalism, which was in a sense not available at the time, but in the contemporary language of political rights. This language of political rights undoubtedly gave a moral elevation to the American claim. It also, however, carried considerable difficulties. One of these difficulties was neatly expressed by the die-hard English Tory, Samuel Johnson: 'How is it,' he asked, 'that we hear the loudest yelps for liberty among the drivers of negroes?' (See Boswell's *Life of Johnson*, 23/9/1777.)]

When, in the course of human events, it becomes necessary for one people to dissolve the political bands which have connected them with another, and to assume among the powers of the earth the separate and equal station to which the Laws of Nature and of Nature's God entitle them, a decent respect to the opinions of mankind requires that they should declare the causes which impel them to the separation.

We hold these truths to be self-evident, that all men are created equal, that they are endowed by their Creator with certain inalienable rights, that among these are life, liberty and the pursuit of happiness. That to secure these rights, governments are instituted among men, deriving their just powers from the consent of the governed. That whenever any form of government becomes destructive of these ends, it is the right of the people to alter or to abolish it, and to institute new government, laying its foundations on such principles and organising its powers in such form, as to them shall seem most likely to effect their safety and happiness. Prudence, indeed, will dictate that governments long established should not be changed for light and transient causes; and accordingly all experience hath shown, that mankind are more disposed to suffer, while evils are sufferable, than to right themselves by abolishing the forms to which they are accustomed. But when a long train of abuses and usurpations, pursuing invariably the same object, evinces a design to reduce them under absolute despotism, it is their right, it is their duty, to throw off such government, and to provide new guards for their future security. Such has been the patient sufferance of these Colonies; and such is now the necessity which constrains them to alter their former systems of government. The history of the present King of Great Britain is a history of repeated injuries and usurpations, all having in direct object the establishment of an absolute tyranny over these [United] States...

[There then follows a list of grievances against the British King.]

... In every stage of these oppressions we have petitioned for redress in the most humble terms: our repeated petitions have been answered only by repeated injury. A prince whose character is thus marked by every act which may define a tyrant is unfit to be the ruler of a free people...

We, therefore, the Representatives of the United States of America, in General Congress assembled, appealing to the Supreme Judge of the world for the rectitude of our intentions, do, in the name, and by the authority of the good people of these Colonies, solemnly publish and declare, that these United Colonies are, and of right ought to be Free and Independent States; That they are absolved from all allegiance to the British Crown, and that all political connection between them and the State of Great Britain is and ought to be totally dissolved; and that as Free and Independent States they have full power to levy war, conclude peace, contract alliances, establish commerce, and to do all other acts and things which independent States may of right do. And for the support of this declaration, with a firm reliance on the protection of Divine Providence, we mutually pledge to each other our lives, our fortunes, and our sacred honour.

3 – J.S. Mill: nationalism, democracy and the problem of 'multi-national' states

[John Stuart Mill (1806-1873) tackled the issue of nationality within the broader context of democracy. The contemporary background of the following chapter on nationality and nationalism, in 1861, was a Europe in which nationalist movements were challenging the large multi-national empires such as the Austrian Empire, and demanding the right to establish their own nation-states. The following is a defence of the right to national self-determination, based on the argument that 'multi-national' states or empires, like the Austrian Empire, have become anachronisms in the new age of nationalism and democracy. It also points, however, to the difficulties of achieving national self-determination in such multi-national states.]

A portion of mankind may be said to constitute a Nationality, if they are united among themselves by common sympathies, which do not exist between them and any others – which make them cooperate with each other more willingly than with other people, desire to be under the same government, and desire that it should be government by themselves or a portion of themselves, exclusively. This feeling of nationality may have been generated by various causes. Sometimes it is the effect of identity of race and descent. Community of language, and community of religion, greatly contribute to it. Geographical limits are one of its causes. But the strongest of all is identity of political antecedents; the possession of a national history, and consequent community of recollections; collective pride and humiliation, pleasure and regret, connected with the same incidents in the past...

Where the sentiment of nationality exists in any force, there is a *prima facie* case for uniting all the members of the nationality under the same government, and a government to themselves apart. This is merely saying that the question of government ought to be decided by the governed. One hardly knows what any division of the human race should be free to do, if not to determine with which of the various collective bodies of human beings they choose to associate themselves. But, when a people are ripe for free institutions, there is a still more vital consideration. Free institutions are next to impossible in a country made up of different nationalities. Among a people without fellow-feeling, especially if they read and speak different languages, the united public opinion, necessary to the working of representative government, cannot exist. The influences which form opinions and decide political acts are different in the different sections of the country. An altogether different set of leaders have the confidence of one part of the country and not of another. The same books, newspapers, pamphlets, speeches do not reach them. One section does not know what opinions, or what instigations, are circulating in another. The same incidents, the same acts, the same systems of government, affect them in different ways; and each fears more injury to itself from the other nationalities than from the common arbiter, the State. Their mutual antipathies are generally much stronger than jealousy of the government. That any one of them feels aggrieved by the policy of the common ruler is sufficient to determine another to support that policy. Even if all are aggrieved, none feel that they can rely on the others for fidelity in a joint resistance; the strength of none is sufficient to resist alone, and each may reasonably think that it consults its own advantage most by bidding for the favour of the government against the rest...

For the preceding reasons, it is in general a necessary condition of free institutions that the boundaries of government should coincide in the main with those of nationalities. But several considerations are liable to conflict in practice with this general principle. In the first place, its application is often precluded by geographical hindrances. There are parts, even of Europe, in which different nationalities are so locally intermingled that it is not practicable for them to be under separate governments. The population of Hungary is composed of Magyars, Slovaks, Croats, Serbs, Roumans [Romanians], and in some districts Germans, so mixed up as to be incapable of local separation; and there is no course open to them but to make a virtue of necessity, and reconcile themselves to living together under equal rights and laws... [Mill is here referring to the Hungarian-administered part of the Austrian Empire.]

The cases in which the greatest practical obstacles exist to the blending of nationalities are when the nationalities which have been bound together are nearly equal in numbers and in the other elements of power. In such cases, each, confiding in its own strength, and feeling itself capable of maintaining an equal struggle with any of the others, is unwilling to be merged in it; each cultivates with party obstinacy its distinctive peculiarities; obsolete customs, and even declining languages, are revived, to deepen the separation; each deems itself tyrannised over if any authority is exercised within itself by functionaries of a rival race; and whatever is given to one of the conflicting nationalities is considered to be taken from all the rest. When nations, thus divided, are under a despotic government which is a stranger to all of them, or which, though sprung from one, yet feeling greater interest in its own power than in any sympathies of nationality, assigns no privilege to either nation, and chooses its own instruments indifferently from all; in the course of a few generations, identity of situation often produces harmony of feeling, and the different races come to feel towards each other as fellow countrymen; particularly if they are dispersed over the same tract of country. But if the era of aspiration to free government arrives before this fusion has been effected, the opportunity has gone by for effecting it. From that time, if the unreconciled nationalities are geographically separate, and especially if their local position is such that there is no natural fitness or convenience in their being under the same government (as in the case of an Italian province under a French or German yoke), there is not only an obvious propriety but, if either freedom or concord is cared for, a necessity, for breaking the connection altogether. There may be cases in which the provinces, after separation, might usefully remain united by a federal tie, but it generally happens that if they are willing to forgo complete independence and become members of a federation, each of them has other neighbours with whom it would prefer to connect itself, having more sympathies in common, if not also greater community of interest.

[from John Stuart Mill, *Considerations on Representative Government* (London, George Routledge and Sons Ltd, 1904, originally published in 1861), pp 285-290, 294-295]

NOTES ON CHAPTER 2

1   Even today, the view that only the responsible and rational citizen should have the right to vote remains: children, convicts and lunatics are normally denied the right to vote.

2   See Immanuel Kant, *Perpetual Peace* (Los Angeles, US Library

Associations Ltd, 1932), p 27 (first published in 1795).

3   John Stuart Mill, *On Liberty, and Considerations of Representative Government* (Oxford, Blackwell, 1948), p 292.

4   See Charles Darwin, *The Origin of Species*, first published by John Murray in 1859; Charles Darwin, *The Descent of Man*, first published in 1871, (London, John Murray, 1913), pp 281-297.

5   For example, see Daniel Corkery, *The Hidden Ireland* (Dublin, M.H. Gill and Son, 1925), chapter 1.

6   In fact, 'nation' comes from the Latin word 'natio', meaning a 'tribe' or 'people'. Natio implied a people who were bound together by birth and custom, as opposed to a civilised, organised 'politeia' (Greek) or 'respublica' (Latin). It has evolved over time into its present meaning.

Chapter 3

National Consciousness and Self-Determination

> O Italy, may you
> Take to your heart the honouring of the dead;
> For now your land is widowed of their like,
> Nor are there any to be honoured now.
> Turn back, and look behind, my Italy,
> On those infinite and immortal ranks,
> And weep and feel disdain for your own self...
>
> from poem written in 1818 by Giacomo Leopardi, 'On Dante's Monument', translated by John Humphreys Whitfield

A definition of terms

In the last chapter, we have examined the process whereby nations were in effect created from above. In these cases, exceptionally powerful states were forged by ruling dynasties in a relatively manageable geographical area over a long period of time. The conscious objective of these dynasties in welding the subjects to the state by substantial administrative reforms and accompanying measures to control religion and centralise the state language was the simple one of enhancing the power of the state. The result of these measures, however, was the creation in these societies of a deep-rooted sense of corporate identity and loyalty that is the essence of modern nationalism. So strong did this sense of national cohesion become that the unity of these states could survive – even be enhanced by – a severe limitation on a dynasty's powers, as in the case of Britain in the seventeenth and eighteenth centuries, or the removal of the dynasty itself, as in the case of the French Revolution. In these cases above, we are seeing states transforming into nations, and thereby becoming what can be called nation-states.

We have also outlined the process where nations were created from below. The French Revolution in particular initiated an era of political awareness among the formerly politically quiescent subjects of states throughout Europe. In part, this political awareness concentrated on the rights of citizens in general; in part, it concentrated on the question of identity. An awareness of differences of identity – of language and custom, for example – had no doubt always existed; what was significant now, however, was that this aware-ness of differences of identity took on a political dimension. In this new climate, just as traditional authoritarian government was rejected as a tyrannical denial of the universal rights of man, so government imposed by people who did not share the identity of their subjects was rejected, not only as tyranny, but as an alien tyranny.

The politics of identity was given a firm grounding by the revival of languages and literatures, and the use of history to discover the former glories of subject peoples. When the assertion of an identity achieved a critical mass of support, then it could be said that a national consciousness had asserted itself. The natural political goal for such a national conscious-ness was to create a state for itself, the nation-state.

The creation of modern nations – whether from above or below – is one of the major historical events of Europe in the period from the late eigh-teenth to the early twentieth centuries. Indeed, the whole history of the twentieth century was to show that this process was neither clear-cut nor easy. In fact, it has probably made the major contribution to the bloodshed and devastation of Europe in the modern era.

We should also note the ambiguities in the relationship between national-ism forged from above, and national consciousness generated from below. The British state provides a very good example. With the incorporation of Wales into England in the sixteenth century, and the union between the monarchies and parliaments of England and Scotland in the seventeenth to eighteenth centuries, a united 'British' state was created. In the eighteenth century in particular, a conscious effort was made to weld together a British identity to match this new state. In Wales and Scotland, however, this process of national integration was never completed, and both countries were affected by the new era of national consciousness in the nineteenth and twentieth centuries. We see, therefore, both in Wales and Scotland a constant and as yet unresolved tension between the processes of integration into a British identity and the counter-tendency towards Welsh and Scottish nationalist separatism.

The development of national-consciousness

In this chapter, what is being specifically considered are the various factors – political, economic and social – that have affected the development of national consciousness in general. What, in other words, are the political and social forces driving the ideology of nationalism?

We describe as 'nationalists' those who seek to define a national identity, to differentiate that national identity from other neighbouring national identities ('I am Welsh, not British') and then to demand political and cultural rights for that national identity, culminating in the demand for complete national sovereignty, the creation of a nation-state. Nationalism, therefore, is in essence 'politicised identity'.

(It should be noted, however, that there is no absolute link between the assertion of a national identity and the demand for national sovereignty. It is possible for a separate national identity to be recognised within a larger state, and it is possible for a nation thus recognised to decide that its national identity can be preserved, and its national interests safeguarded, by sharing sovereignty with other nationalities. This is the existing state of affairs for the Welsh, Scottish and English nations of Britain.

When we talk of 'nationalists', however, we normally refer to those who not only assert a national identity *per se*, but also demand sovereign rights for that identity.)

Nationalist claims, however, are normally only effective if the assertion of a particular national identity can be seen to meet certain objective criteria. The development of a national consciousness and the justification for a nationalist agenda are, therefore, given vital credibility by demonstrable differences: in the area of language and ethnicity (Welsh versus English); of religion (Protestant versus Catholic in Northern Ireland); of geography (The United States versus Britain); or, where it can be defined, of race (Arab versus Turk, for example).

This search for 'fault-lines' of clearly-definable differences between identities is, however, extremely complex. We have already seen in Renan's essay how 'objective' factors like language, ethnicity, religion or geography work in entirely unpredictable ways in the process of defining national identities. Far more decisive for the successful emergence of a national consciousness and a nationalist movement is the 'subjective' factor of will: the will of a particular people to assert their common identity, and claim political rights on the basis of that identity.

Once again, therefore, we return to the dynamic relationship between national identity and democracy. A nation and a national identity cannot be said to exist unless a substantial section of the people so identified support this claim to nationality. In the end, the existence of a nation is not determined by objective criteria; it is self-determined by a particular people. The process of discovering a national identity, defining national goals, and achieving them is therefore described as self-determination. Ultimately, the success or failure of movements for self-determination depends, not on objective criteria, but on 'critical mass': that is, a critical mass of support among the people such a movement for self-determination claims to represent; and a critical mass of power, however defined, directed against forces opposing such a claim for self-determination.

Nationalism and social and economic change

It is, finally, necessary to examine the social, economic and political background to the phenomenon of nationalism. The era of nationalism in Europe, which we can very roughly describe as a period stretching from the French Revolution to the present day, coincides with a period of not just political, but also of profound economic and social, upheaval. The whole revolution of ideas in Europe that we have already examined stimulated that fundamental transformation that is called the Industrial Revolution. Among the most important effects of industrialisation was, first, a massive shift of population from the countryside to the towns and big cities; and, secondly, huge population growth throughout Europe.

The whole process of 'democratisation' that we have already examined had to cope, therefore, with this social and economic convulsion. Although educated and property-owning segments of society could be drawn relatively easily into the enlarging democratic system, there was generally a far greater reluctance to allow 'the masses' – particularly the new urbanised masses – to participate in the political process via an extended suffrage. Hand-in-hand with the enlargement of the vote, therefore, we see an expansion through the nineteenth and early twentieth centuries of education systems, and the introduction of rudimentary programmes of social welfare; one of the main objectives, undoubtedly, was to help turn the uneducated and unpredictable 'masses' into responsible 'citizens'.

The changes brought about by industrialisation, however, did create huge social discontents. Europe at this stage was passing through that most dangerous of all periods – rapid social and economic transition. Though the poverty and living conditions of the new urban masses may in fact have differed little from their former rural situation, and generally improved over time, the fact was that huge numbers of the population had been uprooted from traditional lives where they had in-built strategies for survival. The old certainties and ways of life had been lost, and it would take generations to establish new roots and absorb new strategies for survival. The consequent sense of anxiety and psychological loss affected sections of the middle class as much as the working class. The increasingly relentless process of competition in the new industrial era was to destroy relatively inefficient and small-scale businesses that had hitherto had a solid and valued niche in society. The certainties of the traditional economy and society were breaking up, throwing the educated and the uneducated alike into an unpredictable future.

With increasing mass participation in politics, these discontents were quickly absorbed into the political process. As political activists and political parties sought to mobilise support, they could easily tap these sources of discontent. In order to do so effectively, however, they needed to build a 'world-view' that could provide the disadvantaged with a convincing explanation for their problems, and immediate or long-term solutions. Above all, these world-views had to give to the uprooted and dispossessed a new sense of belonging, new 'roots'.

In nineteenth- and twentieth-century Europe, two main world views have dominated what might be called 'the politics of discontent'. The first of these is socialism, and of the various forms of socialism, the Marxist-Communist version provided the most coherent and appealing world-view. Briefly, Marxism explained the dynamic behind industrialisation as a ruthless, competitive search for profit by an all-powerful bourgeois or capitalist class, which was able to harness the new discoveries of science and technology to the productive process and use its accumulated wealth (capital) to expand their economic activities and 'buy' political power. This process of industrialisation required an ever-expanding work-force in the factories. While industry depended on this work-force, however, the relentless momentum to remain competitive, keep down costs and maintain profits meant that there was a continual – indeed increasing – downward pressure on the wages of this work-force.

The urban working class, or 'proletariat' as Marx called it, was seen by him as absolutely essential to, but at the same time the principle victim of, the phenomenon of industrialisation. The main political objective of Marxism or Communism, therefore, was to show this new urban proletariat the pitiful conditions of its present existence, and compare it with its potential power in the future if its members were to organise politically. The driving-force of industrialisation had drawn millions of people out of the isolation and 'rural idiocy' (Marx's words) of the countryside, and conglomerated them in the big cities and factories. In these conditions, the working class could rapidly develop an awareness of its common suffering and its common interests. In other words, a 'class-consciousness' would eventually emerge, and from this would develop clear political objectives. Eventually, increased revolutionary activity throughout the industrialised world by this mass working class would break the monopoly of power held by the capitalist class and initiate a new era where the benefits of an industrialised economy could be enjoyed by the whole society – in other words, socialism.

The main competing world-view was that of nationalism, which attempted to mobilise support – by means we have already seen – by appealing to a sense of national consciousness. It is vitally important to be aware of this interaction and tension between class-consciousness and national consciousness, since it permeates the mass politics of the nineteenth and particularly twentieth centuries. One of the main problems for socialism, however, was that class-consciousness was essentially an abstract concept. 'Workers of all countries, unite!' the slogan of Karl Marx's international communist organisation, may have appealed to the head and the heart. National consciousness, however, tapped those tribal loyalties, those visceral 'gut-feelings' that have proved to be so effective in mass political mobilisation. Perhaps, in the end, nationalism gave the uprooted and the dispossessed a sense of belonging that the high-minded abstractions of socialism could never match.

Documents

(Nb: in all the following extracts, editorial comments at the beginning of texts, or amendments and explanations in the texts themselves, will be placed in square brackets. Headings and subdivisions will be put in italics.)

1 – Factors in national self-determination: J.G. Fichte and German nationalism

[Elie Kedourie's book, *Nationalism*, first published in 1960, remains one of the most interesting and provocative studies of nationalism, national identity and self-determination. This extract comes from chapter 5, entitled 'National Self-Determination'. Kedourie considers some of the different ingredients that have helped to accentuate national difference, and thereby act as a basis for the assertion of the right to self-determination.

Kedourie examines the attitude to language of the nineteenth- and twentieth-century nationalists, and particularly concentrates on the ideas of the German philosopher J.G. Fichte (1762-1814) whose views on the 'organic' link between language and identity had a crucial impact on the development of nationalist ideas in the nineteenth century.]

The key significance of language for national consciousness

Since men have not continued one flock, but have dispersed over all the earth, and have divided into distinct families, tribes, and nations, their languages bear the imprint of their varying circumstances and distinct identities. 'Only one language,' says [the German theologian] Schleiermacher, 'is firmly implanted in any individual. Only to one does he belong entirely, no matter how many he learns subsequently... For every language is a particular mode of thought and what is cogitated in one language can never be repeated in the same way in another... Language, thus, just like the church or the state, is an expression of a peculiar life which contains within it and develops through it a common body of language.'

This theory has had immense political consequences. The world is a world of diversity, and humanity is divided into nations. Language is the external and visible badge of those differences which distinguish one nation from another; it is the most important criterion by which a nation is recognised to exist, and to have the right to form a state on its own. So crucial is the linguistic criterion that Fichte in his *Addresses to the German Nation* goes so far as to say that 'we give the name of people to men whose organs of speech are influenced by the same external conditions, who live together, and who develop their language in continuous communication with each other'. Fichte devotes a considerable portion of his *Addresses* to discovering and laying bare the intimate and complex relations between language and politics.

Herder had argued that for a man to speak a foreign language was to live an artificial life, to be estranged from the spontaneous, instinctive sources of his personality. With great ingenuity, Fichte works out the political ramifications of this broad and general contention. He tries to show, for instance, that the mere presence of foreign vocables within a language can do great harm, by contaminating the very springs of political morality. When foreign terms relating to political and social life are introduced into a language, those who speak it are unsure of the exact connotations of those terms and they fall into confusions which can lead to great harm. Take for instance, he argues, the words Humanity, Popularity, and Liberality. These words are of Latin origin, and were introduced into German as Humanität, Popularität, and Liberalität. What does Humanity really mean? It means the quality of being a man, and in this there is nothing praiseworthy. But the Romans, because they had a low ethical standard, considered being a man praiseworthy. To introduce then the word Humanität into German is to introduce a low ethical standard among the German people. 'Now,' he says, 'if instead of the word Humanity we had said to a German the word Menschlichkeit, which is its literal translation, he would have understood us without further historical explanation, but he would have said, "Well, to be a man (Mensch), and not a wild beast, is not very much after all"'. In similar fashion, Fichte deals with the words Popularity and Liberality which, to him, only show the degradation of Roman political institutions. 'There is in the word Popularity,' he points out, 'even at the very beginning, something base, which was perverted (in the mouths of the Romans) and became a virtue, owing to the corruption of the nation and its constitution. The German,' on the other hand, 'never falls into this perversion, so long as it is put before him in his own language.' If, instead of introducing these three words into German, writers had confined themselves to proper German vocables, like Menschenfreundlichkeit (friendliness to man), Leutseligkeit (condescension or affability), and Edelmuth (noble-mindedness), the perversions implicit in the Latin terms would have remained unknown to the Germans.

If such is the harm which results from introducing a few foreign words into German, what must it be like when a people abandons its tongue and wholly adopts a foreign language?... Fichte asserts [that] those who speak neo-Latin languages [viz. French] do not, properly speaking, possess a living speech, a mother tongue; they merely make do with a dead language. Fichte's distinction between living and dead languages rests on the theory of the origin of language advanced by Herder in his treatise of 1772, to which currency was also given in the 'Lectures on Literature and Art' delivered by A.W. Schlegel in 1803-4. Original, primitive languages, Fichte says, are superior to composite, derived languages. German is an original language, while French and English are composite, derived languages. Like Herder, Fichte argues that in language abstract ideas are expressed in non-abstract terms, or, as he puts it, 'Language gives a sensuous image of the supersensuous'. Those who speak an original language maintain unbroken the connexion between the abstract ideas and the sense-experience which has given rise to the terms in which abstract ideas are expressed. 'To all who will but think,' he says, speaking of those nations with original languages, 'the image deposited in the language is clear; to all who really think it is alive and stimulates their life,' and this because 'from the time the first sound broke forth among the same people, (such a language) has developed continuously out of the actual common life of this people and... no element has ever entered (into it) that did not express an observation actually experienced by this people, and, moreover, an observation standing in a connexion of widespread reciprocal influence with the other observations of the same people'.

The case is quite the opposite with those who speak in a derived language. Here, the living connexion between abstract ideas and immediate sense-experience is severed – their personality is therefore impoverished, and they cannot attain freedom and fulfilment. For them 'the verbal image contains a comparison with an observation of the senses, which they have either passed over long ago without the accompanying mental development, or else have not yet had, and perhaps never can have... In this way they receive the flat and dead history of a foreign culture, but not in any way a culture of their own. They get symbols which for them are neither immediately clear nor able to stimulate life, but which must seem to them entirely as arbitrary as the sensuous part of the language.' For those, on the other hand, fortunate enough to have it, a primitive language 'does not exert an influence on life; it is itself the life of him who thinks in this fashion... Just because that kind of thinking is life, it is felt by its possessor with inward pleasure in its vitalising, transfiguring and liberating power.'

From this, two conclusions may be drawn: first, that people who speak an original language are nations, and second, that nations must speak an original language. To speak an original language is to be true to one's character, to maintain one's identity, and as German is an original language only the German escapes the artificiality and sterility of those who speak dead languages; and only the German, the original man who is not enmeshed in a lifeless, mechanical organisation, considers Fichte, 'really has a people and is entitled to count on one, and he alone is capable of real and rational love for his nation'. Again, since a nation, *ipso facto*, must speak an original language, its speech must be cleansed of foreign accretions and borrowings, since the purer the language, the more natural it is, and the easier it becomes for the nation to realise itself, and to increase its freedom. All the more, therefore, is it incumbent on a nation worthy of the name to revive, develop and extend what is taken to be its original speech, even though it might be found only in remote villages, or had not been used for centuries, even though its resources are inadequate and its literature poor – for only such an original language will allow a nation to realise itself and attain freedom. Such is the doctrinal foundation of the vast philological labours which have accompanied the spread of nationalism all over the world…

The test, then, by which a nation is known to exist is that of language. A group speaking the same language is known as a nation, and a nation ought to constitute a state. It is not merely that a group of people speaking a certain language may claim the right to preserve its language; rather, such a group, which is a nation, will cease to be one if it is not constituted into a state. Then, says Fichte, 'it is… bound to give up its language, and to coalesce with its conquerors, in order that there may be unity and internal peace and complete oblivion of relationships which no longer exist…'

If a nation is a group of people speaking the same language, then if political frontiers separate the members of such a group, these frontiers are arbitrary, unnatural, unjust. 'Understand me rightly,' says a character in Fichte's dialogue *Patriotism and its Opposite* (1807), 'the separation of Prussians from the rest of the Germans is purely artificial… The separation of the Germans from the other European nations is based on Nature. Through a common language and through common national characteristics which unite the Germans, they are separate from the others.'

From linguistic unity to national unity

Only on this assumption did it make sense to entitle his lectures *Addresses to the German Nation*. For when they were delivered in Berlin in 1807-8 there was, politically, no German nation. The German-speaking parts of Europe had the most diverse political arrangements, and the fact that Prussians and Bavarians, Bohemians and Silesians all spoke German was not considered of great political moment, certainly not enough to warrant the disruption of so many settled institutions. Fichte and his fellow-nationalists strove to prove and convince that the fact of speaking one language was sufficient reason for upsetting all existing political arrangements, and for bringing about a new one in which all who spoke the German tongue would form part of the same state. 'What is the fatherland of the German?' asks Arndt in the well-known poem 'The German Fatherland', 'Name me the great country! Where the German tongue sounds and sings *lieder* in God's praise, that's what it ought to be. Call that thine, valiant German!... that is the fatherland of the German – where anger roots out foreign nonsense, where every Frenchman is called enemy, where every German is called friend – that is what it ought to be. It ought to be the whole of Germany!'

The French Revolution... gave currency to the principle that individuals and communities have the right to secede from one and adhere to another state. No less revolutionary in its consequences is this other principle that the boundaries of states are natural, and correspond with the linguistic map of a territory. 'The first, original, and truly national boundaries of a state,' lays down Fichte, 'are beyond doubt the internal boundaries. Those who speak the same language are joined to each other by a multitude of invisible bonds by nature herself long before any human art begins; they understand each other and have the power to make themselves understood more and more clearly; they belong together and are by nature one and inseparable whole...'

A nation, then, becomes a homogenous linguistic mass which acts as a magnet for groups speaking the same language outside its boundaries, who are tempted to throw off allegiance to their state, and embark on sedition and civil war. Irredentism[1] is a phenomenon which appears following the propagation of nationalism. Again, if states must be formed of linguistically homogeneous nations, then in areas of mixed speech, the unity of the national state is sorely disturbed; for, as Fichte points out, 'such a whole (as the nation), if it wishes to absorb and mingle with itself any other people of different descent and language, cannot do so without itself becoming confused... and violently disturbing the even process of its culture'. This emphasis on language transformed it into what it had seldom been before, into a political issue for which men are ready to kill and exterminate each other. The linguistic criterion also makes extremely difficult the orderly functioning of a society of states. For such a society to function, states must be reasonably stable, well-defined entities, known and recognised by the extent of territory they control, by their clearly delimited frontiers, by the coercive power of which they dispose. If language becomes the criterion of statehood, the clarity essential to such a notion is dissolved in a mist of literary and academic speculation, and the way is open for equivocal claims and ambiguous situations. Such an outcome is inescapable with such a theory as nationalism, invented as it was by literary men who had never exercised power, and appreciated little the necessities and obligations incidental to intercourse between states... Politics to them was... a golden key which gave entrance to fabled realms. But since politics usually deals with actual realms, nationalists must operate in a hazy region, midway between fable and reality, in which states, frontiers, compacts are at once both real and unreal...

It is sometimes argued that there are two or more varieties of nationalism, the linguistic being only one of a number, and the Nazi doctrine of race is brought forward to illustrate the argument that there can be racial, religious, and other nationalisms. But, in fact, there is no definite clear-cut distinction between linguistic and racial nationalism. Originally, the doctrine emphasised language as the test of nationality, because language was an outward sign of a group's peculiar identity and a significant means of ensuring its continuity. But a nation's language was peculiar to that nation only because such a nation constituted a racial stock distinct from that of other nations. The French nationalist writer, Charles Maurras (1868-1952), exemplified this connexion between race and language when he remarked that no Jew, no Semite, could understand or handle the French language as well as a Frenchman proper... It was then no accident that racial classifications were, at the same time, linguistic ones, and that the Nazis distinguished members of the German Aryan race scattered in Central and Eastern Europe by a linguistic criterion. In doing this, the Nazis only simplified and debased the ideas implicit in the writings of Herder and others. Such ideas received great impetus during the nineteenth century owing to the development of ethnological studies...

Education and the national will

National self-determination is, in the final analysis, a determination of the will; and nationalism is, in the first place, a method of teaching the right determination of the will. This indeed is the fundamental subject of Fichte's *Addresses*. These lectures, we must note, were delivered in Berlin in the aftermath of the Prussian humiliation of [the battle of] Jena in 1806; they seek to explain why the Prussian state had been unable to withstand Napoleon, and to indicate what must be done to make good the disaster. Fichte had been an admirer of the French Revolution... What he valued most in the Revolution was the creation of a state where, as he thought, individual freedom would have meaning only in the collective being. Also, he and his contemporaries were impressed by the tremendous collective energy engendered by the Revolution. The revival of Prussia was possible only if the secret of the Revolution were penetrated, and used to generate some of that prodigious collective energy which had enabled the French to subjugate the whole of Europe. Administrative changes, a better organisation of the armed forces, a more efficient bureaucracy, all these, Fichte was quite clear, would not answer. 'It is neither the strong right arm, nor the efficient weapon that wins victory, but only power of the soul... He who sets no limits whatever to himself but, on the contrary, stakes everything he has, including the most precious possession granted to dwellers here below, namely life itself, never ceases to resist, and will undoubtedly win the victory over an opponent whose goal is more limited.' Fichte's quest in the *Addresses* was for this wonderful power of the soul.

The *Moniteur de l'Empire*, the French official gazette, taking notice of the lectures as they were being delivered at the Royal Academy in Berlin, described them as 'public lectures given in Berlin by a celebrated German philosopher on the means for the improvement of education'. To the French censor, education must have seemed an innocuous subject, since he allowed the *Addresses* to be delivered and printed; but he ought to have known better, for had not his master, Napoleon, said, 'There will never be a fixed political state of things until we have a body of teachers instructed on established principles. So long as the people are not taught from their earliest years whether they ought to be republicans or royalists, Christians or infidels, the state cannot properly be called a nation.' For it was to education that Fichte looked to provide him with the key to the power of which he was in search. In his first address, he summed up his programme: 'In a word,' he said, 'it is a total change of the existing system of education that I propose as the sole means of preserving the existence of the German nation.' By this he did not mean that education ought properly to make the pupil familiar with and affectionate towards the traditions of his country, that German education, as it then existed, was not carrying out its duties. His meaning was somewhat different: 'What was lacking in the old system,' he noted, 'namely, an influence penetrating to the roots of vital impulse and action – the new education must supply.' 'By means of the new education,' he added, 'we want to mould the Germans into a corporate body, which shall be stimulated and animated in all its individual members by the same interest.' If this could be done, then the nation as well as all its members would live in freedom.

But how could it be done? Fichte's way was simple; simple because radical. 'The new education must consist essentially in this,' he reveals, 'that it completely destroys freedom of will in the soil which it undertakes to cultivate, and produces, on the contrary, strict necessity in the decisions of the will, the opposite being impossible.' A nation composed of such men is invincible; each of its members 'who has such a stable will, wills what he wills for ever, and cannot, under any circumstances, will otherwise than he always wills. For him freedom of the will is swallowed up in necessity... If you want to influence him at all, you must do more than merely talk to him; you must fashion him, and fashion him in such a way that he simply cannot will otherwise than you wish him to will...'

This is why, on nationalist theory, education must have a central position in the work of the state. The purpose of education is not to transmit knowledge, traditional wisdom, and the ways devised by a society for attending to the common concerns; its purpose rather is wholly political, to bend the will of the young to the will of the nation. Schools are instruments of state policy, like the army, the police, and the exchequer. In his dialogue on *Patriotism and its Opposite*, Fichte says that a state which adapted his educational policy could dispense with any army, for then it 'would have a nation put in arms, which simply could not be defeated by any mortal power'. The purpose of this education is to annex minds to love of the state, and therefore what is taught and how it is taught, what is suppressed and what is changed, is a matter of state policy...

[From Elie Kedourie, *Nationalism* (London, Hutchinson University Library, 1974), pp 63-72, 81-84]

2 – National identity, language and the rediscovery of the past

[The following extract is from Benedict Anderson's highly influential book, *Imagined Communities: Reflection on the Origin and Spread of Nationalism*, which was first published in 1983. What it particularly highlights here is the link between national identity and consciousness and the attempt of philologists, writers and historians to 'retrieve' lost cultures, literatures and histories, and to give a new significance to local languages that had hitherto only had the status of peasant dialects. Enhanced educational opportunities increased the reading public, and thereby gave respectability and mass support for previously submerged ethnic/linguistic identities.]

Rediscovering language and history; nationalism and the vernacular revolution

... The nineteenth century was, in Europe and its immediate peripheries, a golden age of vernacularising lexicographers, grammarians, philologists, and litterateurs. The energetic activities of these professional intellectuals were central to the shaping of nineteenth-century European nationalisms... Monolingual dictionaries were vast compendia of each language's print-treasury, portable (if sometimes barely so) from shop to school, office to residence. Bilingual dictionaries made visible an approaching egalitarianism among languages – whatever the political realities outside, within the covers of the Czech-German/German-Czech dictionary the paired languages had a common status. The visionary drudges who devoted years to their compilation were of necessity drawn to or nurtured by the great libraries of Europe, above all those of the universities. And much of their immediate clientele was no less inevitably university and pre-university students. Hobsbawm's dictum that 'the progress of schools and universities measures that of nationalism, just as schools and universities became its most conscious champions' is certainly correct for nineteenth-century Europe, if not for other times and places.

Examples: the linguistic origins of Greek, Hungarian, Romanian and other nineteenth-century nationalist movements

One can thus trace this lexicographic revolution as one might the ascending roar in an arsenal alight, as each small explosion ignites others, till the final blaze turns night into day.

By the middle of the eighteenth century, the prodigious labours of German, French and English scholars had not only made available in handy printed form virtually the entire extant corpus of the Greek classics, along with the necessary philological and lexicographic adjuncts, but in dozens of books were recreating a glittering, and firmly pagan, ancient Hellenic civilisation. In the last quarter of the century, this 'past' became increasingly accessible to a small number of young Greek-speaking Christian intellectuals, most of whom had studied or travelled outside the confines of the Ottoman Empire. Exalted by the philhellenism at the centres of Western European civilisation, they undertook the 'debarbarising' of the modern Greeks, ie, their transformation into beings worthy of Pericles and Socrates. Emblematic of this change in consciousness are the following words of one of these young men, Adamantios Koraes, in an address to a French audience in Paris in 1803:

> For the first time the nation surveys the hideous spectacle of its ignorance and trembles in measuring with the eye the distance separating it from its ancestors' glory. This painful *discovery*, however, does not precipitate the Greeks into despair. 'We are the descendants of Greeks,' they implicitly told themselves, 'we must either try to become again worthy of the name, or we must not bear it'.

Similarly in the late eighteenth century, grammars, dictionaries and histories of Romanian appeared, accompanied by a drive, successful at first in the Habsburg realms, later in the Ottoman, for the replacement of Cyrillic [the Russian script] by the Roman alphabet (marking Romania sharply off from its Slavic-Orthodox neighbours). Between 1789 and 1794, the Russian Academy, modelled on the Académie Française, produced a six-volume Russian dictionary, followed by an official grammar in 1802. Both represented a triumph of the vernacular over Church Slavonic. Although right into the eighteenth-century Czech was the language only of the peasantry in Bohemia (the nobility and rising middle classes spoke German), the Catholic priest Josef Dobrovsky (1753-1829) produced in 1792 his *Geschichte der bömischen Sprache und ältern Literatur*, the first systematic history of the Czech language and literature. In 1835-39 appeared Josef Jungmann's pioneering five-volume Czech-German dictionary.

Of the birth of Hungarian nationalism Ignotus writes that it is an event 'recent enough to be dated: 1772, the year of publication of some unreadable works by the versatile Hungarian author György Bessenyei, then a resident in Vienna and serving in Maria Theresa's bodyguard... Bessenyei's *magna*

opera were meant to prove that the Hungarian language was suitable for the
very highest literary genre.' Further stimulus was provided by the extensive
publications of Ferenc Kazinczy (1759-1831), 'the father of Hungarian literature,' and by the removal, in 1784, of what became the University of
Budapest to that city from the small provincial town of Trnava. Its first
political expression was the Latin-speaking Magyar [Hungarian] nobility's
hostile reaction in the 1780s to Emperor Joseph II's decision to replace Latin
by German as the prime language of imperial administration.

In the period 1800-1850, as the result of pioneering work by native
scholars, three distinct literary languages were formed in the northern
Balkans: Slovene, Serbo-Croat and Bulgarian. If, in the 1830s, 'Bulgarians'
had been widely thought to be of the same nation as the Serbs and Croats...
a separate Bulgarian national state was to come into existence by 1878. In the
eighteenth century, Ukrainian (Little Russian) was contemptuously tolerated
as a language of yokels. But in 1798 Ivan Kotlarevsky wrote his *Aeneid*, an
enormously popular satirical poem on Ukrainian life. In 1804, the University
of Kharkov was founded and rapidly became the centre for a boom in
Ukrainian literature. In 1819 appeared the first Ukrainian grammar – only 17
years after the official Russian one. And in the 1830s followed the works of
Taras Shevchenko, of whom Seton-Watson observes that 'the formation of
an accepted Ukrainian literary language owes more to him than to any other
individual. The use of this language was the decisive stage in the formation
of an Ukrainian national consciousness'. Shortly thereafter, in 1846, the first
Ukrainian nationalist organisation was founded in Kiev – by a historian!

In the eighteenth century the language-of-state in today's Finland
was Swedish. After the territory's union with Tsardom in 1809, the official
language became Russian. But an 'awakening' interest in Finnish and the
Finnish past, first expressed through texts written in Latin and Swedish in
the later eighteenth century, by the 1820s was increasingly manifested in the
vernacular. The leaders of the burgeoning Finnish nationalist movement
were 'persons whose profession largely consisted of the handling of language:
writers, teachers, pastors, and lawyers. The study of folklore and the redis-
covery and piecing together of popular epic poetry went together with the
publication of grammars and dictionaries, and led to the appearance of periodicals which served to standardise Finnish literary (ie print) language, on
behalf of which stronger political demands could be advanced.' [From Seton-
Watson's *Nations and States*] In the case of Norway, which had long shared a
written language with the Danes, though with a completely different pro-
nunciation, nationalism emerged with Ivar Aasen's new Norwegian grammar

(1848) and dictionary (1850), texts which responded to and stimulated demands for a specifically Norwegian print-language.

Elsewhere, in the latter portion of the nineteenth century, we find Afrikaner nationalism pioneered by Boer pastors and littérateurs, who in the 1870s were successful in making the local Dutch patois into a literary language and naming it something no longer European. Maronites and Copts [Arab Christians], many of them products of Beirut's American College (founded in 1866) and the Jesuit College of St Joseph (founded in 1875) were major contributors to the revival of classical Arabic and the spread of Arab nationalism. And the seeds of Turkish nationalism are easily detectable in the appearance of a lively vernacular press in Istanbul in the 1870s.

Nor should we forget that the same epoch saw the vernacularisation of another form of printed page – the score. After Dobrovsk came Smetana, Dvořák, and Janáček [Czech composers]; after Aasen, Grieg [Norwegian]; after Kazinsky, Bartók [Hungarian]; and so on well into our century.

Nationalism and the reading public

At the same time, it is self-evident that all these lexicographers, philologists, grammarians, folklorists, publicists, and composers did not carry on their revolutionary activities in a vacuum. They were, after all, producers for the print-market, and they were linked, via that silent bazaar, to consuming publics. Who were these consumers? In the most general sense: the families of the reading classes – not merely the 'working father,' but the servant-girded wife and the school-age children. If we note that as late as 1840, even in Britain and France, the most advanced states in Europe, almost half the population was still illiterate (and in backward Russia almost 98 per cent), 'reading classes' meant people of some power. More concretely, they were, in addition to the old ruling classes of nobilities and landed gentries, courtiers and ecclesiastics, rising middle strata of plebeian lower officials, professionals, and commercial and industrial bourgeoisies.

Mid-nineteenth-century Europe witnessed a rapid increase in state expenditures and the size of state bureaucracies (civil and military), despite the absence of any major local wars. 'Between 1830 and 1850 public expenditure per capita increased by 25 per cent in Spain, by 40 per cent in France, by 44 per cent in Russia, by 50 per cent in Belgium, by 70 per cent in Austria, by 75 per cent in the USA, and by over 90 per cent in The Netherlands.' [Eric Hobsbawm's *The Age of Revolution*.] Bureaucratic expansion, which also meant bureaucratic specialisation, opened the gates of official preferment to much greater numbers and of far more varied social origins than hitherto...

[From Benedict Anderson, *Imagined Communities: Reflections on the Origin and Spread of Nationalism* (London, Verso, 1991), pp 71-76]

NOTES ON CHAPTER 3

1   In short, 'irredentism' means the aspiration to return 'unredeemed' ('irrédenta') territory to the national family.

Part II

Case Studies in National Self-Determination

Chapter 4

The First World War and National Self-Determination in Europe

Things fall apart; the centre cannot hold;
Mere anarchy is loosed upon the world,
The blood-dimmed tide is loosed, and everywhere
The ceremony of innocence is drowned;
The best lack all conviction, while the worst
Are full of passionate intensity.

'Second Coming' by W.B. Yeats

The dominance of the nation-state

In 1815, after the defeat of Napoleon and the end of an era of revolutionary turbulence, Europe consisted of a wide variety of state-systems. On the whole, Western Europe was composed of states that had over time evolved into nation-states. Central Europe, on the other hand, was dominated by a medley of small dynastic states and principalities. In Eastern Europe, three sprawling empires – the Russian Empire, the Austrian Empire and the Ottoman Empire – contained within their boundaries a wide variety of peoples and religions, with little or no common identity.

If we compare this picture with the Europe – indeed, the world – of today, the difference is startling. Today, we see an international system completely dominated by the sovereign nation-state. Since the collapse of the multi-national Soviet Union in 1991, and leaving to one side the special case of the Vatican State, there is no state in the world that does not at least claim to be a nation-state, where the essential attribute is a common national affiliation binding its population. The ideology of nationalism and the institution of the nation-state has become a global phenomenon.

The history of Europe between 1815 and 1945 provides the key to this remarkable transformation. In this chapter, an attempt will be made to outline what might be called a 'nationalist history of Europe' in the nineteenth and twentieth centuries. This will try to show how, in some cases, a number of states coalesced in order to form one nation-state; and, in other cases, how aspiring nationalities within larger states broke away from those states, and formed their own independent nation-states. In essence, it is a study of the evolution from national-consciousness to the realisation of the ultimate goal of national-consciousness: the sovereign nation-state. For most of Europe in the modern age, this process has been violent and destabilising, leaving a host of problems in its trail, many of which remain unresolved to this day.

The key difficulty in this process of creating nation-states that match the different ethnic-linguistic identities of Europe is the fact that these ethnic-linguistic groups have not arranged themselves on the map in a tidy and convenient manner, particularly in Eastern Europe. In large areas of Eastern Europe, different ethnic groups have, over the centuries, intermingled with other ethnic groups in the same territory, often occupying a fixed stratum in society and playing a specific role in the economy. The infiltration of national consciousness and nationalist politics has naturally had a devastating effect on these societies. Their intermixed ethnic composition meant that, for every ethnic group that developed a successful nationalist movement and created its own nation-state, there were a number of discontented ethnic minorities with their own unrealised national aspirations. If any of these discontented minorities could look beyond the boundaries of the state they inhabited to an outside state with which they could identify – as the German minorities of Poland, Czechoslovakia and Romania could look to Germany in the years between the First and Second World Wars – then an internal 'minority problem' immediately became a serious source of international tension.

Between 1815 and 1914, the 'nationalist revolution', though it took root throughout Europe, was generally held in check by the international system. It was the First World War, with the resulting collapse of the Russian, Austrian and Ottoman Empires in particular, coupled with the attempt of the victorious allies to introduce a new European international system based on the principle of 'national self-determination', that truly inaugurated the nationalist era. As will be seen in the ensuing chapters, the First World War and its immediate aftermath marked a crucial turning-point, not just for European nationalism, but also for the national idea throughout the globe.

Nationalism before the First World War

After the final defeat of Napoleon in 1815, an attempt was made by the dominant powers of Europe – Russia, Prussia, Austria, Britain and royalist France – to concert measures to prevent the re-emergence of the revolutionary ideas that had originated in France in 1789, and thereafter destabilised the whole of Europe. Dynastic legitimacy was reasserted, and was indeed made into a guiding principle of international relations. The three main revolutionary ideas that threatened this conservative consensus were, of course, 'popular sovereignty' or democracy, nationalism and – increasingly important in the early nineteenth century – socialism.

Gradually, however, the conservative consensus of 1815 broke down, and was replaced by a more fluid 'balance of power' structure. To some degree, this development relaxed the constraints on growing political pressures; the changes of regime in France in 1830 and 1848, and the breakaway of an independent Greek state from the Ottoman Empire between 1821 and 1829 were early examples of this new international flexibility. But, whatever their differences, the big powers of Europe still had a common interest in restraining the turbulent forces of democracy and nationalism, and on the whole – though by no means invariably – resisted the temptation to exploit nationalist forces in order to weaken their international competitors. Generally, nationalist movements could only succeed if, first, they enjoyed the patronage of one or more of the big powers; and, secondly, if the realisation of their national goals did not threaten seriously to disturb the European power-balance.

In terms of the general realisation of the national idea, the most significant upheavals in Europe between 1815 and 1914 were the creations of united nation-states in Germany and Italy. In both cases, the nationalist process generally involved the coalescing of a number of states whose populations shared a common identity. The French revolutionary and Napoleonic era had stirred national aspirations in both the German and Italian regions; aspirations that could not ultimately be contained in the subsequent conservative era.

In the case of Germany, the aspiration to national unity was realised by a dual process; from above, in the sense that the Kingdom of Prussia was able to use its power and its status within the international system to establish a dominance over its weaker neighbouring German states; from below, since there was a substantial consensus among the populations of the various German states in favour of some form of national unity. It was this combination of Prussian power and German nationalist sentiment that helped to forge a united German state. By 1871, the Kingdom of Prussia had extended its sovereignty over the whole German area with the exception of Austria, and transformed itself into the German Empire, or 'Reich'.

The history of the creation of a united Italian nation-state in the 1860s and 1870s has similarities to that of Germany. In the same way, a dominant state within the Italian region – the Kingdom of Sardinia – was able, by a shrewd combination of diplomacy and war, to give a concrete shape to nationalist aspirations that were seething throughout the Italian peninsula, particularly among the educated classes. To a far greater extent than Prussia, however, the Kingdom of Sardinia relied on foreign patronage – that of France in particular - and an ability to exploit the European power-balance to achieve its objectives.

For the other successful nationalist movements of the 1815-1914 period, the achievement of their nationalist goals involved a process of separatism, the breaking away from a larger state. In this sense national 'self-determination' was a direct threat to the international system of nineteenth-century Europe. Despite this fact, however, aspiring national groups within the Ottoman Empire in south-eastern Europe – the Balkan area – benefited from certain specific factors. In the first place, European public opinion had an inherent sympathy for Christian communities struggling for liberation from a despotic, Muslim and therefore essentially 'oriental' and alien Ottoman Empire. More specifically, Tsarist Russia was on the whole prepared in the nineteenth century to promote the interests and rights of Orthodox Christian communities in the Balkans. Moreover, this traditional Russian sense of a religious affiliation with the Balkan nationalities was supplemented in the nineteenth century by the Russian-dominated 'Pan-Slav' movement, which campaigned for the liberation from Ottoman rule of all Slav groups – like the Serbs, Montenegrins or Bulgars – that shared an ethno-linguistic affiliation with the Russian people.

The other great powers of Europe were, of course, intensely suspicious of this potent connection between Russian power and Balkan nationalism. In the face of the growing fact of Ottoman weakness, however, Balkan nationalism could not in the end be checked, but only to some degree managed and controlled by the powers of Europe. By 1914, the greater part of the Balkan region was dominated by newly-emerged nation-states: Serbia, Romania, Bulgaria and Greece.[1] In contrast, aspirant nationalities within the large European states – for example, the Irish in the United Kingdom; the Czechs, Slovaks and 'South Slavs' in the Austrian Empire; or the Poles in the Austrian Empire and Russia – were unable to achieve their national aspirations before 1914.

The significance of the First World War

It was the outbreak of the First World War in 1914 that was to transform Europe and truly inaugurate the nationalist era. Nationalist aspirations played a key role in precipitating hostilities in the first place; both the warring sides – after some initial hesitation – tried during the course of the war to exploit the nationalist difficulties of their opponents; and – at the end of the war – the collapse of the Russian, Austrian and Ottoman Empires enabled aspirant nationalities to establish their own independent nation-states. Furthermore, in the peace settlement that followed the defeat of Germany and its allies, an embryonic international system of nation-states – the so-called League of Nations – was established.

The other epochal event of the First World War period – the Russian Revolution of March 1917 followed by the Communist (Bolshevik) seizure of power in November 1917 – also had profound global consequences. In a fundamental sense, the Union of Soviet Socialist Republics (USSR), or Soviet Union, set up by the communists in Russia and its dependent territories, constituted a challenge to a global system based on the sovereign nation-state. The Russian Communists emphasised class loyalty over national loyalty, and called for world-wide revolution by the working class and other 'oppressed classes' in order to overthrow global capitalism and inaugurate an international socialist system where nation-states would become increasingly redundant. The clash between the two ideologies of nationalism and communism intensified after 1917, and was to have a destructive impact on Europe for most of the remainder of the twentieth century.

The First World War and the building of a new international system

It was Serbian nationalist agitation directed against Austrian rule in neighbouring Bosnia that gave the fatal spark that started the First World War. In the first flush of war-fever, an outburst of patriotic feeling throughout Europe overwhelmed even those socialist political organisations that had hitherto emphasised class loyalties, and thus provided an object-lesson on the depth of 'gut'-feeling that nationalism could evoke in a period of crisis.

In the early months of the war, however, the Germans, Austrians and Ottoman Turks on one side, and the French, British and Russians (the 'Allies') on the other, were both relatively hesitant in their attempts to exploit the national difficulties of their opponents. Both sides were, of course, anxious to invoke broad moral principles that would serve to justify their war-efforts in the eyes of world opinion. France and Britain, for example, talked of defending the rights of 'small nations' such as Serbia, or Belgium, which had been overrun by Germany in the course of its initial attack on France. On the other side, the Ottoman Empire exploited its dominant position in the Islamic world to declare the war against France, Britain and Russia to be a 'jihad' or holy war. But the fact was that both sides were equally vulnerable to any attempt to exploit the issue of nationalism: if the Austrian Ottoman Empires had their turbulent minorities, so too did the British, French and Russian Empires. Nevertheless, the temptation to exploit nationalist aspirations on the opposing side was too strong to be avoided for long. An early example of this, with fateful long-term consequences, was the promise of Britain to the Arabs in 1915 to support the creation of an independent Arab state, in return for Arab military support against the Turkish rulers of the Ottoman Empire.[2]

It was the entry in 1917 of the United States into the war on the side of Britain and France, however, that put the whole question of national rights to the top of the political agenda. In January 1918, President Woodrow Wilson announced his 'Fourteen Points', which were in essence the outline of a new international structure that Wilson wished to see put in place in the event of an Allied victory. At the core of these Fourteen Points were two interlinked principles: that clearly identifiable European nationalities had the right to break away from the existing empires and create their own nation-states; and secondly, that a Europe-wide structure based on the satisfaction of national aspirations and mediated by a 'general association of nations' would be the best possible future guarantee for international stability. At the heart of Wilson's vision was the notion that multi-national empires were a permanent source of international aggression and instability; while the nation-state, with its in-built harmony between the state and its population, formed the 'natural' unit of a stable international system (see document 1 at the end of this chapter).

More important than Wilson's statement of principles, however, were developments on the ground in Europe in 1917 and 1918. During this fateful period, three unwieldy empires – Tsarist Russian, Austrian and Ottoman – collapsed under the strain of conducting a prolonged modern war. In 1917, the Tsarist state in Russia simply disintegrated. V.I. Lenin and his Communist (then Bolshevik) Party were able to exploit the ensuing period of prolonged anarchy and seize power in November 1917. In a calculated gamble designed to trade space in order to gain time to build a socialist state in

Russia, Lenin in March 1918 accepted a hugely-disadvantageous peace agreement with Germany, the Treaty of Brest-Litovsk. This treaty involved nothing less than the removal of the western section of the Tsarist Empire, and the creation of a collection of autonomous states – including Finland, Lithuania, Estonia, Poland and the Ukraine – that were clearly designed to act in the future as German client-states on its eastern flank. (There is, in fact, a remarkable continuity between this settlement and Hitler's arrangements for Eastern Europe in the early 1940s.)

The Germans were, however, unable in the end to exploit Russia's defeat and deal a knockout blow at the Allies in the west. By the autumn of 1918, the Austrian Empire itself began – like the Russian Empire a year earlier – to break up. Nationalist leaders took advantage of the situation to seize control of the areas they dominated in ethnic terms, and declare *de facto* independence. It was in this period of anarchy and civil war, rather than in the subsequent period of prolonged peace negotiations, that the modern Europe of nation-states was created.

In some cases, new nation-states were created out of the ruins of empire. The Czechs and Slovaks coalesced to create the new federal state of Czechoslovakia; the Poles of the Austrin Empire joined their compatriots recently liberated from Russian rule to create an enlarged independent Poland; and the Austrians and Hungarians – shorn of their empire – created their own separate nation-states. In other cases, national groups linked themselves to an already existing state. For example, the 'South Slavs' of the Austrian Empire – the Slovenes, Croats and Bosnians – joined Serbia in the creation of a united state that was later to be called Yugoslavia. For their part, the Romanians took advantage of the general chaos to incorporate within their nation the former Austrian provinces of Transylvania and Bukovina, and Russian Bessarabia.[3]

In a sense, therefore, the victorious Allies were faced with a *fait accompli* when they began their task of arranging a comprehensive peace settlement in 1919. The most powerful and best organised national groups were already in the process of staking out their claims on the ground, and the main task of the Allies was essentially that of adjudicating over disputed areas. In this complex question of deciding the respective national rights over disputed territories, three main criteria were applied. The first was the 'objective' criterion: who were the people of the disputed territory, and what was their ethno-linguistic affiliation? The second was the 'subjective' criterion: to what nation-state did the people of the territory concerned wish to adhere? The means of deciding the second criterion was the so-called 'plebiscite', the equivalent of the modern-day referendum. The third and ultimately most important criterion, however, was the strategic interests of the Allies themselves. It is noticeable that the principles of national self-determination were easily abandoned when what were seen as the 'friendly' states surrounding Germany and Austria required a slice of territory – irrespective of the wishes of its inhabitants – for reasons of 'national security'. It is in this spirit that Italy gained a segment of German-speaking Austria; Czechoslovakia gained predominantly German sections of the Sudetenland; and Poland incorporated manifestly German-inhabited territory within its western frontier. The principles of self-determination, in other words, were not to be allowed to weaken the perceived strategic needs of the victorious Allies.

In other areas, too, the application of the principle of self-determination was severely curtailed. In 1920 and 1921, the civil war in Russia between communists and anti-communists came to an end with the decisive victory of the communists. Although Finland and the Baltic states (Lithuania, Latvia and Estonia) remained independent, the communist leadership was able to reassert its authority over most of the rest of what had been the Tsarist Empire, including the Ukraine, the Caucasian nations, and the Muslim regions of central Asia. In theory, the new state – the Soviet Union – was a voluntary union of independent 'socialist republics'. In practice, real power lay in the hands of a united communist party – the Communist Party of the Soviet Union – that dominated the political systems of all these republics. The Tsarist Empire – shorn, admittedly, of most of its westernmost regions – had been given a new lease of life in a socialist guise.

In addition, the principle of 'self-determination' was not applied beyond Europe. The defeat of Germany and the Ottoman Empire raised the question of the disposal of the territories of the overseas German Empire and of the non-Turkish, Arab-populated sections of the Ottoman Empire. The French and British, of course, rejected the notion that the principles of 'self-determination' should be applied to the colonial areas of Asia and Africa, since the application of that principle could threaten their own extensive empires. Even Woodrow Wilson's Fourteen Points was cautious on this issue, and only asserted that the 'interests' (not the wishes) of colonial populations should be considered, and that the non-Turkish sections of the Ottoman Empire should have the 'opportunity of autonomous development', something that was clearly less than a full right to self-determination. Accordingly, a system was put in place for colonial areas, where the newly-formed League of Nations – in essence, the 'general association of nations' envisaged in Wilson's Fourteen Points – would 'mandate' one of the big powers, mainly

Britain and France, to govern these territories on the League's behalf, until such time as a territory was considered to be 'fit' for self-government (see document 2 at the end of this chapter). The German colonial territories were accordingly disposed of on the basis of this principle and, in the former Ottoman Empire possessions in the Arab world, the French and the British divided the region into 'mandate' territories under their control (Syria and the Lebanon for France; Iraq, Transjordan [later Jordan] and Palestine for Britain).

It should be noted, however, that while the colonial powers tried to limit severely the application of the principle of self-determination in the colonial area, it is precisely at this time that nationalist movements, basing themselves on the right to self-determination, began to take root in Asia and Africa. In some areas – like British India and Burma – the colonial power was prepared to make limited concessions in the decades after the war to the principle of increasing native political participation. In a historic concession made in 1917 – the so-called Montagu Declaration – the British Government announced:

> The policy of his Majesty's Government… is that of the increasing association of Indians in every branch of the administration and the gradual development of self-governing institutions with a view to the progressive realisation of responsible government in India as an integral part of the British Empire.

Though this fell far short of the expression of any right to self-determination for India, it did open the door to pressure for increasing rights to self-government within the empire. In the Arab region, two states – Egypt and Iraq – were granted independence by Britain during the inter-war period, albeit under the shadow of ultimate British military control. But even in areas where no significant political change was permitted by the European colonial power, aspirations to national self-determination were expressed in print, political organisation and – occasionally – revolutionary action. After 1918, the ideology of nationalism became a global phenomenon.

Nationalism, the nation-state and political stability in inter-war Europe

Within a few years of the conclusion of the First World War, the map of Europe clearly shows that, with the exception of the Soviet Union, Europe entirely consisted of states that defined themselves as nation-states. In the central and eastern part of Europe, Finland, the Baltic states, Poland, Czechoslovakia, Hungary, Austria and Yugoslavia had replaced the former Austrian and Russian Empires. At the south-eastern extremity of Europe, the former core of the Ottoman Empire, the Turkish heartland, had formed itself into a nation-state: the modern Turkey of Kemal Ataturk. In the western-most extremity of Europe, the Irish, whose identity had never been absorbed into a British one, gained their independence in 1921.

Although the nation-state had existed in Europe before this time, what was new was that now the nation-state was seen – in Europe at least – as the primary legitimate form of state. To this extent, therefore, Woodrow Wilson's plan outlined in the Fourteen Points had been realised: a system of states based on the principle of self-determination. Moreover, as the 'Fourteen Points' had prescribed, these states formed themselves into a League of Nations, based at Geneva, which would generally regulate their international relations, mediate in their disputes, and collectively protect its members from aggression. The question, therefore, that needs to be asked is: did this new system of government provide greater international stability than the system that had prevailed in Europe before the First World War?

The answer, of course, is 'No'. Within two decades of the First World War, Europe was again embroiled in a conflict which brought about unimaginable destruction. If we try to analyse some of the reasons why an international system based on self-determination failed to bring stability to Europe, it will give an indication of the general problems inherent in allowing the ideology of nationalism to dominate the political sphere.

However, it must in the first place be conceded that there were other factors than the operation of the national idea that brought instability to Europe in the years 1918-1939. There was, first of all, a general collapse of confidence after the terrible experience of the war in existing political and economic systems, particularly what might be called 'liberal capitalist democracy'. The severe economic dislocations of the 1920s and 1930s – above all the world-wide depression that began in 1929 – gave credibility to authoritarian solutions that might, in one form or another, bring certainty to a destabilised generation. While, on one side, various forms of fascism – essentially an explicitly authoritarian and belligerent variant of nationalism – particularly appealed to those who wished to replace the disintegrated *ancien régime* with a new system of order, the communist ideology of the Soviet Union attracted those who aspired to the creation of a entirely new world of social and economic justice that would transcend national divisions. This undercurrent of ideological confrontation became ever more overt in the late

1920s and 1930s, and affected the politics of the whole of Europe during this period.

The general dominance of the national idea made its own particular contribution to the instabilities of the era. One immediate difficulty was that the peace settlement had not applied the national principle even-handedly in deciding the boundaries of states. As we have already seen, there were, in effect, 'winner' nationalities and 'loser' nationalities. Germany, Austria, Hungary and Russia could be described as loser nationalities; large numbers of their fellow-nationals lay outside their own national territories. Poland, Czechoslovakia, Romania and Yugoslavia, on the other hand, were winner nations. Eastern and Central Europe, therefore, was faced at this time with a massive 'irredentist' problem: that is, the desire of nations to reclaim 'unredeemed' ('irridènti') fellow-nationals lying outside the territories of the nation-state, and the converse desire of fellow-nationals outside 'their' nation-state to be included in its territory. This irridentist problem was made even more acute by the fact that Germany and Russia/the Soviet Union were only temporarily weak. Once Germany in particular regained its national strength, conflict over this issue was only a matter of time.

Another key source of national instability in Central and Eastern Europe has already been alluded to. The ethnic groups of this area were not neatly compartmentalised into separate regions, but were intermingled in a manner that was virtually impossible to disentangle. Nearly all these ethnic groups – even the Jews who, though large in number, had no natural 'homeland' in the area – had national aspirations.[4] However, in the chaotic period at the end of the First World War, it was only the most powerful and the best organised that were able to form nation-states. The inevitable result was that these nation-states had large, discontented minorities. These minorities had their own unfulfilled national aspirations. It could be said, therefore, that the 'primary' nationalism of the successful nationalities that were able to create their own nation-states bred 'secondary' nationalisms, and sometimes even 'tertiary' nationalisms. Like a Russian doll, each successful nation-state contained within its boundaries a number of discontented nationalities aspiring to create their own state.

Even among the 'dominant' nations there arose unexpected tensions, and these tensions give an interesting insight into the whole question of defining national consciousness. In the turmoil of the last years of the war, and in the context of the collapse of the *ancien régime* in Europe, a combination of consent and the force of circumstances pushed ethno-linguistic groups together, even though these ethnic groups may have hitherto lived in separate states. It was thus that the Slovenes, Croats and Bosnians, who had been under Austrian rule, joined their fellow South Slavs, the Serbs, Montenegrins and Macedonians, to form Yugoslavia. It soon became apparent, however, that ethno-linguistic similarities could not compensate for huge differences that had become embedded through centuries of living in different states with completely different cultures, traditions and religions. These divergences of historical experience within ethnic groups were exacerbated by political competition for control of the new states, and led inexorably to separatist aspirations among those groups – the Slovaks in Czechoslovakia as against the more powerful Czechs, or the Croats of Yugoslavia – who found themselves at a political disadvantage in the new states. During the Second World War, Hitler was to take advantage of these political tensions, and set up separate client-states in Slovakia and Croatia.

This situation of national and ethnic tension was made worse by the fact that these new nation-states had been founded specifically to promote the interests of a particular national group. It was hardly likely, therefore, that they would cope easily with the reality of a multi-ethnic population, or that they would treat their minorities as equal citizens. Although the post-war peacemakers anticipated this problem, and inserted provisions protecting the minorities in the various treaties that gave international sanction to the new nation-states, attempts to protect minorities were largely ineffective. The new nation-states were, after all, sovereign entities, and therefore had control of their own internal affairs.[5]

It should also be noted that Woodrow Wilson's hope – along with other 'liberal nationalists' – that nationalities would, once they had achieved their goal of creating a nation-state, be content to stay within the boundaries occupied by their own national group, proved to be incorrect. These new nation-states assumed the task, not just of protecting, but also of promoting the interests of the respective nationalities they represented. And, like the dynastic states before them, nation-states equated territorial expansion with strength, and therefore sought to gain strategically or economically important regions, irrespective of the ethnic composition of these regions. In other words, the new nation-states behaved like traditional states.

All these factors explain the instability and volatility of the situation in Central and Eastern Europe in the inter-war years. A cluster of weak states were wedged between two former great powers – Germany and Russia – whose weakness was only temporary, and whose national recovery was only a matter of time. Both had territorial grievances against the new states that they would sooner or later seek to resolve. On top of this, both Russia/the

Soviet Union and – after 1933 – Germany were driven by inherently expansionist ideologies: communism in the Soviet Union, and national socialism – which ultimately saw international relations as a global struggle for racial supremacy – in the case of Nazi Germany.

The inter-war status quo was finally breached in the late 1930s, when the authority of the League of Nations progressively collapsed and the Western democracies demonstrated their reluctance and, indeed, their inability to protect the new states of Eastern Europe. Between 1939 and 1941, Germany and the Soviet Union effectively partitioned Eastern Europe. In the period 1941-1943, after Hitler's invasion of Russia in 1941, Germany dominated Eastern Europe. Hitler's 'New Order' closely resembled the kind of Eastern Europe that the Germans had tried to impose after the defeat of Russia in the First World War: an enlarged Germany, flanked by a series of client-states. It is noticeable that during this period of dominance Germany was able to exploit to its advantage the many ethnic-national tensions that had emerged in the 1918-1939 period.

With the retreat and eventual defeat of Germany in the period 1943-1945, German control of Eastern Europe was directly replaced by that of the Soviet Union. Czechoslovakia, Hungary, Romania and Yugoslavia roughly resumed – with, however, substantial territorial adjustments in favour of the Soviet Union – their 1938 borders. Poland was pushed westwards: the Soviet Union took a large chunk of what before the war had been eastern Poland; Poland, in compensation, moved its border westward at the expense of Germany. The Second World War unleashed all the ethnic hatreds of the region, and the phenomenon that is now called 'ethnic cleansing' – the forcible removal of ethnic groups from their land – took place on a mass scale.[6]

The Soviet Union's control over Eastern Europe – a control that was ultimately guaranteed by the presence of the Soviet 'Red Army' – lasted until 1989, when the communist regimes of Eastern Europe collapsed. A completely new European order was finally ushered in when the Soviet Union itself – the state that had in effect maintained the Tsarist Empire – collapsed in 1991. It is a testimony to the durability of the nationalist idea that, at the end of the twentieth century, the nation-state dominates Europe as never before. The idea that every nationality should have its own state has led to the resurrection or creation of a whole range of new states: Lithuania, Latvia, Estonia, Slovakia, Slovenia, Croatia, Bosnia, Macedonia, Belarus, Ukraine and Moldova; not to mention the complex situation in the Caucasus and Central Asia. The experience of Bosnia, however, or indeed that of

Georgia, Armenia and Azherbaijan in the Caucasus, shows that the problems of defining nationality remain as intractable as they were in the years 1918-1939. The nationality issue remains the principle threat to the future stability of Europe.

After 1945, the nation-state became a global phenomenon. Just as the First World War caused the collapse of the European empires within Europe, so the Second World War did the same – eventually – for the European empires beyond Europe: Italian, British, French, Dutch, Belgian and Portuguese. After 1945, the nationalist movements that had begun to form after the conclusion of the First World War were eventually able to form their nation-states on the ruins of these empires. It is surely one of history's ironies, however, that the essentially anti-European nationalist movements of Asia and Africa adopted a European-based ideology – nationalism – and defined their nation-states on the basis of what were quite often the arbitrary boundaries imposed by the colonial powers when they established their empires. Indeed, the colonial boundaries inherited by the new nation-states beyond Europe have remained mostly – and remarkably – intact, and have in many areas probably made a major contribution to global stability.

Documents

(Nb: in all the following extracts, editorial comments at the beginning of texts, or amendments and explanations in the texts themselves, will be placed in square brackets. Headings and subdivisions will be put in italics.)

1 – Woodrow Wilson and the Fourteen Points

[In April 1917, the United States entered the First World War on the side of the Allies, France and Great Britain. In January 1918, President Woodrow Wilson outlined his Fourteen Points, which he saw as the necessary basis for a 'just and lasting' peace once the war had been won.]

1   Open covenants of peace, openly arrived at, after which there shall be no private international understandings of any kind but diplomacy shall proceed always frankly and in the public view.

2   [Freedom of the seas, except by international agreement.]

3   [Freedom of trade, so far as international conditions permit.]

4   [Reduction of armaments 'consistent with domestic safety'.]

5   A free, open-minded, and absolutely impartial adjustment of all colonial claims, based upon a strict observance of the principle that in determining all such questions of sovereignty the interests of the populations concerned must have equal weight with the equitable claims of the government whose title is to be determined.

6   The evacuation of all Russian territory and such a settlement of all questions affecting Russia as will secure the best and freest cooperation of the other nations of the world in obtaining for her an unhampered and unembarrassed opportunity for the independent determination of her own political development and national policy, and assure her of a sincere welcome into the society of free nations under institutions of her own choosing: and, more than a welcome, assistance also of every kind that she may need and may herself desire. The treatment accorded Russia by her sister nations in the months to come will be the acid test of their good will, of their comprehension of her needs as distinguished from their own interests, and of their intelligent and unselfish sympathy.

7   Belgium, the whole world will agree, must be evacuated and restored, without any attempt to limit the sovereignty which she enjoys in

common with all other free nations. No other single act will serve as this will serve to restore confidence among the nations in the laws which they have themselves set and determined for the government of their relations with one another. Without this healing act the whole structure and validity of international law is forever impaired.

8   All French territory should be freed and the invaded portions restored, and the wrong done to France by Prussia in 1871 in the matter of Alsace-Lorraine, which has unsettled the peace of the world for nearly fifty years, should be righted, in order that peace may once more be made secure in the interest of all.

9   A readjustment of the frontiers of Italy should be effected along clearly recognisable lines of nationality.

10   The peoples of the Austrian Empire, whose place among the nations we wish to see safeguarded and assured, should be accorded the freest opportunity of autonomous development.

11   Romania, Serbia, and Montenegro should be evacuated [by Germany and the Austrian Empire]: occupied territories restored; Serbia accorded free and secure access to the sea; and the relations of the several Balkan states to one another determined by friendly counsel along historically established lines of allegiance and nationality; and international guarantees of the political and economic independence and territorial integrity of the several Balkan states should be entered into.

12   The Turkish portions of the present Ottoman Empire should be assured a secure sovereignty, but the other nationalities which are now under Turkish rule should be assured an undoubted security of life and an absolutely unmolested opportunity of autonomous development...

13   An independent Polish state should be erected which should include the territories inhabited by undisputably Polish populations, which should be assured a free and secure access to the sea, and whose political and economic independence and territorial integrity should be guaranteed by international covenant.

14   A general association of nations must be formed under specific covenants for the purpose of affording mutual guarantees of political independence and territorial integrity to great and small states alike.

[From House Documents, 65th Congress, 2nd Session, vol. CXIII, Document No. 765, pp 3-7]

2 – The League of Nations and the 'Mandate' system for the former German and Ottoman Empires: limitations on the principle of 'self-determination'

[Most of the 'Covenant' of the League of Nations, formulated in 1919, deals with the structure of the League of Nations, with its Assembly and its Council, the objectives of the League in preventing and adjudicating international disputes, and the mechanisms that will enable it effectively to police international affairs. Article 22, however, dealt specifically with the question of the treatment of the colonial (ie Asian and African) territories of Germany and the Ottoman Empire.]

To those colonies and territories which as a consequence of the late war have ceased to be under the sovereignty of the States which formerly governed them, and which are inhabited by peoples not yet able to stand by themselves under the strenuous conditions of the modern world, there should be applied the principle that the well-being and development of such peoples form a sacred trust of civilisation, and that securities for the performance of this trust should be embodied in this Covenant.

The best method of giving practical effect to this principle is that the tutelage of such peoples should be entrusted to advanced nations who, by reason of their resources, their experience, or their geographical position, can best undertake this responsibility, and who are willing to accept it, and that this tutelage should be exercised by them as Mandatories on behalf of the League.

The character of the Mandate must differ according to the stage of development of the people, the geographical situation of the territory, its economic conditions and other similar circumstances.

Certain communities formerly belonging to the Turkish [Ottoman] Empire have reached a stage of development where their existence as independent nations can be provisionally recognised subject to the rendering of administrative advice and assistance by a Mandatory until such time as they are able to stand alone. The wishes of these communities must be a principal consideration of the Mandatory.

Other peoples, especially those of [formerly German] Central Africa, are at such a stage that the Mandatory must be responsible for the administration of the territory under conditions which will guarantee freedom of conscience and religion, subject only to the maintenance of public order and morals, the prohibition of abuses such as the slave trade, the arms traffic, and the liquor traffic, and the prevention of the establishment of fortifications or military and naval bases, and of military training of the natives for other than police purposes and the defence of territory, and will also secure equal opportunities for the trade and commerce of other Members of the League.

There are territories, such as [formerly German] South-West Africa and certain of the South Pacific Islands which, owing to the sparseness of their population, or their small size, or their remoteness from the centres of civilisation, or their geographical contiguity to the territory of the Mandatory, and other circumstances, can be best administered under the laws of the Mandatory as integral portions of its territory, subject to the safeguards above mentioned in the interests of the indigenous population.

In every case of Mandate, the Mandatory shall render to the Council [of the League of Nations] an annual report in reference to the territory committed to its charge.

The degree of authority, control, or administration to be exercised by the Mandatory shall, if not previously agreed upon by the members of the League, be explicitly defined in each case by the Council.

A permanent Commission shall be constituted to receive and examine the annual reports of the Mandatories and to advise the Council on all matters relating to the observance of the Mandates.

[From Parliamentary Papers, Cmd 2300, September 1924, published by HMSO]

3 – Maps showing territorial changes in Europe in the nineteenth and
   twentieth centuries

Map 1: Europe after 1815

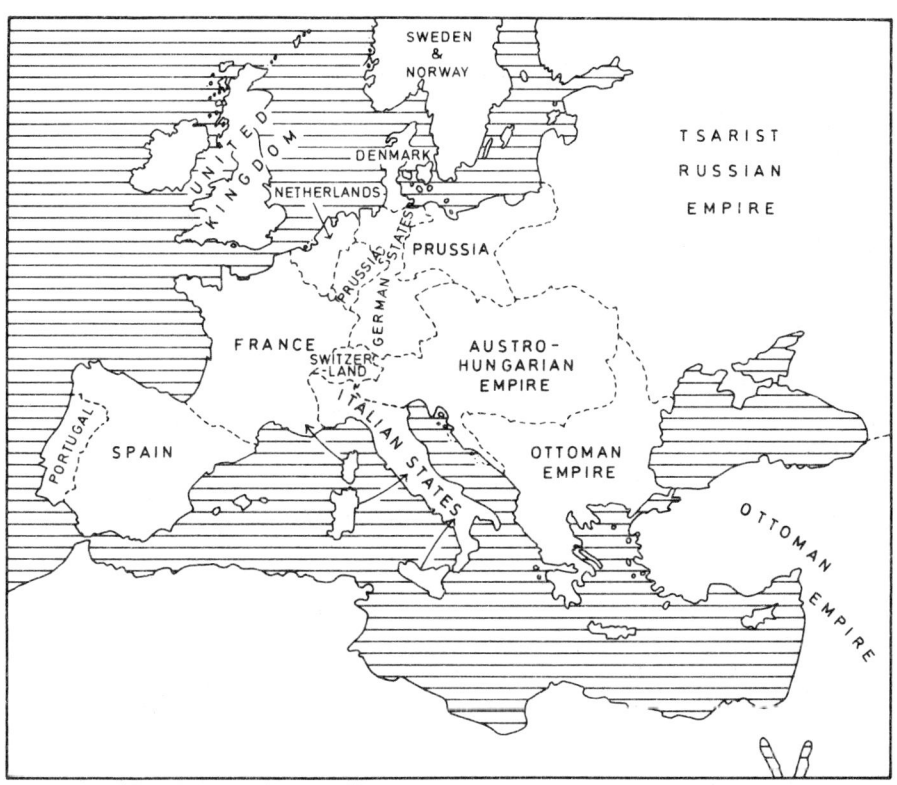

Map 2: Europe in 1914

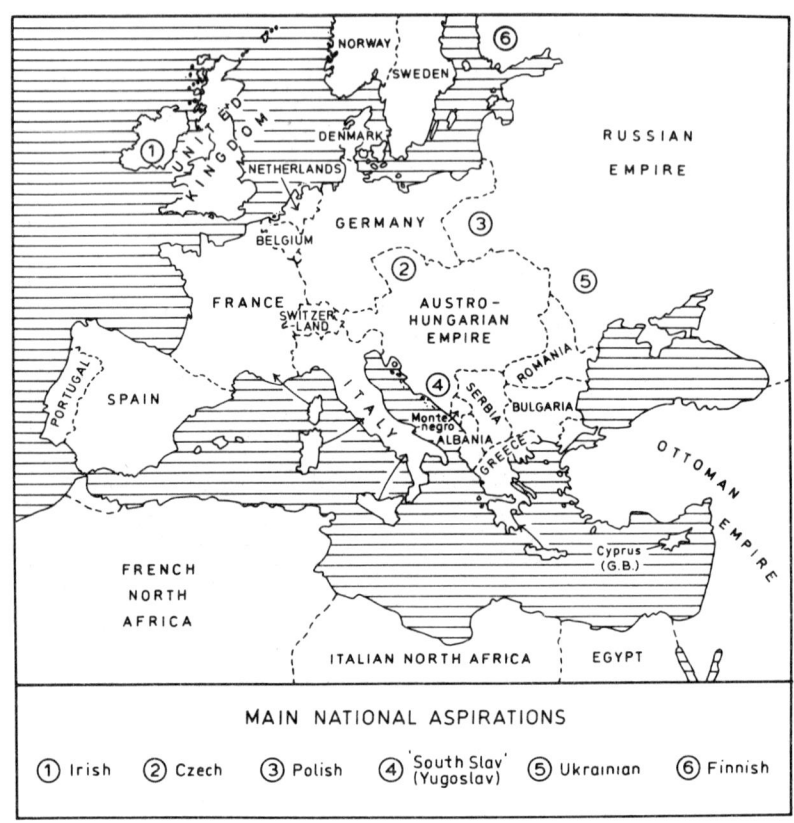

MAIN NATIONAL ASPIRATIONS

① Irish   ② Czech   ③ Polish   ④ 'South Slav' (Yugoslav)   ⑤ Ukrainian   ⑥ Finnish

Map 3: Europe between World War I and World War II

MAIN TERRITORIAL DISPUTES

① Ireland/Britain (Northern Ireland)

② France/Germany (Alsace-Lorraine)

③ Austria/Italy (Tyrol)

④ Italy/Yugoslavia (Istria)

⑤ Germany/Czechoslovakia (Sudetenland)

⑥ Germany/Poland (East Poland)

⑦ Soviet Union/Poland (Western Poland)

⑧ Hungary/Romania (Transylvania)

⑨ Soviet Union/Romania (Bessarabia)

Map 4: Europe after World War II

NEW NATIONS CREATED AFTER COLLAPSE OF
SOVIET UNION AND COMMUNISM (1989 – 1991)

① United Germany   ④ Lithuania   ⑦ Moldova   ⑩ Croatia

② Estonia   ⑤ Belarus   ⑧ Slovakia   ⑪ Bosnia

③ Latvia   ⑥ Ukraine   ⑨ Slovenia   ⑫ Macedonia

NOTES ON CHAPTER 4

1   Albania, a Muslim enclave in the Balkans, emerged as an independent state almost by default in 1913.

2   See chapters 8 and 9. For the British offer of 1915, see Walter Laqueur and Barry Rubin (eds), *The Israel-Arab Reader: A Documentary History of the Middle East Conflict* (London, Penguin Books, 1987), pp 15-17.

3   For a vivid sense of the uncertain atmosphere of these days in Eastern Europe, see Mikhail A. Bulgakov's *The White Guard* (1925), describing the civil war in the Ukraine; and Gregor von Rezzori's *Memoirs of an Anti-Semite* (translated in 1981), describing life in the multi-ethnic province of Bukovina.

4   See chapter 8.

5   See the classic work by C.A. Macartney, *National States and National Minorities* (London, Oxford University Press, 1934), and H.W.V. Temperley (ed.), *A History of the Peace Conference of Paris*, volume V: *Economic Reconstruction and Protection of Minorities* (London, Henry Frowde and Hodder and Stoughton, 1921).

6   As did genocide, or the extermination of an entire ethnic group. See chapters 6 and 7.

Chapter 5

Problems of National Consciousness and Self-Determination: the Case of Ireland

That awful colour problem of the Orange and the Green

from an Ulster song

Ireland provides a useful example of the complexities of defining a national identity. Although it is extremely dangerous to try to constrain the unique history of a country within the straitjacket of some invented model, it is nevertheless the case that a study of nationalism in Ireland – brief though it inevitably must be – will help illuminate many of the points made in the previous chapter. It will demonstrate the importance of the period before, during and after the First World War as a pivotal turning-point in the history of the national idea in Europe. It also shows how the crystallisation of a primary national identity – Catholic, Celtic, Gaelic-speaking Irish nationalism – stimulated a secondary nationalism: the British identity of the Protestants of the province of Ulster. It reveals, furthermore, the problematic relationship between religion and identity, and the way that religion should be seen, not just as a matter of faith, but as a badge of identity. And, finally, it is a useful case-study of the phenomenon of irredentism, or the desire of a minority to be united with their fellow-nationals in another state.

From the twelfth century to the beginning of the twentieth century, Ireland's history was dominated by the attempt, first by the Norman-English state, and then by the Anglo-Scottish ('British') state, to incorporate within its realm the Celtic, Gaelic-speaking people of the island of Ireland.[1] In the sixteenth and seventeenth centuries, the Tudor and Stuart dynasties and the Commonwealth government of Oliver Cromwell resorted to a policy of colonisation or 'plantation' – the granting of land to English and Scottish settlers – as a means of ensuring the 'pacification' of the island. These 'loyal' plantations, however, did not have a sufficient critical mass of numbers and, with a few small exceptions, did not take root in the central, western and southern parts of Ireland. All that was established in these places, in fact, was a thinly-spread, often absentee, land-owning and governing class that was divorced from the native population in terms of culture, language and – given the fact that the native Irish population did not convert to Protestantism – religion. The only place where a successful settlement was established, with substantial landowners and a large Anglo-Scottish peasantry, was the Protestant colony in the north-eastern province of Ulster. It is from 1603, the date of the establishment of this colony, that the origins of the key dilemma of modern Irish national identity can be traced.

Throughout the seventeenth and eighteenth centuries, in fact, Ireland resisted the thoroughgoing nation-building project that was taking place in Britain. Because of this, its religious unassimilability, and the fact that it assumed a strategic importance in the civil conflicts of Britain, Ireland was therefore perceived in the seventeenth century as a serious threat to the stability of the British state. Through the later seventeenth and eighteenth centuries, severe 'penal laws' were directed against Catholics, both against the practice of religion, and in whole areas of education, land-ownership and employment. This had one effect that was to be reinforced by the 'modernising' climate of the nineteenth century: the increasing marginalisation of Gaelic language and culture. This was the era of the so-called Protestant Ascendancy.

By the late eighteenth century, however, Ireland posed a different kind of threat to Britain. As the heat generated by divisive religious and dynastic issues gradually receded in the eighteenth century, a distinctly Anglo-Irish identity began to emerge among the educated classes of the towns of eastern Ireland in particular, mainly settler Protestant in origin, but also containing a growing number of educated urban Catholics. The Irish parliament in Dublin, despite being dominated by the Protestant Ascendancy class of Ireland, and with limited powers in relation to London, came to symbolise in the late eighteenth century the growing sense of Ireland's difference and disadvantage in relation to Britain. In many senses, the discontents of this Anglo-Irish political class were an echo of the confrontation in America between the colonists there and the British state. As in the case of the American colonies, a demand for political rights was linked to the assertion of a separate national identity. This political ferment in Ireland was stimulated

by the added example of the French Revolution, and the French themselves tried to exploit Irish unrest in the revolutionary and Napoleonic wars
against Britain.

This period of revolutionary unrest and intermittent rebellion – with
which the names of Wolfe Tone and Robert Emmet are particularly linked –
has had a symbolic importance in the 'iconography' of subsequent Irish
nationalism, because the leadership was Protestant, and therefore suggested
that an inclusive nationalism that linked Catholic and settler Protestant was
possible. In practice, the revolutionary activity of this period stimulated
religious (or sectarian) conflict between local Protestant and Catholic communities – particularly in Ulster – quite as much as confrontation with
Britain.[2] The British Government, however, was bound to see this unrest as
both a revolutionary threat and a threat to national security. In 1800, therefore, in a new attempt to draw Ireland fully into the British state, an Act of
Union merged Ireland into the parliament at Westminster.

The parliamentary union between Britain and Ireland ushered in the era
of modern Irish nationalism. Prohibitions on Catholic participation in
public life – already substantially whittled away – were ended with the
Emancipation Act of 1829. Subsequently, in Ireland as in Britain, rights to
vote were expanded throughout the nineteenth century to ever wider sections
of the population. These developments enabled the Catholic population of
Ireland to enter into mass politics, and their national aspirations found an
effective voice in the Irish Parliamentary Party at Westminster, headed by the
legendary figure of Charles Stuart Parnell (1846-1891). First and foremost
among its political goals was the restoration of an Irish parliament, but this
time with real political power: the demand for 'home rule', as it was called.

The failure of Parnell and the Irish Parliamentary Party to achieve home
rule through constitutional means in the period 1880-1893 gave greater
prominence to other strands of Irish nationalism: cultural nationalism and
revolutionary nationalism. Violent, secret-society activity had long been a
tradition in Ireland. In the mid-to-late nineteenth century, Irish revolutionary
nationalist organisations spread through Irish communities in the United
States and Britain, as well as in Ireland itself; particularly significant was the
Irish Republican Brotherhood formed in 1858. In the cultural field, various
organisations emerged at this time that were dedicated to the retrieval of
Gaelic cultural traditions, language and literature. This Gaelic culture and
literature had been marginalised almost to vanishing-point by discrimination,
mass evictions from the countryside, the emergence of a modern society and
economy and – not least – by the terrible effects of the potato famine of

1846-1847, and subsequent mass emigration. Most prominent among these cultural nationalist organisations was the Gaelic League, formed in 1893.

Centre-stage in nationalist politics was regained by the Irish Parliamentary Party, however, when the Liberal government in Britain introduced a new Home Rule Bill in 1912. This plan for Irish self-government was, however, challenged by the full force of the Ulster Protestant community. Ever since the foundation of the Ulster plantation in 1603, there had been a long if intermittent tradition of violent confrontation between the local Protestant and Catholic communities. With the creation in the nineteenth century of a mass, Catholic-dominated nationalist movement with the aim of achieving Irish self-government, along with the evocation through cultural nationalism of an Ireland that was essentially defined as ethnically Celtic, Gaelic-speaking and Catholic, it was inevitable that there would be a response in Protestant Ulster. As Ireland seemed inexorably to be moving towards home rule in the period 1912-1914, the Ulster Protestants responded with a mass protest campaign and the creation of an armed force and a shadow government to prevent 'Dublin rule' being imposed on them.

The outbreak in 1914 of the First World War prevented what would otherwise have been a full-scale conflict between the forces of Irish nationalism and those of Ulster Protestant 'Unionism' or 'Loyalism', determined to maintain the link with Britain. With the suspension of political negotiations during the war, the initiative passed once again to the revolutionary nationalists. In Easter 1916, a group of Irish Republican militants, dominated by members of the Irish Republican Brotherhood and headed by the teacher-poet Padraic Pearse, staged an armed uprising in Dublin and declared the creation of an Irish Republic (see document 1 at the end of the chapter). This act of 'propaganda by the deed' could not hope to succeed, and did not initially command public support; but the disproportionate severity of the British response to the rebellion inflamed all the old resentments against British rule, and created patriotic martyrs out of the rebel leaders.

The rebellion of 1916 changed the course of Irish nationalism. At the end of the war, the *impasse* between the Irish nationalist demand for the self-government of a united Ireland, and the determination of the Ulster Protestants to retain the British link remained as unresolved as ever, and was indeed unresolvable within the context of a united Ireland. A hitherto obscure Irish nationalist organisation, Sinn Féin ('Ourselves' or 'Ourselves Alone'), formed itself into a mass organisation in 1917, with the objective simply of proclaiming an independent state, rather than negotiating for self-government with the British parliament. In the British parliamentary elections

of December 1918, Sinn Féin won a crushing majority of seats in the whole
of Ireland except Ulster, thereby illustrating the fundamental divide between
the two Irelands (see document 2 at the end of the chapter). In 1919, the
newly-elected Sinn Féin members of parliament set up their own parliament
in Dublin, the Dail Eireann, and proceeded to administer Ireland as a *de facto*
self-governing republic.

The stage was now set for a two-level confrontation: between the self-
proclaimed Irish Republic in Dublin and the British Government; and
between Irish nationalism and the Ulster Protestants in the north. In 1920,
the British Government – in a move that has been seen by some as a deliberate attempt to sabotage Irish nationalism, by others as a simple recognition
of the logic of the division between two Irelands – created a separate parliament (the so-called Stormont parliament) for what was now officially called
Northern Ireland, made up of six of the nine counties of Ulster. It should be
noted that this was initially regarded as a temporary expedient, pending some
overall agreement between the British government, the Republic in the
south, and the Protestants of Northern Ireland. This Stormont parliament
was to be self-governing in local matters, but subordinate to the British
Parliament in Westminster.

Meanwhile, in the south, an increasingly bloody conflict was fought out
between the forces of the crown and those of the Republic. By 1921, a state
of mutual exhaustion had been reached, and negotiations began between the
two sides. The subsequent Anglo-Irish Treaty of 1921 gave southern Ireland
the substance of independence as the renamed Irish Free State; in return,
however, this Free State had to accept a 'dominion' status within the British
Empire equivalent to that of Canada, which in effect meant that, while it was
self-governing, it still owed allegiance to the British monarch as head of state.
In addition, the free state leaders acquiesced in the right of Northern Ireland
to maintain its separate status if it so wished, and a commission was appointed
to demarcate a mutually-acceptable boundary between Northern Ireland and
the Irish Free State. The recommendations of this boundary commission were
not, however, implemented, and the 'six counties' remained the boundary
between Northern Ireland and the Irish Free State: an arrangement that left
large numbers of Catholics within Northern Ireland, and a significant number
of Protestants within the Irish Free State.

There then followed a particularly bloody civil war in the free state (1922-
1923) between pro- and anti-Treaty forces. The main dispute was not, it
should be noted, over the partition of Ireland, but over the issue of allegiance
to the British crown. Though the pro-Treaty leadership prevailed, this war

left a long legacy of bitterness. In particular, it nurtured among the losing side the 'republican' myth that lies at the heart of the political agenda of the Provisional Irish Republican Army (IRA) and Provisional Sinn Féin to this day: the notion that the only legitimate Irish state was the republic proclaimed by the 1916 rising and installed in 1919, a completely sovereign all-Ireland (32 county) republic. Till the work of 1916 was completed by means of the 'armed struggle' against Britain, no state in Ireland – north or south – could be regarded as legitimate. It has been, and to a degree still is, a potent myth.

Ever since 1921, all Irish nationalists have aspired to unify Ireland: the difference has been over the question of means, not ends. All hopes for unity, however, have foundered on the bed-rock of the determination of the Ulster Protestants to stay outside the Irish state. Though attempts have been made, particularly by the nationalists of the republican tradition, to paint the Ulster Protestants as a colonial remnant – similar to the white settlers in former Rhodesia (now Zimbabwe), Kenya or French Algeria – who must either bow to the national will for unity or leave, this view ignores the sheer length of time that the Ulster Protestant community has been settled in Ireland. Outside the republican camp, there is a general if reluctant acceptance that nearly 400 years of settlement in Ulster has created a community with deep roots and a separate identity.

There has been much debate as to whether it is possible to talk of an Ulster Protestant 'nationalism'. The issue of the national identity of the Ulster Protestants has been confused by the fact that their principle political aspiration has been and still is to remain linked to a British identity and a British state, and that this aspiration has been termed 'loyalism' or 'unionism' rather than nationalism. Nomenclature does not, however, alter the fact that there is in Ireland a confrontation between two separate national identities: a classic case, in fact, of a 'primary' nationalism activating a 'secondary' nationalism.

The twin questions of the link with Britain and that of unity dogged Ireland after 1921. The aspiration to unite all the 32 counties of Ireland (including, that is, the six counties comprising Northern Ireland) remained absolutely central in southern Irish politics. Indeed, it was embodied in the Irish constitution of 1937: article 2 declared that 'The national territory consists of the whole island of Ireland, its islands and territorial seas'; and article 3 reserved the right of the Irish Government to exercise its authority over the whole of Ireland. At the same time, paradoxically, the other main aspirations – to create a sovereign state completely separate from Britain (article 1 of the Irish Constitution), and to retrieve Ireland's lost cultural identity – worked against the objective of unity. Eamon de Valera, who headed the Irish government before and during the Second World War, made particular efforts to resuscitate Ireland's distinctive identity (see document 3 at the end of this chapter). The very things that he emphasised, however – the Catholic religion, the Gaelic language and the traditional Irish way of life – reinforced what might be called the 'alien-ness' and outside status of the Ulster Protestants. When, in 1948-1949, southern Ireland declared itself a republic and broke all residual constitutional links with Britain and the British Commonwealth, any remaining chances of negotiating some kind of 'umbrella' agreement for Ireland that would satisfy Irish and Ulster Protestant national aspirations within a loose framework of unity was lost. In 1949, Northern Ireland effectively had its right to self-determination guaranteed when the British government agreed that its status could not be changed without its consent.

1949 did not solve the issue of unity and national identity in Ireland, however, for the simple reason that there was – and is – in Northern Ireland a very sizeable minority of Catholics (see document 1 at the end of this chapter). Like most states formed on a national principle – in this case resistance to Irish nationalism – the Protestant-dominated mini-state of Northern Ireland did not treat this minority well.[3] From 1968, a campaign to assert the civil rights of this Catholic minority largely achieved its aims after a prolonged and bitter campaign. This campaign for civil rights rapidly slid, however, into a wider campaign for outright Irish unity (the Sinn Féin/republican position) or, at the very least, a substantial redefinition of the relationship between the two Irelands that would take into account the national aspirations of the Catholics in Northern Ireland (the 'nationalist' position of the Social Democratic and Labour Party, or SDLP).

While on the whole the Ulster Protestant leadership (mainly the Ulster Unionist Party) have reluctantly accepted the idea of a restructuring of government within Northern Ireland that would allow the Catholic minority greater participation in the government of Northern Ireland ('power-sharing'), they have resisted all attempts to redefine the relationship between Britain and Northern Ireland, or Northern Ireland and the Irish Republic. It has always been a core belief of the Ulster Protestants that any such process of redefinition would open the door to an irresistible slide towards a united Ireland.

At the higher levels of relations between Britain and Ireland, there has been at least a degree of consensus. Both the Anglo-Irish Agreement of 1985 and the 'Framework Document' for inter-party negotiations set out in 1994 emphasise that any settlement to the problem of Northern Ireland must be based on the principle of the right of the people of Northern Ireland to self-determination: the right, that is, for Northern Ireland to remain in the United Kingdom so long as a majority so wishes. The consensus position of both governments is the hope that, under the protection of this guarantee, a power-sharing political structure can be created in Northern Ireland that would ensure proportionate Catholic participation in government, and that there can be a process of increased constitutional links and cooperation between the two Irelands. The Irish Government's acquiescence in the notion of Northern Ireland's right to self-determination is possibly to a degree based on the expectation that the rising Catholic proportion of the population in Northern Ireland, coupled with growing connections between the north and south, will eventually lead to a peaceful unification by consent.

Any student of the phenomenon of nationalism would be bound to regard these well-meaning hopes with caution. The persistence of the 'troubles' since 1968 precisely reflects the fact that the Catholic minority in Northern Ireland has not accepted the verdict of the Protestant majority. Is there any more likelihood that a future Protestant minority would accept the verdict of a Catholic majority? Since 1600, Ulster has seen a violent 'turf-war' between two communities and two identities. This turf-war intensified in the period before, during, and after the First World War, and has done so again in the present troubles. The main protagonists in this turf-war are the Protestant 'paramilitaries' (mainly the Ulster Defence Association, or UDA, and the Ulster Volunteer Force, or UVF) and the Catholic paramilitaries (principally the Provisional IRA); the main characteristics of this bitter confrontation are murder, arson, intimidation, and local 'ethnic-cleansing'. That this turf-war has not reached the level of the ethnic wars in the Balkans and the Caucasus is almost certainly not due to any greater inherent moderation in Ireland, but to the ubiquitous British security and police presence.

The whole problem of Ulster begins and ends with the fundamental difference of national identity between the two communities in Northern Ireland. This conflict has variously been described as sectarian, religious, or as a conflict between two 'traditions'. At the heart, however, it is a conflict of national identity and loyalty between two communities that live apart but share the same territory. In such a situation, democracy or popular sovereignty cannot operate in the normal way, any more than it has done in Bosnia since the breakdown of Yugoslavia. Political alignments in a Northern Ireland or a Bosnia are overwhelmingly based simply on allegiances of identity:

Protestants vote for Protestant parties, Catholics vote for Catholic parties. In such circumstances, democracy becomes demography, and the key determinant of politics becomes the population census. The community with the greatest number will impose its national will on the other community.

A solution, therefore, requires a redefinition of the concept of national sovereignty and a redefinition of the concept of popular sovereignty. Possible solutions along these lines might well involve the imposition of some form of permanent Irish-British joint sovereignty over Northern Ireland, and an agreement that this status could not be changed unless a majority of both communities wished it. Political structures – along the lines of the so-called 'consociational' model – would then have to be put in place in Northern Ireland that would guarantee equal rights and political participation between two co-existing but separate communities.

Unfortunately, such a solution flies in the face of the absolute global dominance of the concept of national sovereignty. The alternatives are, however, bleak. These might involve a separation of the two communities – supervised or unsupervised – into 'coherent' areas, and repartition. If, on the other hand, a united Ireland was in any way imposed on the Ulster Protestants against their will, then the likelihood is that decades of Catholic armed struggle against the British state would simply be replaced by future decades of Protestant armed struggle against the Irish state.

Documents

(Nb: in all the following extracts, editorial comments at the beginning of texts, or amendments and explanations in the texts themselves, will be placed in square brackets. Headings and subdivisions will be put in italics.)

1 – Padraic Pearse and the Republican tradition

[Padraic Pearse was the main inspiration behind, and the leader of, the Easter Rising of 1916: he was executed by the British after the collapse of the insurrection. In many ways Pearse – teacher, writer, poet and nationalist revolutionary – was a classic example of that familiar figure in nineteenth-century European nationalism, the romantic nationalist. The romantic qualities in his nationalism are illustrated in the extracts below from an essay, entitled 'Ghosts', that he wrote in December 1915, shortly before the Easter Rising. It also illustrates what might be described as a sentimental version of Irish nationalism: that is, the obvious divisions of identity within Ireland are not addressed by Padraic Pearse, but are simply by-passed in his evocation of an 'ideal' nation which can be forged out of the example of struggle by past generations, and an iron exercise of will by the present generation. What Pearse and others of the republican tradition most deprecated was the attempt just before the First World War of the Irish Parliamentary Party and other moderates to try to reach a negotiated settlement with the British Government, rather than simply demand separation from Britain, pure and simple. This latter position has remained a key tenet of the Republican tradition.

The proclamation of the Irish Republic encapsulates this romantic and sentimental vision of a united Irish people, and the republican notion that this nation can only be resuscitated by uncompromising armed struggle, not by negotiation with the British.

The names referred to in the following passage by Padraic Pearse are those of Irish-language writers.]

'Ghosts'

['The ghosts of a nation sometimes ask very big things: and they must be appeased, whatever the cost...']

Like a divine religion, national freedom bears the marks of unity, of sanctity, of catholicity, of apostolic succession. Of unity, for it contemplates the nation as one; of sanctity, for it is holy in itself and in those who serve it; of catholicity, for it embraces all the men and women of the nation; of apostolic succession, for it, or the aspiration after it, passes down from generation to generation from the nation's fathers. A nation's fundamental idea of freedom is not affected by the accidents of time and circumstance. It does not vary with the centuries, or with the comings and goings of men or of empires. The substance of truth does not change, nor does the substance of freedom. Yesterday's definition of both the one and the other is today's definition and will be tomorrow's. As the body of truth which a true church teaches can neither be increased nor diminished – though truths implicit in the first definition may be made explicit in later definitions – so a true definition of freedom remains constant; it cannot be added to or subtracted from or varied in its essentials... If the definition can be varied in its essentials, or added to, or subtracted from, it was not a true definition in the first instance...

The Irish mind is the clearest mind that has ever applied itself to the consideration of nationality and of national freedom. A chance phrase of Keating's might almost stand as a definition. He spoke of Ireland as 'domhan beag innti féin,' a little world in herself. It was characteristic of Irish-speaking men that when they thought of the Irish nation they thought less of its outer forms and pomps than of the inner thing which was its soul. They recognised that the Irish life was the thing that mattered, and that, the Irish life dead, the Irish nation was dead. But they recognised that freedom was the essential condition of a vigorous Irish life. And for freedom they raised their ranns; for freedom they stood in battle through five bloody centuries...

Irish nationalism is an ancient spiritual tradition, one of the oldest and most august traditions of the world. Politically, Ireland's claim has been for freedom in order to [achieve] the full and perpetual life of that tradition. The generations of Ireland have gone into battle for no other thing. To the Irish mind for more than 1,000 years freedom has had but one definition. It has meant not a limited freedom, a freedom conditioned by the interests of another nation, a freedom compatible with the suzerain authority of a foreign parliament, but absolute freedom, the sovereign control of its destinies. It has meant not the freedom of a class, but the freedom of a people. It has meant not the freedom of a geographical fragment of Ireland, but the freedom of all Ireland...

And the freedom thus defined has seemed to the Irish the most desirable of all earthly things. They have valued it more than land, more than wealth, more than ease, more than empire.

[As] Angus Mac Daighre O'Daly [wrote], 'Better to be on the tops of the old bens keeping watch, short of sleep yet gladsome, urging fight against the foreign soldiery that hold your fathers' land'. And Fearflatha O'Gnive spoke for the generations that preferred exile to slavery: 'If thou has consented (O God) that there be a new England named Ireland, to be ever in the grip of a foe, then to this isle we must bid farewell'.

I make the contention that the national demand of Ireland is fixed and determined; that the demand has been made by every generation; that we of this generation receive it as a trust from our fathers; that we are bound by it; that we have not the right to alter it or abate it by one jot or tittle; and that any undertaking made in the name of Ireland to accept in full satisfaction of Ireland's claim anything less than the generations of Ireland have stood for is null and void, binding on Ireland neither by the law of God nor by the law of nations.

A nation can bind itself by treaty to do or to forego specific things, as a man can bind himself by contract; but no treaty which places a nation's body and soul in the power of another nation, no treaty which abnegates a nation's nationhood, is binding on that nation, any more than a contract of perpetual slavery is binding on an individual. If in a drunken frolic or in mere abject unmanliness I sell myself and my posterity to a slaveholder to have and to hold as a chattel property to himself and his heirs, am I bound by the contract? Are my children bound by it? Can any legal contract make a wrong thing binding? And if not, can a contract executed in my name, but without my express or implied authority, make a wrong thing binding on me and on my children's children?

Ireland's historic claim is for Separation. Ireland has authorised no man to abate that claim. The man who, in the name of Ireland, accepts as 'a final settlement' anything less by one fraction of an iota than Separation from England will be repudiated by the new generation as surely as O'Connell [the parliamentary nationalist of the early nineteenth century] was repudiated by the generation that came after him...

[From Padraic Pearse, *Collected Works: Political Writings and Speeches* (Dublin, Maunsel and Roberts Ltd, 1922), pp 226-232]

The Proclamation of the Irish Republic, 24 April 1916

The Provisional Government of the Irish Republic to the People of Ireland

Irishmen and Irishwomen: in the name of God and of the dead generations
from which she receives her old tradition of nationhood, Ireland, through us,
summons her children to her flag and strikes for her freedom.

Having organised and trained her manhood through her secret revolutionary organisation, the Irish Republican Brotherhood, and through her
open military organisations, the Irish Volunteers and the Irish Citizen Army,
having patiently perfected her discipline, having resolutely waited for the
right moment to reveal itself, she now seizes that moment and, supported by
her exiled children in America and by gallant allies in Europe, but relying in
the first on her own strength, she strikes in full confidence of victory.

We declare the right of the people of Ireland to the ownership of Ireland,
and to the unfettered control of Irish destinies, to be sovereign and inde-
feasible. The long usurpation of that right by a foreign people and government
has not extinguished the right, nor can it ever be extinguished except by the
destruction of the Irish people. In every generation the Irish people have
asserted their right to national freedom and sovereignty; six times during the
past 300 years they have asserted it in arms. Standing on that fundamental
right and again asserting it in arms in the face of the world, we hereby pro-
claim the Irish Republic as a sovereign independent state, and we pledge our
lives and the lives of our comrades-in-arms to the cause of its freedom, of its
welfare, and of its exaltation among the nations.

The Irish Republic is entitled to, and hereby claims, the allegiance of
every Irishman and Irishwoman. The Republic guarantees religious and civil
liberty, equal rights and equal opportunities to all its citizens, and declares its
resolve to pursue the happiness and prosperity of the whole nation and of all
its parts, cherishing all the children of the nation equally, and oblivious of all
the differences carefully fostered by an alien government, which have divided
a minority from the majority in the past.

Until our arms have brought the opportune moment for the establishment of a permanent national government, representative of the whole people
of Ireland, and elected by the suffrages of all her men and women, the
Provisional Government, hereby constituted, will administer the civil and
military affairs of the Republic in trust for the people. We place the cause
of the Irish Republic under the protection of the Most High God, whose
blessing we invoke upon our arms, and we pray that no-one who serves the

cause will dishonour it by cowardice, inhumanity or rapine. In this supreme hour the Irish Nation must, by its valour and discipline, and by the readiness of its children to sacrifice themselves for the common good, prove itself worthy of the august destiny to which it is called.

2 – Democracy, demography and national identity: the demographic basis of the 'two Irelands' 1918-1920

Map 5: Political map of Ireland, 1920-present day

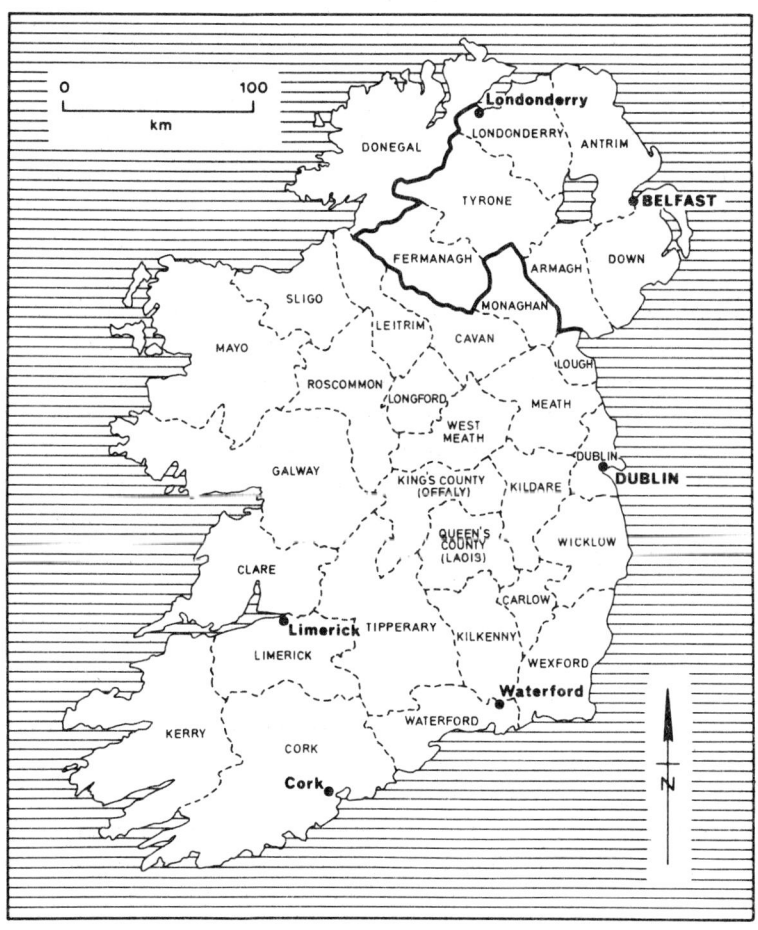

Results of the general election held in the United Kingdom (including Ireland) in December 1918

[December 1918 saw the last election which included the whole of Ireland. The results of that election – indicated below county by county – were, of course, part of the general election held throughout the United Kingdom at that date.

In 1920, as has been related in this chapter, a separate parliament was set up for six of the counties of the province of Ulster in the north-east. The boundary between these six counties (henceforth known as Northern Ireland) and the rest of Ireland is indicated on the map.

It can be seen from the figures below that, in effect, 'two Irelands' emerged from the general election of 1918. The north-eastern corner of Ireland was dominated by the Ulster Unionists, while the rest of Ireland over-whelmingly voted for Sinn Féin. It is worth noting, however, that if proportional representation had been used, the representation of the Nationalist Party (formerly the Irish Parliamentary Party) would have been far more respectable.

In the following election results, the area that was later to become Northern Ireland is listed first.]

> Belfast: 9 Unionist; 1 Nationalist (approximately 26% Catholic in 1918)
> Londonderry: 1 Sinn Féin (approximately 58% Catholic in 1918)
> Antrim: 2 Unionists; 1 Nationalist (approximately 21% Catholic in 1918)
> Armagh: 2 Unionists; 1 Nationalist (approximately 45% Catholic in 1918, but in 1990s approximately 51% Catholic)
> Down: 4 Unionists; 1 Nationalist (approximately 31% Catholic)
> Fermanagh: 1 Unionist; 1 Sinn Féin (approximately 55% Catholic, but in 1990s approximately 61% Catholic)
> County Londonderry: 2 Unionists (approximately 42% Catholic)
> Tyrone: 1 Unionist; 1 Nationalist; 1 Sinn Féin (approximately 55% Catholic, but in 1990s approximately 57% Catholic)

[In the above constituencies, the approximate proportion of Catholics is noted. For the border county areas (Fermanagh, Armagh and Tyrone) the change in the percentage of Catholics since 1918 is also noted.

In these areas, and elsewhere in Northern Ireland, there has been a steady increase in the Catholic population over the past decades.]

Results for the rest of Irelend

Dublin: 8 Sinn Féin; 1 Unionist; 1 Independent
Waterford: 1 Nationalist
Limerick: 1 Sinn Féin
Cork: 2 Sinn Féin
Carlow: 1 Sinn Féin
Cavan: 2 Sinn Féin
Clare: 2 Sinn Féin
Cork: 7 Sinn Féin
Donegal: 3 Sinn Féin; 1 Nationalist
County Dublin: 1 Unionist; 3 Sinn Féin
Galway: 4 Sinn Féin
Kerry: 4 Sinn Féin
Kildare: 2 Sinn Féin
Kilkenny: 2 Sinn Féin
King's County; 1 Sinn Féin
Leitrim: 1 Sinn Féin
Limerick: 2 Sinn Féin
Longford: 1 Sinn Féin
Louth: 1 Sinn Féin
Mayo: 4 Sinn Féin
Meath: 2 Sinn Féin
Monaghan: 2 Sinn Féin
Queen's County: 1 Sinn Féin
Roscommon: 2 Sinn Féin
Sligo: 2 Sinn Féin
Tipperary: 4 Sinn Féin
Waterford: 1 Sinn Féin
West Meath: 1 Sinn Féin
Wexford: 2 Sinn Féin
Wicklow: 2 Sinn Féin

3 – Eamon de Valera and Irish national identity

[In 1932, de Valera was elected Prime Minister of the Irish Free State. He represented more than any other figure in the nationalist movement the view that Ireland's nationalism was unfulfilled in three vital areas: the island of

Ireland remained divided; full Irish sovereignty had not been achieved; and Ireland had not retrieved its own clear identity, expressed in terms of language and what might be called its distinctive national culture and character. The key ingredient for de Valera of this national culture and character could be described as an adherence to traditional rural values and to the moral authority of the Catholic Church.

The national aspirations of de Valera are clearly outlined in his St Patrick's Day radio broadcast address in 1943. The problem for de Valera, as for other nationalists seeking to create a clear national identity for a new nation-state, was that the more he defined and emphasised Ireland's core values and identity, the more he was bound to exclude minorities – such as the Ulster Protestants – from this narrow and exclusive vision of the nation. Furthermore, the more he tried to break the tie with Britain, the less likely it was that the Ulster Protestants – who defined themselves as British – could be drawn into the national community.]

De Valera's Patrick's Day broadcast to the nation, 1943

[This broadcast took place during the height of the Second World War. Eire (southern Ireland) remained neutral during the war, although a significant number of its nationals enlisted in the British forces.]

Before the present war began I was accustomed on St Patrick's Day to speak to our kinsfolk in foreign lands, particularly those in the United States, and to tell them year by year of the progress being made towards building up the Ireland of their dreams and ours – the Ireland that we believe is destined to play, by its example and its inspiration, a great part as a nation among the nations.

Acutely conscious though we all are of the misery and desolation in which the greater part of the world is plunged, let us turn aside for a moment to that ideal Ireland that we would have. That Ireland which we dreamed of would be the home of a people who valued material wealth only as the basis of right living, of a people who were satisfied with frugal comfort and devoted their leisure to the things of the spirit – a land whose countryside would be bright with cosy homesteads, whose fields and villages would be joyous with the sounds of industry, with the romping of sturdy children, the contests of athletic youths and the laughter of comely maidens, whose firesides would be forums for the wisdom of serene old age. It would, in a word, be the home of a people living the life that God desires that man should live.

With the tidings that make such an Ireland possible, St Patrick came to our ancestors 1,500 years ago, promising happiness here as well as happiness hereafter. It was the pursuit of such an Ireland that later made our country worthy to be called the Island of Saints and Scholars. It was the idea of such an Ireland, happy, vigorous, spiritual, that fired the imagination of our poets, that made successive generations of patriotic men give their lives to win religious and political liberty, and that will urge men in our own and future generations to die, if need be, so that these liberties may be preserved.

One hundred years ago the Young Irelanders, by holding up the vision of such an Ireland before the people, inspired our nation and moved it spiritually as it had hardly been moved since the golden age of Irish civilisation. Fifty years after the Young Irelanders, the founders of the Gaelic League similarly inspired and moved the people of their day, as did later the leaders of the Volunteers [in the Easter Rising of 1916]. We of this time, if we have the will and the active enthusiasm, have the opportunity to inspire and move our generation in like manner. We can do so by keeping this thought of a noble future for our country constantly before our minds, ever seeking in action to bring that future into being, and ever remembering that it is to our nation as a whole that future must apply.

... For many the pursuit of the material is a necessity. Man, to express himself fully and make the best use of the talents God has given him, needs a certain minimum of comfort and leisure. A section of our people have not yet this minimum. They rightly strive to secure it, and it must be our aim and the aim of all who are just and wise to assist in the effort. But many have got more than is required and are free, if they choose, to devote themselves more completely to cultivating the things of the mind, and in particular those which mark us out as a distinct nation.

The first of these latter is the national language. It is for us what no other language can be. It is our very own. It is more than a symbol; it is an essential part of our nationhood. It has been moulded by the thought of a hundred generations of our forebears. In it is stored the accumulated experience of a people, our people, who even before Christianity was brought to them were already cultured and living in a well-ordered society. The Irish language spoken in Ireland today is the direct descendant without break of the language our ancestors spoke in those far-off days.

As a vehicle of three thousand years of our history, the language is for us precious beyond measure. As the bearer to us of a philosophy, of an outlook on life deeply Christian and rich in practical wisdom, the language today is worth far too much to dream of letting it go. To part with it would be to abandon a great part of ourselves, to lose the key of our past, to cut away the roots from the tree. With the language gone we could never aspire again to being more than half a nation.

For my part, I believe that this outstanding mark of our nationhood can be preserved and made forever safe by this generation. I am indeed certain of it, but I know that it cannot be saved without understanding and co-operation and effort and sacrifice. It would be wrong to minimise the difficulties. They are not slight. The task of restoring the language as the everyday speech of our people is a task as great as any nation ever undertook. But it is a noble task. Other nations have succeeded in it, though in their case, when the effort was begun, their national language was probably more widely spoken among their people than is ours with us. As long as the language lives, however, on the lips of the people as their natural speech in any substantial part of this land we are assured of success if – *if* we are in earnest.

It is a task in which the attitude of the individual is what counts most. It is upon the individual citizen, upon you who are listening to me, that the restoration of the language finally depends. The State and public institutions can do much to assist, but if the individual has not the inclination or the will-power to make the serious efforts initially required or to persevere till reasonable fluency is attained, outside aids will be of little use. The individual citizen must desire actively to restore the language and be prepared to take the pains to learn it and to use it, else real progress cannot be made.

... Each additional person who speaks the language makes the task of all the others easier. Each one who opposes the language and each one who knowing it fails to use it makes the task of those striving to restore it more difficult. For those who can speak it, to neglect doing so, whenever and wherever it can be understood, is a betrayal of those who gave their lives so that not merely a free but an Irish-speaking nation might be possible. Were all those who now have a knowledge of the language to speak it consistently on all occasions when it could reasonably be spoken, our task would be easy.

Let us all, then, do our part this year. The restoration of the unity of the national territory and the restoration of the language are the greatest of our uncompleted national tasks. Let us devote this year especially to the restoration of the language; let the year be one in which the need for this restoration will be constantly in our thoughts and the language itself as much as possible on our lips.

The physical dangers that threaten, and the need for unceasing vigilance in the matters of defence as well as unremitting attention to the serious day-to-day problems that the war has brought upon us, should not cause us to neglect our duty to the language. Time is running against us in this matter of the language. We cannot afford to postpone our effort. We should remember also that the more we preserve and develop our individuality and our characteristics as a distinct nation, the more secure will be our freedom and the more valuable our contribution to humanity when this war is over.

[From Seamus Deane (general editor), *The Field Day Anthology of Irish Writing*, Volume 3 (Derry, Field Day Publications, Faber and Faber, 1991), pp 747-750

Note: A very readable satire on the overemphasis on Irish language and culture was written by Flann O'Brien in 1941, and translated in English in 1973 as *The Poor Mouth (An Béal Bocht): A Bad Story about the Hard Life* (London, Hart-Davis, MacGibbon Ltd). A similar concern as that of de Valera's for the survival of the Irish language was expressed about the Welsh language by the writer and Welsh nationalist Saunders Lewis in a BBC broadcast of 1962, entitled 'The Fate of the Language', which can be found in Alun R. Jones and Gwyn Thomas (eds), *Presenting Saunders Lewis* (Cardiff, University of Wales Press, 1983), pp 127-141.]

NOTES ON CHAPTER 5

1   The Gaelic languages also include Manx and the native language of the highlands and islands of western Scotland; they are one branch of the Celtic language family, of which the other is that which comprises the Welsh, Cornish and Breton languages.

2   It was in 1795 that the Orange Order was formed in County Armagh, to defend Protestantism in Ireland. Orange Lodges spread throughout Ulster, and remain a powerful influence in the province.

3   Curiously, though, the number of this minority has risen significantly since 1921, whereas the Protestant minority in the south has drastically dwindled in the same period.

Part III

Race and Nation: the Phenomenon
of Antisemitism

Chapter 6

Antisemitism in Nineteenth-Century Europe

And we cried unto the Lord, the God of our fathers;
the Lord heard our voice, and observed our affliction,
our sorrow and our oppression.

from the service for the first nights of the Passover

Nationalism and racism

In the vocabulary of nationalism, the concept of 'race' has very rarely had any real connection with truly scientific investigations of race. Those who were interested in developing a 'racial' basis for national differences were – and are – quite happy, however, to exploit any scientific findings on race that might work to their benefit.

The uses of race in political discourse have been many and contradictory. Sometimes, it has been used as a kind of rhetorical flourish: for instance, patriotic British writers and politicians used to boast – before the use of the word 'race' became sensitive after the Second World War – of the achievements of the British or the English 'race' in a rather indiscriminate manner. The concept of race was also used in the nineteenth century to make distinctions of class rather than of nation: to justify the distance between a ruling 'caste' and the mass of the people in European states, through the assertion of an inherent racial superiority. Comte de Gobineau (1816-1882), the 'father' of modern racism, claimed, for example, that there was a fundamental racial distinction between the 'Aryan' aristocracy of France, and the 'Gallo-Roman' population as a whole.

Attempts have been made to define the difference between the main European language-groups – Germanic, Latin, Slav and Celtic – in racial terms. Adolf Hitler and the Nazis, for example, drew a distinction between the German race and the 'racially inferior' Slavs of Eastern Europe. Even the Nazis, however, were never entirely confident or consistent in their handling of the immensely complex relationship between language, culture and ethnic roots. There were, for example, many Germans of manifestly Slav ethnic origins who were nevertheless fully German in terms of language and culture: the Nazis did not discriminate against such people. Moreover, these wide racial-linguistic categories never fitted in well with the actual patterns of national conflict and cooperation in Europe. The 'Germanic' nations have never formed a natural bloc, as can be shown by British-German or Dutch-German relations in the twentieth century; equally, the reality of Polish-Russian relations has tended to make a nonsense of the idea of a natural 'pan-Slav' unity.

Generally, in fact, the ideology of 'race' has tended to destabilise rather than strengthen the concept of the nation. Where race has acted as a divisive political force, the racial confrontation concerned has been far wider than that of the nation, and it has tended either to divide (black versus white in South Africa) or to supersede national loyalties (the white world versus the non-white world). The assertion of racial difference has generally only been made where there are clearly observable differences of skin-colour – as in the 'black-white' confrontation in the history of the United States – or where there is a fundamental divergence between very broadly defined cultures and civilisations, as in the case of 'Christian' Europe and 'Muslim' North Africa and West Asia. The latter divergence has been given scientific credence by the linguistic distinction between the Indo-European language group that includes most of the European languages (but also those of Iran and northern India), and the Semitic language group which includes Arabic and Hebrew. This linguistic difference was turned into a racial difference with political significance when, in the nineteenth century, the European 'Aryan' race was differentiated from the non-European 'Semitic' race.

In Europe, the concept of race has ultimately tended to centre on the distinction between European and non-European. At the global level, the notion of the racial superiority of Aryan-European civilisation served as a justification for colonial expansion into areas peopled by 'inferior' races. Within Europe itself, however, the issue of race and racial difference focused – up to the time of mass non-European immigration after the Second World War – on the status and identity of the 'Semitic' Jewish community of Europe.

In order to understand the background to European antisemitism, it is therefore necessary to look at the broad identity of the Jewish people and at the history of Jewish settlement in Europe.

The Jews in Europe

It is hard to imagine a people with firmer roots of identity than the Jewish people. The key to Jewish identity is to be found in the Jewish Bible, known as the Torah (the Law), though this strictly speaking only refers to the first section of the Bible. This is written in the Hebrew language that has survived as the language of the Jewish religion (Judaism), and has been revived in the twentieth century as the national language of everyday use in modern Israel. In the Torah, Jewish origins and history are traced in strict genealogical fashion from Adam to Shem, the son of Noah, and thence to Abraham, Isaac and Jacob. The religious core of Jewish identity is of course the notion of a special relationship between the Jewish people and the one universal God, and the Jewish Bible is fundamentally a history of that turbulent relationship. The books of Moses outline in exact detail the terms of the covenant between God and the Jewish people, including strict rules to ensure that Jewish identity should not evaporate through the otherwise natural process of inter-marriage with neighbouring communities. The notion of the Jews as a special and separate people dedicated to God through a covenant demanded the maintenance by the Jews of a complex set of rules. The principle emphasis of these rules was the maintenance of purity: in terms of food, of marriage and connections with other communities, and of religious ritual. These rules, embodied in the covenant, form the basis for Jewish culture and custom.

It was fundamental to the covenant between God and the Jews that the one area where the Jews did not have roots was in land. The land of Israel ('eretz Israel' in Hebrew) – also known in the Bible as Canaan or Palestine – was essentially a loan from God to the formerly nomadic Jewish people, but only on the condition that the Jewish people maintained the covenant. The history of the Jews outlined in the Bible is a story of settlement in Israel/Palestine, exile and return: it is a morality play on the relationship between God and humanity, with the Jews playing the role of humanity. It was in post-Biblical times, however, in 70AD, that the Romans forced the most recent exile, when it ejected the Jews from Palestine after an unsuccessful rebellion.[1] As a consequence, the Jews were dispersed (the so-called diaspora or in Hebrew 'galuth') around and beyond the Mediterranean.

Thereafter, the history of the Jewish people is that of obstinate survival despite relentless discrimination and persecution. The basis for their persecution was religious, first from Christendom and later – though to a slightly lesser extent – from the Islamic world. In Christian areas, the Jews were persecuted for their failure to convert, and for their perceived role in Christ's death. The nature of persecution shaded from discrimination (severe restrictions on employment and areas of settlement) to forcible expulsion and outright massacre. Through the Middle Ages and the early modern era, Jewish communities were pushed in a haphazard fashion from one state to another, as persecution intensified here and slackened there. The main consequence of this process of expulsion and migration was a gradual concentration of Jewish communities in a large area between Russia and Germany, a zone of relative tolerance centring on Poland.

Clearly, the very pressure of persecution and exclusion helped to bind the Jewish communities together and preserve their separate identity. In the urban areas of Europe – where they were not excluded altogether, that is – Jews lived in separate areas known as ghettos. Within these ghettos, the community was sustained by a strict adherence to traditional religious custom and ritual, and leadership for the community was provided by the rabbis, or religious scholars. Exclusion from land-ownership and whole areas of economic activity meant that the Jews concentrated on certain professions, particularly those shunned by mediaeval Christianity, most notoriously money-lending or 'usury'.[2]

In the Polish area of Europe, where there was the largest concentration of Jews with the widest measure of freedom, a distinctively European-Jewish cultural identity emerged. Here Jewish communities were not only concentrated in urban ghettos, but also spread out through the countryside in villages known as 'shtetls'.[3] While Hebrew remained the language of religious ritual and learning, Yiddish – a dialect of German, with an admixture of Polish, Hebrew and other languages, and written in the Hebrew script – became the language of everyday communication between Jews.

In the late eighteenth century, a slow change began in relations between the Jewish communities of Europe and their host nations. The gradual growth of secularisation and religious tolerance in gentile (non-Jewish) society had the natural effect of reducing the traditional religious antagonism between Jew and Christian. Conversely, a religious reform movement was initiated by some Jewish religious scholars in the late eighteenth century. In essence, this involved the drawing of a distinction between the fundamentals of Judaism on the one side – embodied in the sacred Hebrew texts – which were of enduring importance, and the huge accumulation of ritual and tradi-tion that dominated Jewish everyday life on the other, which was considered to be inessential. This outlook on the part of the so-called enlightened ('maskilim') Jews and the Reform branch of Judaism sparked a fundamental confrontation in the Jewish community between the traditionalists, who argued that Judaism was a comprehensive and exclusive way of life, and those who argued that, while the fundamentals of religious observance should be maintained, Jews could in all other respects engage in the social, economic and political life of the gentile societies in which they lived.

Engagement between Jewish communities and European societies increased dramatically with the enacting of Jewish emancipation legislation in the nineteenth century. Jewish communities were able to benefit from the ideals that had inspired the American and French Revolutions: those of equal citizenship and equal political rights within the nation. In the course of the nineteenth century, legislation to give the Jews equal rights in employment, land ownership, access to education and the professions, and rights of poli-tical participation, spread through much of Europe. Only in Russia did the political structure of autocracy remain intact, along with substantial restrictions on the employment, rights and even movement of the Jews. Since, after 1815, Russia had absorbed within its territory the major areas of Jewish settlement in Europe – the so-called Pale of Settlement to which Jews of the Russian Empire were mostly restricted – a large number of the Jews in Europe did not in fact benefit directly from the era of emancipation (see document 1 at the end of the chapter).

Nevertheless, where emancipation did occur, it generated a huge change in Jewish society. On the whole, Jewish society split three ways. The more liberal and 'Europeanised' section of the Jewish community moved into mainstream society, but maintained their Jewish links through the Synagogue and observation of the main Jewish festivals. However, as traditional Jews had feared, this movement out of the ghetto led inevitably to a creeping process of assimilation, where Jews abandoned their identity and their religion, intermarried with non-Jews, and merged completely into the wider society. Traditional Jewish communities in the ghettos remained, however. But their way of life was increasingly threatened by the lures of secular soci-ety, and leadership of Jewish communities quite often shifted from the rabbis to successful Jewish entrepreneurs and financiers.

Paradoxically, however, while the concept of liberal democracy helped to emancipate the Jews, simultaneously the growing strength of the ideology of nationalism initiated a new and altogether more savage era of persecution, which was to culminate in the genocide of the European Jews in 1939-1945. The whole process of developing national consciousness among a people was both inclusive and exclusive: it defined – by language, ethnicity, religion or whatever – those who belonged to the national family, and those who did not. Out of this process of national definition, a new and more deadly form of prejudice against the Jews took shape: a prejudice that was not based on religion, but rather on racial identity. This racial discrimination against the 'non-indigenous' Jews was more implacable in its effect than the religious discrimination of previous centuries. It was at least possible to escape from religious persecution by the expedient of conversion to Christianity: it was not possible to escape from one's skin and one's blood. Even the most assimilated Jew could not escape racially-based discrimination. When, in 1840, the German Jew Moses Hess set a German patriotic hymn to music, he was chillingly reminded, 'Du bist ein Yid' ('You are a Yid'); as such, it was implied, he had no right to interfere in matters that were only the concern of 'real' Germans.[4] As racial outsiders, the Jews had no place in a world of nation-states. This was the foundation of the modern phenomenon known as 'antisemitism'.

The antisemitism inherent in the new nationalism was reinforced by the effects of mass democracy. In the search of politicians and parties for a broad basis of support among newly-enfranchised populations, the appeal of ethnic politics soon became apparent. The mobilisation of populations on the basis of ethnic loyalties, and political programmes directed against a racial outsider, particularly a racial outsider that could be depicted as a threat, enabled antisemitism to become a major political force in Europe. One classic example of the mass appeal of antisemitism – in an age, of course, when antisemitic views and programmes could be openly propagated – was Karl Lueger's overtly antisemitic Christian-Social Party, which administered Vienna from 1897 to 1910.

The actual impact of antisemitism was wide-ranging. At one end of the social scale, there was the genteel antisemitism of the upper and middle classes: the exclusion of Jews from certain élite professions, from rarefied sections of high society, or the informal rather than legal restrictions on the career advancement of Jews for what were politely called 'denominational considerations'.[5] At the other end of the social scale, there were outbreaks of violence - generally known as pogroms, the Russian word for mass violence – directed against Jews in the ghettos. The evidence of nineteenth and early twentieth century Europe shows that antisemitism intensified during periods of economic or financial upheaval (Germany in 1873, and Europe generally after 1929); military defeat (France after 1870, Russia after 1905, Germany after 1918); revolutionary turmoil (Russia and the whole of central and Eastern Europe after 1917); or a long-term era of national decline, as in the case of Tsarist Russia in the nineteenth and early twentieth centuries.

Russian antisemitism and the slavophile ideal

The 'heartland' of antisemitism in nineteenth century Europe was not Germany but Tsarist Russia. The main ingredients in Russian antisemitism during this period were a combination of traditional religious sentiment, peasant grievances, and that very specific expression of Russian nationalism: slavophilism. The mainly Russian, Belorussian and Ukrainian peasantry of the Pale of Settlement area in particular resented the perceived economic power exerted by the Jewish community there; but peasant antisemitism was also sustained by traditional religious-inspired hatred directed against the 'killers of Christ'.

A more sophisticated form of antisemitism emerged out of a fundamental debate between intellectuals in nineteenth-century Russia on the question of Russia's future. On the one side, a group that could broadly be called the westernisers argued that Russia had to look westwards and learn from Europe if it was to liberate itself from its condition of perceived political and economic backwardness. It was argued by the westernisers that only by absorbing the whole panoply of Enlightenment ideas – particularly liberalism and socialism – that had transformed Europe could Russia escape from its traditional world symbolised by the Tsarist regime, the Orthodox Church and a virtually mediaeval peasantry.

On the other side, the 'slavophiles' – particularly the conservative variety represented by the writer Feodor Dostoevsky (1818-1881) – argued that it was precisely through these three 'pillars' that Russia could eventually tap its own inner resources of spiritual, national and social renewal. Dostoevsky went further, and asserted in his *Diary of a Writer* (written between 1873 and 1881) that the spiritual values embodied in traditional Russia, particularly the Church and the long-suffering peasantry, would by some unspecified process bring about the redemption, not only of Russia, but also of a Europe under threat of moral disintegration from precisely the ideas that the westernisers wished to import into Russia.[6]

For Dostoevsky, the battle between the westernisers and the slavophiles was, therefore, not just a struggle for the soul of Russia, but for the soul of

Christian Europe itself. In his eyes, the Jews of Europe were in the front rank of those seeking to undermine the Christian foundations of Europe, and he saw the Jewish community in Russia as a fundamental threat to Russian society, subverting Russia with the weapons of 'cosmopolitanism, materialism, financial power and corruption, liberalism and socialism, influence over the press and publishing, and the creation of anti-Russian feeling in other countries'.[7]

In *Diary of a Writer*, Dostoevsky – in a series of notorious polemic essays written in 1877 – accused the Jews of Russia of deliberately setting themselves apart from the rest of the community: what he called maintaining a 'status in statu' (state within a state). He ascribed this 'status in statu' mentality not to the persecution and exclusion of the Jews by the rest of society, but to an inherent tendency on the part of the Jewish community to stay aloof from Russian and European society and promote its own separate interests. He then went further, and suggested that the Jews of Russia and of Europe as a whole were in fact conspiring to exploit the spiritual and social upheavals of the time in order to weaken Christian civilisation from within:

... It goes without saying that man always, at all times, has been worshipping materialism and has been inclined to perceive and understand liberty only in the sense of making his life secure through money hoarded by the exertion of every effort and accumulated by all possible means. However, at no time in the past have these tendencies been raised so cynically and so obviously to the level of a sublime principle as in our nineteenth century. 'Everybody for himself, and only for himself, and every intercourse with man solely for oneself' – such is the ethical tenet of the majority of present-day people, not even bad people, but on the contrary, laboring people who neither murder nor steal. And mercilessness for the lower classes, the decline of brotherhood, exploitation of the poor by the rich – oh, of course all this existed also before and always; however, it had not been raised to the level of supreme truth and science – it had been condemned by Christianity, whereas at present, on the contrary, it is being regarded as a virtue.

Thus it is not for nothing that over there [in Western Europe] the Jews are reigning everywhere over stock-exchanges; it is not for nothing that they control capital, that they are the masters of credit, and it is not for nothing – I repeat – that they are also the masters of international politics, and what is going to happen in the future is known to the Jews themselves; their reign, their complete reign is approaching! We are approaching the complete triumph of ideas before which the sentiments of humanity, thirst for truth, Christian and national feelings, and even those of national dignity, must bow. On the contrary, we are approaching [the age of] materialism, a blind, carnivorous craving for personal material welfare, a craving for personal accumulation of money by any means - this is all that has been proclaimed as the supreme aim, as the 'reasonable thing', as liberty, in lieu of the Christian idea of salvation only through the closest moral and brotherly fellowship of men.

People will laugh and say that this is not brought about by the Jews. Of course, not only by them, but if the Jews have completely triumphed and thriven in Europe precisely at the time when these new principles have triumphed there to the point of having been raised to the level of a moral principle, it is impossible not to infer that the Jews, too, have contributed their influence to this condition.

[See F.M. Dostoevsky, *The Diary of a Writer*, translated and annotated by Boris Brasol (New York, George Braziller, 1954), pp 649-650]

It need hardly be said that Dostoevsky's antisemitism is the darkest part of what is in any case a rather murky and confused political vision; occasionally shot through, however, as the Russian writer Alexander Solzhenitsyn has emphasised, with piercing insights.[8]

Documents

(Nb: in all the following extracts, editorial comments at the beginning of texts, or amendments and explanations in the texts themselves, will be placed in square brackets. Headings and subdivisions will be put in italics.)

1 – Map 6: The 'Pale of Settlement'

[In this map, the area of the Jewish 'Pale of Settlement' of pre-1917 Tsarist Russia is superimposed on the map of Europe during the inter-war period 1919-1939. The approximate number of Jews in each country in the 1919-1939 period is indicated below.]

Countries which had territories in the former Pale of Settlement area:

Soviet Union: 3,000,000	Romania: 1,000,000
Poland: 3,150,000	Lithuania: 177,000

Other European countries with large Jewish populations, a number of whom fled from the 'Pale of Settlement' in the decades after 1882:

Hungary: 440,000	Yugoslavia: 70,000
Czechoslovakia: 380,000	Belgium: 63,000
Germany: 375,000	Italy: 52,000
Britain: 350,000	Bulgaria: 47,000
France: 230,000	Switzerland: 17,000
Austria: 180,000	Denmark: 7,000
Netherlands: 115,000	Sweden: 7,000
Latvia: 97,000	Estonia: 4,000
Greece: 75,000	

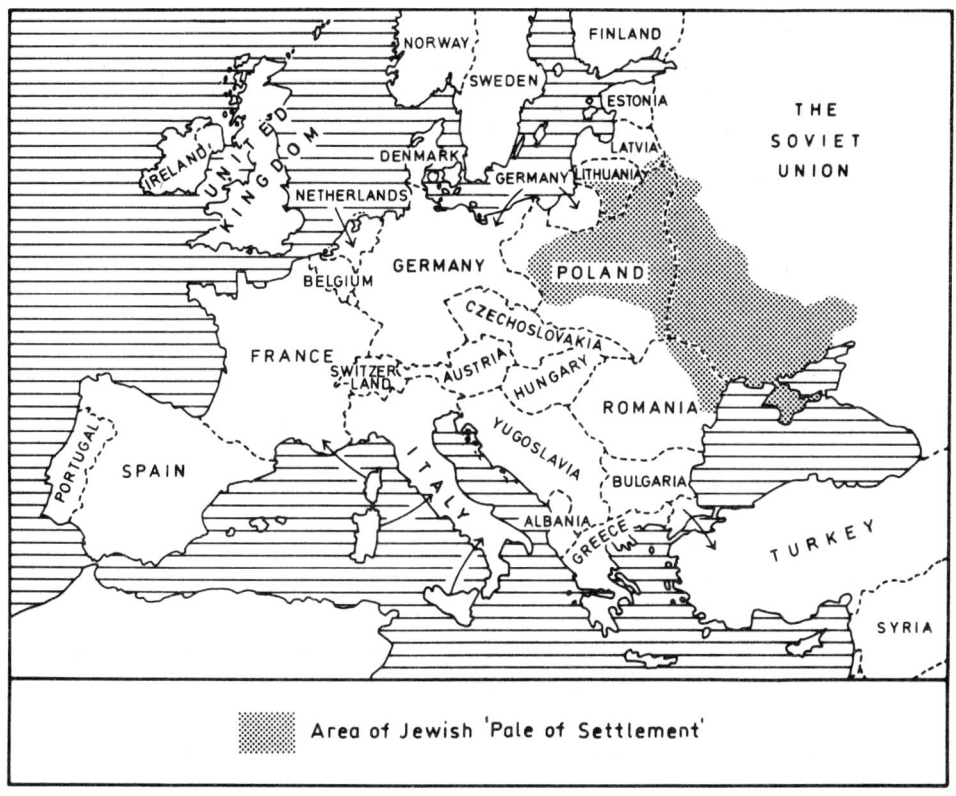

Area of Jewish 'Pale of Settlement'

2 – Edouard Drumont and the 'Jewish conspiracy'

[That the relationship between antisemitism and nationalism was – is – always uneasy, is demonstrated in the following passage taken from Edouard Drumont's *La France Juive* (1886). Edouard Drumont (1844-1917), a French politician and journalist, was mainly noted for his single-minded dedication to the cause of antisemitism. What was notable about his antisemitism, however, was its pan-European, or 'Aryan', rather than specifically French, standpoint. His view reflected a general shift in the course of the nineteenth century from an essentially limited form of antisemitism, which simply argued that the 'alien' Jew could not fit into this or that nation-state, to the notion that the Jews were an active threat to all European nations and to European civilisation in general.

This is the essence of the 'Jewish conspiracy' theory that underpins modern antisemitism. There are clear indications of this in Dostoevsky's antisemitic outbursts, but in Drumont's writing the motives and the purpose of this supposed Jewish conspiracy are outlined in full. In many ways, this conspiracy theory is a re-statement in a modern political form of an ancient fear – latent in much European writing – of the perceived threat of the Orient to Europe.

The passage below is of importance, not only for understanding the 'world-view' of antisemitism in the late nineteenth century, but also as an indication of the world-view that influences European racism in general.]

Aryan versus Jew

Our central task in this book is to try to analyse that unique and perennial human type, so completely different from other human types: the Jew.

At first sight, this task would seem simple. No other race has a more clearly delineated physiognomy; none has kept more faithfully the distinctive characteristics of its original ancestors. What, in truth, has prevented us from understanding and depicting the Jew clearly has been our own ways of thinking, our own tendency to see him from a point of view that is entirely different from his own.

We must avoid broad generalisations. We should rather concentrate on the essential traits that differentiate the Jew from other peoples, and we should start our work by an ethnographic, physiological and psychological comparison between the Jew and the Aryan, two distinct racial groups irremediably hostile to each other, whose mutual antagonism has shaken the world in the past, and will disturb it even more in the future.

The generic term Aryan (or Aryas) - which comes from a Sanskrit word which means 'noble', 'illustrious', 'honourable' – is ascribed to that superior branch of the white race, the Indo-European family which has its cradle in the huge plains of Iran.

The Aryan race spread out across the world through successive waves of migration. The Greeks and Romans made their home on the edges of the Hellespont and the Mediterranean, while the Celts, the Slavs and the Germans headed westwards, swarming round the Caspian Sea and crossing the Danube.

All the nations of Europe are therefore closely connected to the Aryan race, which has been the origin of all the great civilisations.

The Semites, represented by diverse groups – Aramaic, Hebrew and Arab – seem to have originated from the plains of Mesopotamia.

No doubt Tyre, Sidon and Carthage for a while reached a high degree of material prosperity; at a later date, the Arab Empire had its fleeting moment of glory; but nothing about these ephemeral empires resembles the glorious and enduring civilisations of Greece and Rome, or the admirable civilisation of Christendom in the Middle Ages. Only the Aryan, Indo-European race possesses the notion of Justice, the feeling for Freedom, and the concept of Beauty.

From the very beginning of history we see the Aryan locked in mortal combat with the Semite. This conflict has continued through the ages, and it is almost always the Semite who provokes these hostilities – before eventually being defeated.

In fact, it is the constant objective of the Semite – his obsession, in fact – to reduce the Aryan to slavery, and to bind the Aryan to servitude on the land.

The Jewish conspiracy

Nowadays, however, the Semites have replaced violence by cunning in order to achieve their ends. They have replaced open invasion by silent, cautious step-by-step infiltration. It is no longer a case of rampaging invading hordes, but of separate individuals joining together into groups, stealthily advancing their cause, unobtrusively moving into all the key positions, all the main jobs of a particular country, from the humblest to the most important. Instead of assaulting Europe directly, the Semites have attacked it from the rear and outflanked it. In the area around Vilna [modern-day Lithuania], that *vagina Judaeorum* ['womb of Jewry'], organised exoduses have infiltrated Germany, and have crossed the Vosges and conquered France.

It should be emphasised that no direct violence has been used in this process. It is rather a case of a sort of gentle 'take-over', a process of gradually dispossessing the indigenous inhabitants of their houses and their jobs; a process of gently stripping them, first of their property, and then of their traditions, their customs, and – eventually – of their religion itself. It is this last area, however, which will, I believe, be a decisive stumbling-bloc.

[Drumont asserts that Aryans are inherently spiritual, creative, generous, naive, but – if provoked – warlike. The Semites, on the other hand, are pragmatic, imitative, calculating and exploitative. Because of the Aryan's generosity and naiveté, the Semitic plan of infiltration will initially succeed. At a certain point, however, the Aryan's pride will be stung beyond endurance, and he will take up his sword and inflict 'terrible revenge' ('châtiments terribles') on the Jews. The Semite will then go 'underground', 'où il rumine une nouvelle combinaison pour recommencer quelques siècles après'.]

The Jewish strategy against Europe

The Jewish army [of infiltration] has three main divisions:

> The true Jews, the obvious and undisguised Jews... who publicly venerate Abraham and Jacob, and who are willing to take the chance of making their fortune while at the same time remaining faithful to their God;
> The Jews disguised as free-thinkers... who hide their Jewish identity, and persecute Christians in the name of the 'glorious' principles of tolerance and the 'sacred' rights of liberty;
> Conservative Jews, who, though Christian to all outward appearances, are in fact closely linked to the two former categories, and pass to their compatriots any secrets that might help their common cause...

The power of the Jews lies in their solidarity. All Jews are indissolubly linked one to another, a fact that is symbolised by the Alliance Israélite [a Jewish-French charitable organisation] which has taken for its emblem two clasped hands under a halo.

The solidarity between Jews throughout the world is truly touching.

One can easily grasp the advantage, from the human point of view, that this principle of solidarity gives the Jew over the Christian; who, while he practises the virtue of charity, does not understand the value of solidarity.

Don't think that anyone admires more than I do the sublime flower of charity that Christianity implants in the human soul: untiring, inexhaustible, ardent charity, which always gives, gives without cease, which does not only give away money, but the heart itself, as well as all the time and understanding in the world. Nevertheless, I am duty bound to point out in this book, which is a work of unflinching analysis, the fundamental difference which exists between the solidarity of the Jew and the charity of the Christian.

Christians generously open their arms to all misfortunes; they respond to every appeal to help, and they do not confine their help to their own kind. Since they quite naturally feel themselves to be unthreatened in the country which they inhabit, and which belongs to them, it does not occur to them to build a defensive wall against Jewish infiltration.

Accordingly, the Jews strikes at Christians one at a time. Today it is a merchant whose capital is coveted by a Jew; combined Jewish commercial interests will conspire to lure him gradually into bankruptcy. Tomorrow, it will be a writer who opposes the Jews, and whom the Jews will reduce to despair and drive into drunkenness or madness. At another time, it will be an aristocrat with a noble name who had snubbed a baron of dubious origins at the races: it will be 'arranged' for the unfortunate man to acquire a Jewish mistress; a broker - fellow member of the Jewish conspiracy – will recommend to him a 'good bargain'; the victim is then lured on by an initial gain, and eventually he will be simultaneously ruined and disgraced.

If the merchant, the writer and the nobleman had been aware of each other's circumstances, if they had been united, they would have escaped their fate, they could have come to each other's defence; each would have been a support for the others; but – and this is the point – each one was destroyed separately, without in the least suspecting who their real enemy was.

On the other hand, thanks to their solidarity, whatever happens to one Jew, even in the most distant corner of the desert, becomes a major crisis for all Jews.

The Jew as 'inexorable universalist'

The fatherland ('La patrie'), in the sense that we understand the term, has no meaning for the Jew. The Jew – as the forceful expression of the Alliance Israélite puts it – is an 'inexorable universalist'.

I don't quite understand why the Jew should be blamed for this. What, after all, does 'fatherland' mean? The land of one's fathers. Feeling for the fatherland is engraved on the heart like a name engraved on the bark of a tree; with each year that passes, as the tree grows older, so that name will deepen itself into the bark, so that the name and the tree become inextricably linked. One cannot improvise patriotism; it is in the blood; in the marrow of the bones.

How can a Semite, that perpetual nomad, experience such durable feelings?

Besides, the Jew has his own fatherland which he will never forget; that is, the holy and mysterious city of Jerusalem. Outside Jerusalem, any country, be it France, Germany or England, is for the Jew simply a temporary residence, 'any old place', a mere social agglomeration where he can make good, where it may perhaps for a short time be profitable to promote his interests, but where he never sees himself as anything more than a free associate, a temporary member…

France, Germany, Russia will never be fatherlands for the Jews; and they are perfectly justified, in my opinion, to refuse to be patriots, but rather to follow, wherever they may be, their own distinct political interests, their *Jewish* political interests.

[It is because of this, Drumont asserts, that Jews do not feel any compunction about betraying the countries in which they live.]

Antisemitism

The Semites, restless agitators that they are, delight in destroying the foundations of ancient civilisations. They hope that, with the money that they can extort from it, they can then build their own new society. They have created a social crisis; but it will be resolved at their expense. All their ill-gotten gains will be distributed to those who will play a part in the great struggle that is to come; just as, in the past, land and fiefdoms were given to the most courageous.

In Germany, in Russia, in the Austrian empire, in Romania, even in France, where the movement is still lying dormant, noblemen, bourgeois, intelligent workers; all those, in a word, who have a Christian background – even if sometimes they are not practising Christians – have reached agreement. The universal Antisemitic Alliance ('L'Alliance anti-israélite universelle') has been set up, and the Universal Jewish Alliance ('L'Alliance israélite universelle') will not prevail against it.

... This century will not end before history will witness the repetition of a phenomenon that has been constantly repeated: the Jew, profiting from the divisions that he himself has created by his cunning plans to dominate entire nations; scheming to uproot the ideas, customs and traditional beliefs of these countries; will, precisely because of his over-confident insolence, force people who had hitherto been at each other's throats to club together and set upon the Jews with wholehearted zeal.

As for me, I am only a modest prophet of these strange events which will soon take place. Maybe I will die insulted, defamed and misunderstood – though I doubt it – before witnessing these events which I consider inevitable. So what? I would have done my duty, and accomplished my task. As events unfold in the future, the correctness of my predictions will be confirmed...

I have only tried to undertake this task in a spirit of good will, in order to demonstrate by what an insidious and cunning enemy France has been infiltrated, corrupted, stupefied, to the point of robbing her of everything that has up till now made her powerful, respectable and happy. Have I written our epitaph? Have I prepared the way for our rebirth? That I cannot tell.

[Translated by C.J. Christie from Edouard Drumont, *La France Juive* (Paris, Librairie Victor Palmé, 1890), pp 7-15, 25-30, 58-61, 529-530]

NOTES ON CHAPTER 6

1   See the classic history of this event, Flavius Josephus, *History of the Jewish War*, in many translations and editions.

2   For an insight into mediaeval attitudes towards the Jews, see St Thomas Aquinas, 'On the Government of the Jews', in A.P. d'Entrèves (ed.), *Selected Political Writings* (Oxford, Basil Blackwell, 1959), pp 84-95.

3   For a vivid description of Jewish life in the shtetl, see Sholom Aleichem's *Inside Kasrilevke* (London, Robson Books, 1973).

4   See Sir Isaiah Berlin, *The Life and Opinions of Moses Hess* (The Jewish Historical Society of England, 1959), p 19.

5   See anecdotal references in Sigmund Freud, *The Interpretation of Dreams*
     (London, George Allen and Unwin Ltd, 1961), especially p 136.
6   These themes are pursued in two of Dostoevsky's novels: *The Possessed
     or The Devils* (1871-2); and *Crime and Punishment* (1866).
7   Robert F. Byrnes, *Pobedonostsev: His Life and Thoughts* (Bloomington,
     Indiana University Press, 1968), p 104.
8   Alexander Solzhenitsyn, 'One Word of Truth...' (London, The Bodley
     Head, 1970), pp 7, 18-19. The most measured expression of
     Dostoevsky's slavophile views is to be found in his speech in 1880 on
     Pushkin, which can be found in F. Dostoevsky, *The Diary of a Writer*,
     translated by Boris Brasol (New York, George Braziller, 1952),
     pp 959-980.

Chapter 7

Antisemitism and the Origins of Genocide in Twentieth-Century Europe

In the nightmare of the dark
All the dogs of Europe bark,
And the living nations wait,
Each sequestered in its hate.

Intellectual disgrace
Stares from every human face,
And the seas of pity lie
Locked and frozen in each eye.

from 'In memory of W.B. Yeats' by W.H. Auden

If the basis for the antisemitism of modern Europe could be encapsulated in a term, it would be that the Jews were seen as 'rootless cosmopolitans'. The hypothetical rootlessness of the Jewish communities – hypothetical, because the Jews had a history of centuries of residence in Europe – was a cardinal offence against the link between nationality, ethnicity and land that under-pinned the ideology of nineteenth-century nationalism in Europe. To pursue the 'roots' metaphor further, in the eyes of the antisemite the Jewish communities of Europe had roots in the blood, but not in the land; and Jewish affiliation through blood, coupled with their dispersal through the nations of Europe, was seen by the antisemite as a danger to the nationalist principle. Antisemitism, therefore, was likely to be particularly virulent in areas where ethnic nationalism pervaded the political agenda and political rhetoric. Its impact was magnified by the introduction of democratic politics or, in areas where democracy operated imperfectly or not at all, the growth of what could be called 'mass politics': a situation, that is, where governments sought to enlist the general loyalty of the people without necessarily soliciting their votes.

It was precisely the cosmopolitanism attributed to Jewish communities – the notion that they had 'horizontal' links throughout Europe rather than 'vertical' links with a particular land – that was used to identify them, not just as outsiders, but as a positive threat. They therefore became an easy target for those who felt themselves to be, in one way or another, victims of the massive social and economic upheaval that accompanied the processes of industrialisation and political change in Europe. In this period of rapid change, the landed gentry of the *ancien régime* saw their economic power and political influence seeping away to a new middle-class urban bureaucracy and to a new financial and industrial élite.[1] Lower down the social scale, what Karl Marx described in *The Communist Manifesto* as the 'lower-middle class' of 'small manufacturers, small traders, handicraftsmen, peasant proprietors' found themselves squeezed out of the modern economy, and sliding into the general conglomeration of the urban poor.[2] Such groups, facing the threat or the reality of dispossession from their social status, would find a focus for their resentment, and perhaps an explanation for their plight, in the apparent economic power and international connections of the Jews of Europe.

The notion of a 'Jewish conspiracy' cut across class and political lines. Socialists would often see a sinister Jewish role in the networks of international capitalism, symbolised by the Rothschild family that straddled Europe and America. Conversely, the political and financial establishment linked Jews – symbolised by such figures as Karl Marx or Leon Trotsky – with revolutionary conspiracies and international socialism. Antisemitism, therefore, was not the exclusive preserve of either the educated or uneducated; it did, however, provide a coherent yet simple world-view for what might be described as the semi-educated and the 'semi-intellectual' (see document 2 at the end of the chapter). In general, as has been observed in the previous chapter, European antisemitism would tend to crystallise in a time of perceived national weakness, during a period of revolutionary upheaval, or after a national defeat.

At the core of the antisemitic world-view was the notion that the 'Jewish conspiracy' was seeking to undermine – by guile rather than direct force – the foundations of European civilisation. Europe's political foundations would be undermined by the incitement to war between nations; its economic foundations by the simultaneously destructive impact of revolutionary activity from below and financial juggling from above; and its cultural foundations by the encouragement of literary and artistic fashions that would destabilise the traditional values and norms of literature, art and music. Antisemites were generally vague as to what this gigantic conspiracy was supposed to achieve, apart from some obscure notion of 'Jewish domination'. For the antisemite, the role of the Jews was ultimately seen as destructive *per se*.

All of these ingredients of antisemitism can be seen in 'The Protocols of the Elders of Zion', a forged document purporting to be the outline of an international Jewish conspiracy to destroy European civilisation. This forgery was concocted in 1903 by Russian agents in Paris, and was publicised in court circles in Russia in 1905. However, it did not have a great impact until the aftermath of the First World War, that fatal turning-point in European and global history. The 'conspiracy' outlined in this forgery was hopelessly muddled and utterly preposterous, almost as if the forgers had actually written a deliberate satire on antisemitism, embellished with some sub-Hammer Horror details. But its contents perfectly merged with the anxieties generated by – above everything else – a Europe-wide fear of revolution after 1917. Antisemitic fears and fantasies were to play a key role in a vicious spiral of hatred and fear that would reach its climax in the Second World War (see document 1 at the end of this chapter).

It was in the last decades of the nineteenth century, however, that anti-semitism acquired Europe-wide significance, mainly because of its impact in Tsarist Russia. In 1881, Tsar Alexander II was assassinated by revolutionaries. The Jews of the Tsarist Empire had always been associated with revolutionary activity by the conservative establishment; although there is no direct evidence of an official Tsarist conspiracy, the assassination was followed by a whole series of savage pogroms in the Pale of Settlement that were for a long period largely unchecked by officialdom. Intermittent pogroms had always been an ever-present threat in the shtetls and ghettos of Eastern Europe. But the sheer scale and persistence of the 1881-1882 pogroms indicated a much more fundamental assault on Jewish communities in Russia. The pogroms were followed, therefore, by waves of emigration westwards out of the Pale of Settlement.

In the long term, this was the beginning of the demographic shift of the heartland of the Jewish world community from Europe to America and Israel (see next chapter). Roughly between 1800 and 1900, the world-wide Jewish population, in line with the general spectacular rise in the population in Europe during this period, increased from some two-and-a-half million to around ten-and-a-half million. Of these, by the last half of the nineteenth century, at least five million lived in the Tsarist controlled Pale of Settlement,

and some 300,000 lived to the east in Russia proper. As a consequence of
successive pogroms that regularly hit the Jews in the Pale of Settlement in
the period 1881-1914, no less than two million Jews left the Tsarist Empire.
Although large numbers of these refugees went, either directly or indirectly,
to the United States, this wave of Jewish emigration took large numbers of
mainly traditional Jewish communities to Central and Western Europe.
Their alien appearance and culture – very distinct from the settled and often
assimilated Jews already living in Central and Western Europe – gave a new
lease of life to antisemitism in countries such as Austria, Germany, France
and Britain.[3]

Another seminal event – the Dreyfus scandal in France – illustrated the
pervasiveness of antisemitism throughout Europe, even in the land that had
set the example of Jewish emancipation a century earlier. During the nineteenth century, France passed through a profound political crisis, stimulated
in part by a bitter struggle between competing versions of the French nation:
a republican, liberal and secular version on one side; and a monarchist, conservative and Catholic version on the other. This struggle for the 'soul' of the
nation was exacerbated by France's relative decline in Europe vis-à-vis
Germany, a decline that was highlighted by France's humiliating defeat by
Germany in the war of 1870-1871. The confrontation between liberal and
conservative forces in France came to a head in 1894 when a French army
officer of Jewish origin, Captain Alfred Dreyfus, was accused of espionage for
the Germans, convicted and imprisoned. Although the manifestly innocent
Dreyfus was eventually exonerated in 1906, the affair unleashed all the antisemitic passions of the French right, which generally believed that the Jews
of France, even – perhaps particularly – assimilated Jews like Dreyfus, were
seeking to weaken France and undermine her traditional values.[4]

The relationship between national crisis and intensified antisemitism
was shown once again in 1905, when the defeat of Russia by Japan and an
outbreak of revolutionary unrest was followed by pogroms throughout south-
western Russia. The worst pogroms, however, took place after the collapse of
Tsarist Russia in the 1917 Revolution. The years 1918 to 1920 saw economic
and social collapse, a bitter civil war between conservative forces and revolutionaries, and the unleashing of nationalist passions in areas like the
Ukraine. These events were the perfect setting for antisemitic pogroms, and
it is estimated that up to 300,000 Jews were killed during this period, particularly in the Ukraine and Belorussia.

In fact, after the First World War, a confluence of three developments
contributed to the heightening of antisemitic sentiment throughout Europe.

The first of these was the emergence of a general revolutionary threat in the wake of the seizure of power by the Bolsheviks in 1917, the defeat of Germany and the collapse of the Austrian Empire. It was widely assumed that Jews dominated the Bolshevik/Communist Party of the Soviet Union, and this impression of a link between international revolutionary activity and Jews was reinforced by the prominent roles that Jews played in the short-lived revolutions in 1919-1920 in Munich, Berlin and Budapest. Another development was, as has already been seen in chapter 4, the creation of a number of small, unstable and insecure nation-states in East and Central Europe. These nation-states were founded on the principle of ethnic nationalism, and therefore regarded any minority as a threat to national security, but particularly the Jews. The third factor destabilising inter-war Europe and encouraging antisemitism was the impact of the global economic depression that was triggered in 1929.

When we turn, therefore, to the rise to power of Adolf Hitler and his National Socialist German Workers' Party (NSDAP, or 'Nazi' Party for short), it is important to understand the extent to which antisemitism was a general feature of the politics of east and central Europe in the years between the First and Second World Wars. Hitler's youth in Vienna before the First World War provides a classic example, both of the kind of mentality that might be drawn to antisemitism, and of the kind of social and political milieu in which antisemitism took root and flourished (see document 2 at the end of this chapter).

It was through the Nazi Party that Adolf Hitler brought antisemitism into the mainstream of German politics after the First World War. Precisely because antisemitism was such a pervasive element of European populist politics in the early twentieth century, it was easy for contemporaries to dismiss Hitler's antisemitism as an ancillary element in his political strategy, to be used or shrugged off as occasion demanded.[5] Antisemitism was, however, the very core of his world-view. Hitler saw world history as a ceaseless 'biological' struggle between races, governed by a Darwinian law of the survival of the fittest, in which the very existence of racial civilisations – such as 'Aryan' Europe – was at stake. For Europe, the primary confrontation was with 'international Jewry' ('Das internationale Judentum'). According to Hitler, international finance and international socialism were two key weapons used by the Jews to destabilise and subvert Europe. After 1917, however, Hitler saw international socialism in the form of Bolshevism/Communism as the principal threat to Aryan Europe, because of its explicit use of the 'class struggle' as a weapon to weaken Aryan racial unity.

As a counter to the 'international' socialism of the Bolsheviks, therefore, Hitler relied on 'national socialism' as a means of welding together all classes in a common national and racial purpose.

Within this very broad world-view, Nazi ideology was muddled and opportunist. What, for example, was the relationship between race and nation? between the German 'volk' and Aryan Europe as a whole? Or, indeed, how was the Aryan race or any other race to be defined? Were the semitic Arabs, for example, to be considered a race enemy, and treated accordingly? The very imprecision of the concept of race allowed Hitler considerable scope to vary his policy according to political expediency. The only areas of absolute consistency in his outlook were, however, clear: the racial threat of 'international Jewry', combined with the ideological threat of Bolshevism/Communism. For Hitler, these two threats were symbiotically linked, and the fact that the epicentre of the global Bolshevik conspiracy was the Soviet Union linked Nazi ideology to that persistent strand in European thinking that saw 'the East' in general as a threat to European civilisation (see document 3 at the end of this chapter).

If this was the basis of Hitler's world-view, then genocide – the complete extermination of a race or people – was the logical consequence.[6] Initially, Hitler's treatment of the Jews was constrained by his need to win over, or at least neutralise, world opinion while he consolidated his power-base in Germany. Subsequently, as Hitler gained increasing confidence between 1933 and 1938, so his treatment of the Jews became correspondingly harsh. Generally, however, his Jewish policy up to 1938 was that of persecution and expulsion rather than extermination. The policy of genocide effectively began with the invasion of Poland and the outbreak of the Second World War. From then on, the very existence of Jews could be portrayed as a threat to national (perhaps one should say racial) survival. With the invasion in 1941 of the Soviet Union – the heartland of the 'Jewish-Bolshevik conspiracy' – the whole Pale of Settlement was opened up to Germany. Genocide against the Jews became an automatic part of a racial endeavour that involved Germany and all its racial and ideological allies throughout Europe. Later, the project of extermination was to a degree withdrawn from the public view, carried out by an ideological élite, systematised and bureaucratised. By the end of the war, it is estimated that up to six million Jews were murdered by the Nazi regime and its allies.

Those who are astonished at the fact that the Nazis were prepared to waste resources and choke up vital logistics during a life-and-death war for the sake of such a hideous and pointless exercise are missing the essence of

Hitler's racial logic. For Hitler and the Nazis, Auschwitz and the other death camps were a crucial front-line of the war effort.

1939-1945 saw the natural consequence of the antisemitism and racial ideology that had taken root in Europe in the nineteenth and twentieth centuries: systematic genocide. The 'Holocaust' – as it was called from the Hebrew word 'shoah', meaning devastation – wiped out the distinctive, centuries-old Jewish civilisation of the Pale of Settlement: its culture, religion and language, as well as its people. The same thing happened to Jewish communities throughout Europe, and – it must not be forgotten – to a large number of people who, despite their Jewish origins, did not identify themselves as Jewish, but as Germans, Dutch, French or Italians, etc. The Nazi version of antisemitism had linked up with the nationalist and traditional religious versions of antisemitism that pervaded Europe during that time. The nationalist view that Jews could not be part of the nation had fused with the much more apocalyptic racial view that the Jews were a mortal enemy to European civilisation.

It is not too much to say that the Holocaust of 1939-1945 was the most significant event in Europe in the twentieth century. The death trains, the camps, the mass burial-pits of the Eastern Front have haunted Europe since the end of the war. The issue of the general complicity of the German people; the ancillary complicity of many people in Europe as a whole, where anti-semitism had seeped into the political culture; the cowardly silence of the Churches; the fact that major intellectual, literary and artistic figures throughout Europe lent their reputation and support to the depraved political climate of the time; the unrestrained sadism that was unleashed and justified by racial ideology: all these have raised tormenting but ultimately unanswerable questions. Above all, the Holocaust raised a question-mark over the optimistic Enlightenment view that humanity could, through the operation of reason, create a better world for itself. Eighteenth- and nineteenth-century thinkers had dreamed of the heights which humanity could reach if it was liberated from the constraints of tradition and religion. The twentieth century showed – through the Nazi regime and its ideological counterpart, the communist state in the Soviet Union – the unfathomable depths of barbarity that could be plumbed.

'Ice will rise from the dead,' wrote the Romanian-born Jewish poet Paul Celan. After 1945, Europe knew its own potential for barbarism, and was in consequence frozen in self-doubt, with a more pessimistic and cautious view of human nature and the potential for human progress. Paradoxically, this has probably helped make Europe a safer and a more civilised place.

Documents

(Nb: in all the following extracts, editorial comments at the beginning of texts, or amendments and explanations in the texts themselves, will be placed in square brackets. Headings and subdivisions will be put in italics.)

1 – Céline and the 'Protocols of the Elders of Zion'

[Louis-Ferdinand Céline was one of the most eminent French writers of the early-to-mid-twentieth century. His literary genius, however, went hand-in-hand with an almost deranged antisemitism, which was most fully expressed in a book published in 1937, *Bagatelles pour un Massacre*. Although this book in general is little more than a confused and rambling compendium of the usual themes of antisemitism, it is interesting to note the emphasis it places on the combined danger posed by the Jewish, the Anglo-American and the Russian-Bolshevik worlds to European civilisation: the threat to Europe posed by 'Moscow' on one side, and 'Hollywood' and 'Jewish-Negro' culture on the other, linked by a common Jewish conspiracy. This was a favourite theme of a certain strand of the French intelligentsia of the inter-war period, and served – as in the case of Céline himself – to justify collaboration with Nazi Germany. In post-1945 France, French obsession with the 'Anglo-Saxon' threat to Europe and to France shared many of the characteristics of France's pre-war antisemitism, as the language of Céline's book clearly reveals.

For the purposes of this study of antisemitism, the main interest in *Bagatelles pour un Massacre* is the rough summary that Céline gives in it of the main aspects of the 'global Jewish conspiracy' outlined in the forged document, 'The Protocols of the Elders of Zion'. What is immediately apparent from this document is that the major fear that antisemitism was able to exploit – particularly after the trauma of the First World War – was that of political, economic and social instability.]

The Jewish conspiracy against Europe: Céline's summary of the 'Protocols of the Elders of Zion'

'Gold managed by expert hands will always be the most useful lever for those who possess it, and an object of envy for those who do not possess it.

'With gold, one can buy off the most stubborn consciences, fix the worth of things, and bring into debt states which can then be held at one's mercy.

'Already the principal banks, the Stock Exchanges world-wide, the debts of all governments is in our hands. The other great power is that of the press. By repeating endlessly certain ideas, the press can eventually convert these into truths. The theatre can do the same. Everywhere, the theatre and the press obeys our directions.

'By continuously praising the democratic system, we will divide the Christians into political parties. We will destroy the unity of their nations, and we will spread discord. Powerless, they will be subjected to the power of our banks, who are always united in their devotion to our cause.

'We will push the Christians into war by exploiting their pride and their stupidity. They will massacre each other and destroy each other wherever and whenever it suits us.

'The possession of land has always procured influence and power. In the name of social justice and equality, we will parcel out large estates; we will give these fragments to the peasantry, who want them so much, and who will soon get into debt because of our exploitation. We will use our capital to snare them.

'We will become major landowners in our turn, and the possession of land will consolidate our power.

'We will go all-out to replace the circulation of gold by that of paper-money: our own coffers will absorb all the gold, and then we will regulate the value of paper-money, which will put us in control of the very means of existence.

'We can count among our ranks orators capable of feigning enthusiasm and persuading the masses. We will spread them out among the masses in order to campaign for changes which will "benefit humanity".

'By gold and flattery, we will win over the proletariat, who will commit themselves to destroy *Christian* capitalism. We will promise to the workers salaries that they would never have dared dream of, but we will at the same time raise the price of essentials, so that our profit will be all the greater.

'In this way, we will prepare the way for revolutions which the Christians will direct against each other, and we will reap the fruits.

'By our mockery and our attacks, we will make their priests first ridiculous, and then hateful, and their religion as ridiculous and as harmful as their clergy. Then we will be masters of their souls – because our pious attachment to *our* religion, to *our* religious ceremonies, will prove to [the people] the superiority of our souls.

'We have already placed our people in all the important positions. Let us now make an effort to infiltrate lawyers and doctors among the *goyim* ['gentiles', non-Jews]; the lawyers will keep in touch with everything that's going on; and doctors – once they are in a house, they can become father-confessors and guides for behaviour. But above everything else we must monopolise teaching. In this way, we will spread ideas that are useful to us, and we will bend minds to our way of thinking.

'If one of us should unfortunately fall into the claws of Christian justice, we must all rush to his aid: find as much evidence as will be needed to save him from his judges – until such time that we ourselves will become the judges.

'Christian monarchs, swollen with ambition and vanity, surround themselves with luxury and huge armies. We will supply them with all the money that their stupidity requires, and thus we will put them on our leash...'

The aim of the 'Jewish conspiracy' is to:

'Encourage uninhibited luxury, outrageous fashions, crazy expense; and, in this way, gradually eliminate the capacity to enjoy the simple and healthy joys of life.

'Distract the masses by popular amusements, games, sporting competitions etc.; amuse the populace, so as to prevent them from thinking.

'Poison the spirit with baneful theories; ruin the nervous system by an endless hubbub, and enfeeble the body by the spreading of viruses.

'Create a universal discontent, and provoke hatred and distrust between the classes.

'Despoil the aristocracy of their traditional rights and their land, and weigh them down with huge taxes, thus forcing them to contract debts: take over as business tycoons, and disseminate the cult of money.

'Poison the relationship between bosses and workers by strikes and "lock-outs", and thus eliminate any possibility of good relations, from which could result a harmonious industrial cooperation.

'Demoralise the upper classes by all means available and provoke fury among the masses at the perceived depravity and stupidity of the rich.

'Allow industry to squeeze out agriculture, and gradually transform industry into a system of crazy speculation. Encourage all kinds of utopian visions in order to lead the masses into a labyrinth of impractical ideas. Increase the salaries of workers; without any benefit to them, however, because of the simultaneous hiking up of the cost of living.

'Encourage "incidents", provoking suspicion between nations; envenom even further conflicts between peoples; unleash hatred and encourage a destructive arms race.

'Support universal suffrage, so the destinies of nations may be entrusted to the least well-educated sections of the population.

'Overthrow all monarchies, and establish republics everywhere, intrigue to ensure that the most important posts may be entrusted to people with disreputable secrets, in order to be able to have a hold on them because of their fear of a scandal.

'Gradually abolish all industrial restraints, in order to put in place the absolute control of a communist system.

'Organise huge monopolies in which vast fortunes will lie hidden, until the time that the political crisis reaches a climax.

'Destroy all financial stability; multiply economic crises, and prepare the way for global bankruptcy; stop the wheels of industry; bring about a collapse of the financial system; concentrate all the world's gold in a few hands; leave huge sums of capital in stagnation; and, at a given moment, suspend all credit and provoke a panic. Prepare for the final death throes of states, exhaust humanity by suffering, anguish and privation – because hunger creates slaves.'

This [concludes Céline] is the exact substance [of the Jewish plot]. In the great hour of destiny, when the cards are finally down... Mr Rothschild and Mr Marx, previously at odds, will find themselves completely in accord in their plot to entice us, 'all comrades together', to shoot each other up like fish in a barrel, and turn each other into mincemeat. This is the final Jewish endgame, the last act in their grand conspiracy...

[Translated by C.J. Christie from Louis-Ferdinand Céline, *Bagatelles pour un Massacre* (Paris, Editions Denoel, 1937), pp 165-172]

2 – Adolf Hitler: antisemitism and the 'philosophy of the doss-house'

[Adolf Hitler (1889-1945) was the son of a minor official in the Austrian Government. In 1908, he moved to Vienna, but was unable either to enter the Academy of Fine Arts as a student, or find a steady job. Though he had an artistic 'temperament', he lacked anything more than a mediocre artistic talent. From 1907 to 1913, when he moved to Germany, he lived the life of a drifter, refusing to accept work that did not live up to his notion of his worth and his social status.[7] It is in this period that he came into contact with the political life of Vienna, and developed his political outlook. In his classic biography, *Hitler: A Study in Tyranny*, Alan Bullock made the following analysis of the link between Hitler's political ideas and his psychological make-up. All the quotes in the following passage are from Hitler's own book, *Mein Kampf (My Struggle)*.

It should be noted that Hitler wrote *Mein Kampf* after the First World War. The passages from *Mein Kampf* relating to his youth, therefore, should not necessarily be seen as an exact indication of the views that he held while he was in Vienna, but rather as a general picture of his political, particularly antisemitic, views up to the time that he embarked on his political career in the early 1920s.

It should also be noted that the Austrian Social Democratic Party referred to below was essentially Marxist in its programme, a forerunner of the Communist movement that emerged in the post-First World War era.]

'The idea of struggle is as old as life itself, for life is only preserved because other living things perish through struggle... In this struggle, the stronger, the more able, win, while the less able, the weak, lose. Struggle is the father of all things... It is not by the principles of humanity that man lives or is able to preserve himself above the animal world, but solely by means of the most brutal struggle... If you do not fight for life, then life will never be won.'

This is natural philosophy of the doss-house. In this struggle any trick or ruse, however unscrupulous, the use of any weapon or opportunity, however treacherous, are permissible. To quote another typical sentence from Hitler's speeches: 'Whatever goal man has reached is due to his originality plus his brutality'. Astuteness; the ability to lie, twist, cheat and flatter; the elimination of sentimentality or loyalty in favour of ruthlessness: these were the qualities which enabled man to rise; above all, strength of will. Such were the principles which Hitler drew from his years in Vienna. Hitler never trusted anyone; he never committed himself to anyone, never admitted any loyalty. His lack of scruple later took by surprise even those who prided themselves on their unscrupulousness. He learned to lie with conviction and dissemble with candour. To the end he refused to admit defeat and still held to the belief that by the power of will alone he could transform events.

Distrust was matched by contempt. Men were moved by fear, greed, lust for power, envy, often by mean and petty motives. Politics, Hitler was later to conclude, is the art of knowing how to use these weaknesses for one's own ends. Already in Vienna Hitler admired Karl Lueger, the famous Burgomaster of Vienna and leader of the Christian Social Party, because 'he had a rare gift of insight into human nature and was very careful not to take men as something better than they were in reality'. He felt particular contempt for the masses: 'everybody who properly estimates the political intelligence of the masses can easily see that this is not sufficiently developed to enable them to form general political judgements on their own account'. Here again was material to be manipulated by a skilful politician. As yet Hitler had no idea of making a political career, but he spent a great deal of time reading and arguing politics, and what he learned was an important part of his political apprenticeship.

In the situation in which he found himself in Vienna, Hitler clung tenaciously to the conviction that he was better than people with whom he was now driven to associate. 'Those among whom I passed my younger days belonged to the petit bourgeois class... The ditch which separated that class, which is by no means well-off, from the manual labouring class is often deeper than people think. The reason for this division, which we may almost call enmity, lies in the fear that dominates a social group which has only just risen above the level of the manual labourer − a fear lest it may fall back into its old condition or at least be classed with the labourers...'

Although Hitler writes in *Mein Kampf* of the misery in which the Vienna working class lived at this time, it is evident from every line of the account that these conditions produced no feeling of sympathy in him. 'I do not know which appalled me most at that time: the economic misery of those who were then my companions, their crude customs and morals, or the low level of their intellectual culture'. Least of all did he feel any sympathy with the attempts of the poor and the exploited to improve their position by their own efforts. Hitler's hatred was directed not so much against the rogues, beggars, bankrupt business men, and *déclassé* 'gentlemen' who were the flotsam and jetsam drifting in and out of the hostel in the Meldemannstrasse [Hitler's lodging between 1910 and 1913], as against the working men who belonged to organisations like the Social Democratic Party and the trade unions, and who preached equality and solidarity of the working classes. It was these, much more than the former, who threatened his claim to superiority. Solidarity was a virtue for which Hitler had no use. He passionately refused to join a trade union, or in any way to accept the status of a working man.

The whole ideology of the working-class movement was alien and hateful to him:

> All that I heard had the effect of arousing the strongest antagonism in me. Everything was disparaged – the nation because it was held to be an invention of the capitalist class (how often I had to listen to that phrase!); the Fatherland, because it was held to be an instrument in the hands of the bourgeoisie for the exploitation of the working masses; the authority of the law, because this was a means of holding down the proletariat; religion, as a means of doping the people, so as to exploit them afterwards; morality, as a badge of stupid and sheepish docility. There was nothing that they did not drag in the mud... Then I asked myself: are these men worthy to belong to a great people? The question was profoundly disturbing; for if the answer were 'Yes,' then the struggle to defend one's nationality is no longer worth all the trouble and sacrifice we demand of our best elements if it be in the interest of such a rabble. On the other hand, if the answer had to be 'No,' then our nation is poor indeed in men. During these days of mental anguish and deep meditation I saw before my mind the ever-increasing and menacing army of people who could no longer be reckoned as belonging to their own nation.

Hitler found the solution of his dilemma in the 'discovery' that the working men were the victims of a deliberate system for corrupting and poisoning the popular mind, organised by the Social Democratic Party's leaders, who cynically exploited the distress of the masses for their own ends. Then came the crowning revelation: 'I discovered the relations existing between this destructive teaching and the specific character of a people, who up to that time had been almost unknown to me. Knowledge of the Jews is the only key whereby one may understand the inner nature and real aims of Social Democracy.'

There was nothing new in Hitler's antisemitism; it was endemic in Vienna, and everything he ever said or wrote about the Jews is only a reflection of the antisemitic periodicals and pamphlets he read in Vienna before 1914. In Linz there had been very few Jews – 'I do not remember ever having heard the word at home during my father's lifetime'. Even in Vienna Hitler had at first been repelled by the violence of the antisemitic press. Then, 'one day, when passing through the Inner City, I suddenly encountered a phenomenon in a long caftan and wearing black sidelocks. My first thought was: is this a Jew? They certainly did not have this appearance in Linz. I watched the man stealthily and cautiously, but the longer I gazed at this strange countenance and examined it section by section, the more the question shaped itself in my brain: is this a German? I turned to books for help in removing my doubts. For the first time in my life I bought myself some anti-Semitic pamphlets for a few pence.'

The language in which Hitler describes his discovery has the obscene taint to be found in most antisemitic literature: 'Was there any shady undertaking, any form of foulness, especially in cultural life, in which at least one Jew did not participate? On putting the probing knife carefully to that kind of abscess one immediately discovered, like a maggot in a putrescent body, a little Jew who was often blinded by the sudden light.'

Especially characteristic of Viennese antisemitism was its sexuality. 'The black-haired Jewish youth lies in wait for hours on end, satanically glaring at and spying on the unsuspicious girl whom he plans to seduce, adulterating her blood and removing her from the bosom of her own people... The Jews were responsible for bringing negroes into the Rhineland with the ultimate idea of bastardising the white race which they hate and thus lowering its cultural and political level so that the Jew might dominate.' Elsewhere Hitler writes of the 'nightmare vision of the seduction of hundreds of thousands of girls by repulsive, crooked-legged Jew bastards'. More than one writer has suggested that some sexual experience – possibly the contraction of venereal disease – was at the back of Hitler's antisemitism.

In all the pages which Hitler devotes to the Jews in *Mein Kampf* he does not bring forward a single fact to support his wild assertions. This was entirely right, for Hitler's antisemitism bore no relation to facts, it was pure fantasy: to read these pages is to enter the world of the insane, a world peopled by hideous and distorted shadows. The Jew is no longer a human being, he has become a mythological figure, a grimacing, leering devil invested with infernal powers, the incarnation of evil, into which Hitler projects all that he hates and fears – and desires. Like all obsessions, the Jew is not a partial, but a total explanation. The Jew is everywhere, responsible for everything – the Modernism in art and music Hitler disliked; pornography and prostitution; the anti-national criticism of the Press; the exploitation of the masses by Socialism; not least for his own failure to get on. 'Thus I finally discovered who were the evil spirits leading our people astray... My love for my own people increased correspondingly. Considering the satanic skill which these evils counsellors displayed, how could their unfortunate victims be blamed?... The more I came to know the Jew, the easier it was to excuse the workers.'

Behind all this, Hitler soon convinced himself, lay a Jewish world conspiracy to destroy and subdue the Aryan peoples, as an act of revenge for their own inferiority. Their purpose was to weaken the nation by fomenting social divisions and class conflict, and by attacking the values of race, heroism, struggle, and authoritarian rule in favour of the false internationalist, humanitarian, pacifist, materialist ideals of democracy. 'The Jewish doctrine of Marxism repudiates the aristocratic principle of nature and substitutes for it and the eternal privilege of force and energy, numerical mass and dead weight. Thus it denies the individual worth of the human personality, impugns the teaching that nationhood and race have a primary significance, and by doing this takes away the very foundations of human existence and human civilisation.'

In Hitler's eyes the inequality of individuals and races was one of the laws of Nature. This poor wretch, often half-starved, without a job, family, or home, clung obstinately to any belief that would bolster up the claim of his own superiority. He belonged by right, he felt, to the *Herrenmenschen* ('Supermen'). To preach equality was to threaten the belief which kept him going, that he was different from the labourers, the tramps, the Jews and the Slavs with whom he rubbed shoulders in the streets.

Hitler had no use for any democratic institution: free speech, free press, or parliament. During the earlier part of his time in Vienna he had sometimes attended the sessions of the Reichsrat, the representative assembly of the Austrian half of the empire, and he devotes 15 pages of *Mein Kampf* to expressing his scorn for what he saw. Parliamentary democracy reduced government to political jobbery, it put a premium on mediocrity and was inimical to leadership, encouraged the avoidance of responsibility, and sacrificed decisions to party compromises. 'The majority represents not only ignorance but cowardice... The majority can never replace the man.'

All his life Hitler was irritated by discussion. In the arguments into which he was drawn in the hostel for men or in cafés he showed no self-control in the face of contradiction or debate. He began to shout and shower abuse on his opponents, with an hysterical note in his voice. It was precisely the same pattern of uncontrolled behaviour he displayed when he came to supreme power and found himself crossed or contradicted. This authoritarian temper developed with the exercise of power, but it was already there in his twenties, the instinct of tyranny.

[From Alan Bullock, *Hitler: A Study in Tyranny* (Penguin Books, Harmondsworth, 1962), pp 36-41]

3 – Hitler and the link between antisemitism and anti-'Bolshevism'

[Like other believers in the 'Jewish conspiracy', Hitler saw the threat of world Jewish domination as a kind of pincer movement between Jewish financial interests on the one side and a Jewish-dominated international socialist movement on the other. But it is noticeable that Hitler was particularly obsessed by what he saw as the link between Jewish interests and socialism, particularly of the Marxist variety. This explains his particular loathing before 1914 for the Social Democrats in Vienna.

After the First World War, of course, leadership of world Marxism or International Socialism passed to the Bolshevik Party – later Communist Party – of the Soviet Union. Hitler accordingly turned his attention to Bolshevism as the main Jewish instrument for the destruction of European civilisation. The continuity of Hitler's thinking on this is evident in the three following passages: the first is an extract from Hitler's *Mein Kampf*, written in 1924-1925; the second is a memorandum written by Hitler in August 1936, roughly three years after he had gained power, and three years before the outbreak of the Second World War; and the third is an extract from his final 'Political Testament' composed just before his death in April 1945.

Though there can be no doubt that Hitler's immediate decisions were often determined by pragmatic rather than ideological considerations, what should be noted in the documents below is his underlying world-view, which remained consistent throughout his political career.]

Hitler in Vienna before the First World War: the link between the Jewish conspiracy and Marxism

… Under the inducement of my everyday experience, I now began to seek out the sources of the Marxian doctrine. Its workings were clear to me in individual instances; my observant eye daily marked its successes, and with a little imagination I was able to figure out the consequences of it…

Thus I began to make myself acquainted with the founders of the doctrine in order to study the principles of the Movement. The fact that I achieved my object quicker than I dared hope at first was thanks to the knowledge I had gained of the Jewish question, though at that time it had not gone very deep. Nothing but that made possible to me a practical comparison of its realities with the theoretic claims of the first apostles of Social Democracy, since it had taught me to understand the verbal methods of the Jewish people, whose aim is to hide, or at least cloak, their ideas; their real objective is not to be read on the lines, but is tucked away well concealed between them.

It was at this time that the greatest change took place in me that I was ever to experience. From being a feeble world citizen, I became a fanatical antisemite.

During my long study of the influence of the Jewish nation throughout long periods of human history, the gloomy question suddenly occurred to me whether possibly inscrutable destiny, for reasons unknown to us poor mortals, had not decreed the final victory of that little nation. But this question was answered in the negative by the Jewish doctrine itself.

The Jewish doctrine of Marxism rejects the aristocratic principle in nature, and in place of the eternal privilege of force and strength sets up the mass and dead weight of numbers. It thus denies the value of the individual among men, combats the importance of nationality and race, thereby depriving humanity of the whole meaning of its existence and *Kultur*. It would, therefore, as a principle of the Universe, conduce to an end of all order conceivable to mankind.

If the Jew, with the help of the Marxian creed, conquers the nations of this world, his crown will be the funeral wreath of the human race, and the planet will drive through the ether once again empty of mankind as it did millions of years ago.

Eternal nature takes inexorable revenge on any usurpation of her realm.

Thus did I now believe that I must act in the sense of the Almighty Creator: by defending myself against the Jews I am doing the Lord's work.

[From Adolf Hitler, *Mein Kampf* (*My Struggle*) (London, Hurst and Blackett Ltd, 1938), pp 34-36]

Memorandum by Adolf Hitler on the threat facing Germany in 1936

The political situation

Politics are the conduct and the course of the historical struggle for life of the peoples. The aim of these struggles is the assertion of existence. Even the idealistic ideological struggles (*Weltanschauungskampfe*) have their ultimate cause and are most deeply motivated by nationally (*volklich*) determined purposes and aims of life. Religions and ideologies are, however, always able to impart particular harshness to struggles of this kind, and therefore also to give them great historical impressiveness. They leave their imprint on the content of centuries. In such cases it is not possible for peoples and States living within the sphere of such ideological or religious conflicts to dissociate or exclude themselves from these events. Christianity and the migration of peoples determined the historical content of centuries. Mohammedanism too convulsed the Orient, and with it the Western world, for half a millennium. The Reformation caught up the whole of Central Europe in its wake. Nor was it possible for individual States – either by skill or by deliberate non-participation – to steer clear of events. Since the outbreak of the French Revolution, the world has been moving with ever-increasing speed towards a new conflict, the most extreme solution of which is called Bolshevism, whose essence and aim, however, is solely the elimination of those strata of mankind which have hitherto provided the leadership and their replacement by world-wide Jewry.

No State will be able to withdraw or even remain at a distance from this historical conflict. *Since Marxism, through its victory in Russia, has established one of the greatest empires in the world as a forward base for its future operations, this question has become a menacing one. Against a democratic world ideologically rent within itself stands a unified aggressive will founded upon an authoritarian ideology.* The means of military power available to this aggressive will are meantime increasing rapidly from year to year. One has only to compare the Red Army as it actually exists today with the assumptions of military men 10 or 15 years ago to realise the menacing extent of this development. Only consider the result of a further development over 10, 15 or 20 years and think what conditions will be like then!

Germany

Germany will, as always, have to be regarded as the focal point of the Western world in face of the Bolshevist attacks. I do not regard this as an agreeable mission but rather as a handicap and encumbrance upon our national life regrettably resulting from our position in Europe.

We cannot, however, escape this destiny.

Our political situation results from the following: Europe has at present only two states which can be regarded as standing firm in the face of Bolshevism: Germany and [fascist] Italy. The other countries are either disintegrated through their democratic form of life, infected by Marxism, and thus likely themselves to collapse in the foreseeable future, or ruled by authoritarian Governments whose sole strength lies in their military means of power; this means, however, that, being obliged to secure the existence of their leadership in the face of their own peoples by means of the armed hand of the Executive, they are unable to direct this armed hand outwards for the preservation their States. All these countries would be incapable of ever conducting a war against Soviet Russia with any prospects of success. In any case, apart from Germany and Italy, only Japan can be regarded as a Power standing firm in the face of the world peril.

It is not the aim of this memorandum to prophesy the time when the untenable situation in Europe will become an open crisis. I only want in these lines to set down my conviction that this crisis cannot and will not fail to arrive and that it is Germany's duty to secure her own existence by every means in the face of this catastrophe, and to protect herself against it, and that from this compulsion there arises a series of conclusions relating to the most important tasks that our people have ever been set. *For a victory of Bolshevism over Germany would not lead to a Versailles Treaty but to the final destruction, indeed to the annihilation of the German people.* [The Versailles Treaty was signed by Germany after her defeat in 1918.]

The extent of such a catastrophe cannot be foreseen. How, indeed, would the whole of densely populated Western Europe (including Germany), after a collapse into Bolshevism (*nacht einem bolschewistischen Zusammenbruch*), live through probably the most gruesome catastrophe for the peoples which has been visited upon mankind since the downfall of the States of antiquity? *In the face of the necessity of defence against this danger, all other considerations must recede into the background as being completely irrelevant.*

Germany's defensive capacity

Germany's defensive capacity is based upon several factors. I would give pride of place to the intrinsic value of the German people *per se*. A German people with an impeccable political leadership, a firm ideology and a thorough military organisation certainly constitutes the most valuable factor of resistance which the world of today can possess. Political leadership is ensured by the National Socialist Party; ideological solidarity has, since the victory of National Socialism, been introduced to a degree that had never been previously attained. It must be constantly deepened and hardened on the basis of this concept. This is the aim of the National Socialist education of our people.

Military development is to be effected through the new Army. *The extent and pace of the military development of our resources cannot be made too large or too rapid!* It is a capital error to think that there can be any argument on these points or any comparison with other vital necessities. However much the general pattern of life of a people ought to be a balanced one, it is nonetheless imperative that at particular times certain disturbances of the balance, to the detriment of other, less vital, tasks, must be adopted. *If we do not succeed in developing the German Army within the shortest possible time into the first Army in the world, in training, in the raising of units, in armaments, and, above all, in spiritual education as well, Germany will be lost!*

All other desires must therefore be unconditionally subordinated to this task. For this task is life and the preservation of life, and all other desires – however understandable they may be in other periods – are, by comparison, of no account or are even mortally dangerous and therefore to be rejected. Nor will posterity ever ask us by what methods or by what concepts, views, etc, which are valid today, we achieved the salvation of the nations, but only *whether* we achieved it. Nor would it one day be an excuse for our downfall were we to point to the measures, be they never so well tried, which had nevertheless unfortunately caused that downfall.

Germany's economic position

Just as the political movement among our people knows only one goal – to make good the claim to life of our people and Reich, that is to say to secure all the spiritual and other prerequisites for the self-assertion of our people – so too the economy has but this one purpose. The people do not live for the economy or for economic leaders or economic or financial theories; on the contrary, finance and economy, economic leaders and theories must all exclusively serve this struggle for self-assertion in which our people are engaged...

... I therefore draw up the following programme for a final solution of our vital needs.

Like the military and political rearmament and mobilisation of our people, there must also be an economic one, and this must be effected in the same tempo, with the same determination, and, if need be, with the same ruth-lessness as well.

In future, the interests of individual gentlemen can no longer be allowed to play any part in these matters. There is only one interest and that is the interest of the nation, and only one single view, which is that Germany must be brought politically and economically into a state of self-sufficiency...

... I consider it necessary that now, with iron determination, 100 per cent self-sufficiency should be attained in all those spheres where it is feasible, and not only should the national requirements in [the] most important raw materials be made independent of other countries but that we should also thus save the foreign exchange which in peacetime we require for our imports of foodstuffs...

But I further consider it necessary to make an immediate investigation into the outstanding debts in foreign exchange owed to German business abroad. There is no doubt that the outstanding claims of German business are today quite enormous. Nor is there any doubt that behind this in some cases there lies concealed the contemptible desire to possess, whatever happens, certain reserves abroad which are thus withheld from the grasp of the domestic economy. I regard this as deliberate sabotage of our national self-assertion and of the defence of the Reich, and for this reason I consider it necessary for the Reichstag to pass the following two laws:

1   A law providing for the death penalty for economic sabotage, and
2   A law making the whole of Jewry liable for all damage inflicted by individual specimens of this community of criminals upon the German economy, and thus upon the German people.

... I thus set the following task:
1   The Germany Army must be operational (*einsatzfahig*) within four years.
2   The Germany economy must be fit for war (*kriegsfahig*) within four years.

[From *Documents of German Foreign Policy 1918-1945*, Series C (1933-1937), *The Third Reich: First Phase*, Volume V, 5 March-31 October 1936, pp 853-856, 859, 861-862]

Hitler's Political Testament, written just before his suicide in the Berlin bunker, April 1945

...It is untrue that I or anybody else in Germany wanted war in 1939. It was wanted and provoked exclusively by those international statesmen who either were of Jewish origin or worked for Jewish interests.

... I have never wished that after the appalling First World War there should be a second one against either England or America. Centuries will go by, but from the ruins of our towns and monuments the hatred of those ultimately responsible will always grow anew. They are the people whom we have to thank for all this: international Jewry and all its helpers.

... Three days before the outbreak of the German-Polish war, I suggested to the British Ambassador in Berlin a solution of the German-Polish question... It was rejected only because the ruling political clique in England wanted war, partly for commercial reasons, partly because it was influenced by propaganda put out by international Jewry.

... I also made it quite plain that, if the peoples of Europe were again to be regarded merely as pawns in a game played by the international conspiracy of money and finance, they, the Jews, the race that is the real guilty party in this murderous struggle, would be saddled with the responsibility for it.

... I left no-one in doubt that this time not only would millions of grown men meet their death and not only would hundreds of thousands of women and children be burned and bombed to death in cities, but this time the real culprits would have to pay for their guilt even though by more humane means than war.

After six years of war, which, in spite of all setbacks, will one day go down in history as the most glorious and heroic manifestation of the struggle for existence of a nation, I cannot forsake the city that is the capital of this state ... I wish to share my fate with that which millions of others have also taken upon themselves by staying in this town. Further, I shall not fall in the hands of the enemy, who requires a new spectacle, presented by the Jews, to divert their hysterical masses.

[But the armed forces and the people, strengthened by the 'National Socialist belief', must continue the 'nation's struggle' to the end. The Testament concludes...]

... Above all, I enjoin the government of the nation and the people to uphold the racial laws to the limit and to resist mercilessly the poisoner of all nations, international Jewry.

Berlin, 29 April 1945, 0400 hours

[From William R. Shirer, *End of a Berlin Diary* (London, Hamish Hamilton, 1947), pp 180–181, 183]

NOTES ON CHAPTER 7

1   For an insight into the antisemitic attitudes of many of the landed gentry in Europe, see chapter entitled 'The Father', in Gregor von Rezzori, *The Snows of Yesteryear: Portraits for an Autobiography* (London, Chatto and Windus, 1990).

2   Karl Marx and Frederick Engels (1848), *The Communist Manifesto*, Section I: 'Bourgeois and Proletarians'.

3   For a fascinating picture of life in the Jewish ghetto in the East End of London at the beginning of the twentieth century, see Israel Zangwill's novel, *Children of the Ghetto* (London, J.M. Dent and Sons, 1909).

4   The 'Dreyfus Affair' is a vitally important underlying theme in Marcel Proust's novel, *Remembrance of Things Past*, translated by C.K. Scott Moncrieff and Terence Kilmartin, 3 volumes (London, Penguin Books, 1989).

5   For example, Hermann Rauschning's contemporary analysis of Nazism, *Germany's Revolution of Destruction*, shrewdly highlighted what might be called the nihilist-revolutionary elements in Hitler's ideology, but missed the central role that antisemitism played in his political thinking. See Hermann Rauschning, *Germany's Revolution of Destruction* (London, William Heinemann, 1939).

6   It is significant that the other main group that was a victim of genocide under Hitler's regime were the Gypsies who, like the Jews, were categorised as non-European.

7   As has recently been noted by George Steiner ('On the Edge of Hunger', *TLS*, 31 January 1997, p 3), there is a strong resemblance between the psychological makeup of the fictional protagonist of Knut Hamsun's novel *Hunger* (1890), and that of the young Hitler in Vienna. Hamsun's novel had a profound impact on European literature.

Part IV

Race, Nation and Colonialism

Chapter 8

Zionism

'By the rivers of Babylon, there we sat down;
yea, we wept, when we remembered Zion.'

By the river of Bâle we sit down, resolved to weep no
more.

Israel Zangwill, writing about the First International
Congress of Zionists in Basel, Switzerland, 1897; from
Israel Zangwill, *Dreamers of the Ghetto* (London, William
Heinemann, 1897), p 391

Zionism

At the core of Judaism, the Jewish religion, is the notion of a covenant
between the Jews and God. The essence of the covenant is the understanding
that, if the Jews remain faithful to God and his laws, then they will eventually
be 'redeemed' from their 'captivity' or exile in foreign lands, and allowed to
return once again to the land that had once been given by God to the children
of the Jewish patriarch Jacob or, as he was also called, 'Israel': hence, 'the land
of Israel' ('eretz Israel'). This aspiration for redemption was given the name
'Zionism', after Mount Zion in Jerusalem. This hope for spiritual redemption
and return was, however, entirely subject to God's will. To attempt to 'force'
a return to Israel without God's sanction was – and is – for 'spiritual' Zionists
a violation of the most fundamental aspect of the Jewish religion: absolute
submission to God's authority.

In the course of the nineteenth century, a quite different kind of Zionism
emerged, namely nationalist Zionism or Jewish nationalism. The leaders of

this new movement were largely secular Jews, and their objective was to create a 'national home' in Palestine, not, like the 'spiritual' Zionists, in 'God's time', but through their own efforts.

Two crucial factors stimulated the emergence of this modern Zionist movement. The first, and probably the most important, was the persistence – indeed intensification – of antisemitism in the nineteenth century. The various measures for the civic emancipation of the Jews throughout most of Europe had seemed to offer secular Jews in particular a new era in which they would be able to become full citizens of the states they inhabited, with equal rights and equal opportunities. The late nineteenth century showed, however, that traditional Christian religious prejudice against the Jews had been replaced by a new and more virulent form of antisemitism. The antisemitism of the new nationalism was more implacable than traditional religious anti-Jewish prejudice, since it was directed against the racial origin of the Jewish people rather than their faith. The bleak logic of racially based antisemitism removed even the option of full-scale assimilation as a means of escaping discrimination and persecution. Even if the Jews were to 'disappear' as a people – that is, if they were to renounce their religion and all aspects of their culture and identity – they could not meet a racially-based criterion of belonging. Racially-based antisemitism determined that the Jews as a race were inherently outsiders; they had no place, therefore, in Europe. Europe-wide incidents, such as the 1881-1882 pogroms in Tsarist Russia and the Dreyfus affair in France, also demonstrated that they had no hiding-place.

This pessimistic vision of the future of the Jews in Europe was comple-mented by the pervasive influence of the national idea. At a time when ethnic groups throughout Europe were discovering their national identities and building nationalist movements with the objective of creating nation-states, it was natural that many Jewish intellectuals, particularly in the face of anti-semitism, should follow the same road. The Jewish people, after all, had all the requisite ingredients of national identity; their history, their ethnic 'roots', their religion, their culture and their language. Secular Zionists argued that what ultimately bound Jews together in the modern age was not so much their faith – Judaism, that is – but the sense of a common identity. What had previously been seen in religious terms - the Bible, Hebrew, Jewish customs and festivals - should now be seen in the new nationalist era as 'badges' of a national identity.

Zionism and the question of territory

The main problem that confronted the Zionist nationalist project was that of land. The Jews of Europe had no land they could call their own. One nationalist solution to this problem was promoted by a movement known as the Jewish 'Bund', formed in the Pale of Settlement in 1897. Essentially, the Bundists argued that a Jewish nation could be created out of the dispersed Jewish communities of the Pale of Settlement. This nation would have no territorial core: but an archipelago of Jewish communities, linked by their cultural identity rather than possession of land, would collectively regulate their own social and legal affairs within European states. This concept of the non-territorial 'cultural nation' was borrowed from ideas that were current at the time in the Austrian Empire as a possible solution to the complex 'nationalities' problem within that empire. The Bundists were secular and socialist in their outlook, and linked their aspirations with the general revolutionary aspiration of the time to replace the *ancien régime* in Europe with an entirely new socialist order. In terms of identity, their aim was to build this Jewish confederation on the basis of the Yiddish-speaking, European-influenced culture of the existing Jewish communities of the Pale of Settlement, not to reach back to the Biblical and Hebrew roots of Jewish identity.[1] The Jewish Bund flourished in Poland in the inter-war years, but lost its *raison d'être* after the Holocaust. Even before the Russian Revolution, it had to face the hostility of the Bolsheviks, particularly that of Joseph Stalin, the Bolshevik 'expert' on the question of nationalism. For Stalin – himself a Georgian – the only 'genuine' nations of the Soviet Union were those that had a territorial base: as an instinctive centralist, not to say instinctive anti-semite, Stalin recoiled from the divisive Bundist concept of a 'rootless' cultural nationalism.[2]

The Zionist nationalists fundamentally disagreed with the Bundists on two counts. They absolutely rejected the idea of basing a Jewish national identity on the 'mongrel' culture of Yiddish: for them, it was essential to build on the historic roots of the Jewish people; indeed, one of the most remarkable of the Zionist endeavours was the restoration of a modified Biblical Hebrew as an everyday, spoken national language. On the issue of land, it was a crucial element of Zionist thinking that the Jews could neither be safe, nor build a genuinely independent national identity, unless they had control over their own land and their own nation-state. Theoretically, some of the secular Zionists were happy to establish such a nation-state wherever it was practical so to do. In practice, a sense of historic right stretching back to Biblical times pointed to Palestine as the only choice that would be acceptable to the Jewish world community as a whole, and that might even help lure religious Zionists into supporting the nationalist plan.

Zionism and colonialism

Although the Zionists were prepared to enlist the Jewish religious tradition to strengthen their claim to Palestine, what gave Zionism the essential impetus and justification for its territorial claim was the prevailing nineteenth-century ethos of European colonialism. Throughout nineteenth-century Europe, socialist, utopian, national, religious or purely commercial enterprises were planning, promoting and raising money for the resettlement of European communities in areas beyond Europe. One justification for these widespread ventures of colonial settlement was a fashionable notion – stolen from Charles Darwin's observations on the 'survival of the fittest' in the natural world – that humanity as a whole could only 'progress' if the most advanced, well-organised and enterprising races were given free scope for their activity. This racial version of what was called Social Darwinianism echoed the Old Testament command to humanity to 'go forth, be fruitful and multiply'; an injunction that, in the eyes of many in the nineteenth century, gave religious sanction to European colonial expansion and settlement.

Whether it based itself on Darwinian theory or Biblical injunction, Zionism must be understood first and foremost as a classic project of colonial settlement, a typical phenomenon of the colonial era. Like other European colonial projects of the time, the interests – the existence, indeed – of the indigenous inhabitants was not taken into account. This omission should be seen, therefore, not as a specific Zionist trait, but rather as an intrinsic aspect of the notion of European racial superiority that pervaded the colonial mentality of the time. As in the case of other projects of colonial settlement in the nineteenth century, the question of the interests and the future of the inhabitants on whose land it was intended to settle was so intrinsically unanswerable that it had to be ignored. When the issue was addressed, it was generally argued – for instance by the plain-speaking 'ultra-nationalist' Zionist Vladimir Jabotinsky (d. 1940) – that the Palestinian Arabs would benefit economically and culturally from the presence of essentially 'European' Jewish settlers.[3]

Apart from this fundamental question of land, there were other debates among the founders of the Zionist movement that still have their reverberations today. Key among these was the issue of the relationship between secular Zionism and religious Judaism, and between the projected Jewish homeland and the Jewish diaspora that did not move to the homeland. Many of the secular Zionists believed that the question of religion had be put on one side and that, ultimately, the Jewish community as a whole should abandon their religious-based sense of a 'special' status, and instead aim to become simply one nation among the nations. For matter-of-fact Zionists like Theodor Herzl, the choice for the Jews was simple: those who wished to retain their identity as Jews should join the colonial project of Zionism and settle in their national home; the remaining Jews of the diaspora should merge into the identities of the states they inhabited and, eventually, abandon their Jewish identity.[4] Herzl argued that experience made clear that the half-way house of trying to maintain a Jewish identity while living within a non-Jewish society was the main stimulus for antisemitism and persecution – and worse.

Against this position, some Zionists, particularly Ahad Ha'am (1886-1927), argued that Zionism could never renounce the essential spiritual core within Jewish identity. For him, the national homeland should fulfil two principle goals: it should serve as a national haven for Jewish settlers, but also as a spiritual focus for the world Jewish community as a whole. Jewish identity, in other words, could not be pigeon-holed within a mere national identity: it combined national and spiritual elements.

The formation of the Zionist movement

In the last two decades of the nineteenth century, Zionist organisations sprang up in the Pale of Settlement with the object of encouraging, financing and organising Jewish-Zionist settlement in Palestine. Zionism, however, did not emerge as a substantial national and colonial project until 1897, when the Hungarian-born Herzl, following on the publication of his outline idea of a Jewish state (*Der Judenstaat*) a year earlier, spearheaded the organisation of the first International Congress of the World Zionist Organization, whose general aims were defined as follows:

> ... To create for the Jewish people a home in Palestine secured by public law.
> ... The promotion, on suitable lines, of the colonisation of Palestine by Jewish agricultural and industrial workers.

... The organisation and binding together of the whole of Jewry by means of appropriate institutions, local and international, in accordance with the laws of each country.

... The strengthening and fostering of Jewish national sentiments and consciousness.

... Preparing steps towards obtaining government consent, where necessary, to the attainment of the aim of Zionism.[5]

Up until the First World War, however, Zionists remained a tiny minority in the world Jewish community, the 'dreamers of the ghetto', eccentric zealots with little or no practical chance of achieving their objectives. The main – seemingly insurmountable – obstacle was the fact that Palestine not only had over half a million mostly-Arab, mostly-Muslim inhabitants, but that the region formed part of the Turkish-dominated Ottoman Empire, whose head of state was also the symbolic leader of the world Islamic community. The primary objective of Herzl and the World Zionist Organisation was to nego-tiate some kind of deal with the Ottoman Empire that would permit the creation of a self-governing Jewish 'homeland' in Palestine, but one that owed loyalty to the Ottoman Empire. Herzl used ingenious arguments to try to persuade the Ottoman Government that such a Jewish enclave would be beneficial to the empire; ultimately, and not surprisingly, to no avail.

However, despite the failure of this larger strategic objective of Zionism, a drip-feed of small-scale Zionist immigration – aided by the corruption or occasional indifference of local officials – managed in the years before 1914 to infiltrate and gain a foothold in Palestine. By the time of the outbreak of the First World War, there was a significant Zionist community of some 85,000 in Palestine, with its own agricultural settlements, commercial enter-prises and schools, increasingly bound together by the revived and modernised Hebrew language.

Zionism and the First World War

Ultimately, Zionism was to gain its objective in Palestine not through the consent but through the collapse of the Ottoman Empire at the end of the First World War. For various reasons – genuine enthusiasm for the 'Biblical' Zionist objective; an anxiety that Jewish refugees from the Pale of Settlement be diverted from Britain itself – Britain of all the European powers had responded most positively to Zionism before 1914. In 1914, the Ottoman

Empire aligned itself with Germany and the Austrian Empire against Britain, France and Russia. This was the turning-point for Zionism. In November 1917 the British Government made a historic promise – the 'Balfour Declaration', so-called after Arthur Balfour, the British Foreign Secretary – to the Zionist leadership in Britain that, in the event of a British victory in the Middle East over the Ottoman Empire, Britain would encourage the creation of a vaguely-defined Jewish 'homeland' in Palestine. From the British point of view, this was designed to promote two objectives: support from the world Jewish community for the British war effort; and the establishment of a strongly pro-British Jewish settlement in a strategically vital area guarding a flank of the Suez Canal.

As is so often the case, promises made in the heat of battle seem less attractive once victory has been achieved. In their anxiety to gain Arab support for their war effort against the Turkish-dominated Ottoman Empire, the British had in 1915 also promised the Arab leadership in Mecca that they would support the 'independence of the Arabs' in the Arab part of the Ottoman Empire (which consisted of the Damascus and Baghdad regions, and the coastal areas of western Arabia) if they aided the British war effort. With the defeat and collapse of the Ottoman Empire in 1918, the British – who, along with the French, dominated the Middle East – now had to reconcile their promise to satisfy Arab national aspirations with their 1917 promise to create a Jewish 'homeland' in Arab Palestine.

It is crucial at this point to remember (see chapter 4) that, while the victorious Allies of 1918 encouraged the application of the principle of self-determination in Europe, they regarded areas beyond Europe as not sufficiently advanced, in political or economic terms, to be fit for self-determination. The application of the principle of self-determination beyond Europe would, of course, have undermined the legitimacy of the extensive French and British Empires. The newly-created League of Nations therefore settled on an interim solution: namely, that control over the overseas territories of the German Empire, and the Arab territories of the Ottoman Empire, would in effect be handed over to the victorious powers, who would be 'mandated' by the League of Nations to administer these territories until they should be deemed by the League of Nations to be ready for self-government.

It was on these terms that France established mandates in Syria and Lebanon, and Britain likewise established their mandate governments in Mesopotamia (later Iraq), Jordan and Palestine. In Palestine, however, Britain had a dual obligation: it was supposed to lead the population as a whole to eventual self-government, but at the same time it was obliged to

create, as it had promised, a Jewish 'homeland' in Palestine. These irreconcilable objectives, both within the Balfour Declaration itself, and in the terms
of the British mandate, are outlined in document 2 at the end of this chapter.

Zionism and the British Mandate

When the British took over the administration of Palestine and their
Mandate responsibilities, they found themselves faced on the one side by a
well-organised Jewish community backed by a World Zionist Organisation
absolutely determined to use the obligation written into the Balfour
Declaration and the terms of the mandate (see document 2 at the end of this
chapter) as a first step to achieving their ultimate goal: a self-governing
Jewish state in Palestine. On the other side, the vast majority of the inhabitants of Palestine were Arabs – mainly Muslim, but with a strong Christian
presence – who had been politicised as never before by the events of the war
and the threat implicit in the Balfour Declaration, and were determined to
assert their national rights as the indigenous inhabitants and as the majority
of the population. The strength of the Palestinian Arab case was not, however, equalled by the statecraft of the traditional Arab leadership in Palestine,
which proved to be no match for the astuteness and influence of the Zionist
leadership. Using the Balfour obligation as a lever, Zionists within and outside
Palestine organised mass Jewish immigration and created what was in effect
a state within a state, with its own administration, economy, educational
structure and defence force. Ultimately, however, the success of the Zionist
project depended on numbers. Here, the 'pull' factor of the Zionist dream
was increasingly matched in inter-war Europe by the 'push' factor of antisemitism, particularly in inter-war Poland and, after 1933, Nazi Germany
(see previous chapter).

In 1920, the Jewish population of Palestine had probably fallen from its
pre-war number of around 85,000 to 50,000; Jewish sympathies for the
Allied cause had contributed in one way or another to this exodus. In the
period 1920-1935, however, around 230,000 Jewish immigrants entered
Palestine. In subsequent years, this rate of entry was significantly slowed by
increasing British immigration controls, and in the period 1936-1939,
around 90,000 Jews entered Palestine. Overall, therefore, the Jewish population
probably increased by over 300,000 during the inter-war period. Although
the Arab population of Palestine also increased considerably from its approximate pre-1914 total of 600,000 to around 1 million, the population gap

between the two communities was significantly narrowed during the mandate period.

Partition

The Palestinian Arab revolt of 1936 revealed to the British the full extent of Palestinian alarm at this huge level of Jewish immigration, and their determination to block the creation of a Jewish state in their own land, and to force the immediate creation of a self-governing Palestinian Arab state in line with the universally-accepted principle of self-determination. It was in this context that the British 'Peel Commission' of 1936, headed by Lord Peel, tried to come up with a solution that would reconcile the Palestinian Arab majority's right to self-determination with the Balfour obligation to create a Jewish homeland. The solution of the Peel Commission – published in 1937 – was the proposed partition of Palestine between a self-governing Jewish state established in the principal areas of Jewish settlement, and a self-governing Arab state elsewhere, and an 'internationalised' Jerusalem (see documents 3 and 4 at the end of this chapter). With the luxury of hindsight, it could be argued that a historic opportunity was lost at this time: up to the present-day, partition has remained the most viable solution to the problem of Palestine. The Arab leadership, however, was determined – for understandable reasons – to block a plan that would imply acceptance of the right of the Zionists to create a Jewish state in Arab land. The Zionists themselves, incidentally, were less than enthusiastic about a partition solution that would have given them a tiny state with a very large Arab minority.

In any case, the partition plan was immediately overtaken by events in Europe. By 1938, Britain was gearing up for what seemed to be an inevitable war with Hitler's Germany; in any such war, the Middle East – with its oil supplies and strategic position – would be vital. The cynical but reasonable calculation of the British was that the Jews – in Palestine and world-wide – would have no option but to support Britain against Nazi Germany. The all-important objective, therefore, was to ensure Arab support; or, at the very least, neutralise Arab hostility. To this end, the British in 1939 in effect ditched their 'Balfour' obligation to create a Jewish homeland, severely restricted Jewish immigration to Palestine and Jewish rights to buy land, and undertook to 'do everything in their power to create conditions which will enable the independent Palestine state to come into being within ten years'. Henceforth, until 1947, when the British abandoned all attempts to resolve the Palestine problem, Britain was effectively committed to the creation of an independent Arab Palestine.

Zionism, the Second World War, and the creation of the State of Israel

The new British policy was, however, itself overtaken by events. During the course of the Second World War, two major developments were ultimately to ensure the success of Zionism. In the first place, Zionism, deprived as it now was of official British support, turned increasingly to the United States as its major international patron; henceforth, the very large Jewish community in the United States was to play a crucial role in ensuring official American support for Zionism. In the second place, there can be no doubt that the Holocaust created a world-wide surge of sympathy for the tragic plight of the Jews in Europe: a sympathy that tended, on the issue of Palestine, to obscure the question of Palestinian Arab rights. Europe in particular assuaged its guilt over the Jews at the expense of the Palestinian Arabs. During the course of the Second World War, up to six million European Jews were slaughtered; many of the remnant that survived were resolutely determined to seek safety in Palestine despite the British restrictions on Jewish immigration, and were supported in this objective by Zionist networks. The fate of these Jewish refugees became a major international issue after 1945, an issue that inevitably worked to the advantage of the Zionist cause and discredited official British policy.

It soon became apparent after the end of the war that Britain had neither the will nor the means to continue to govern a Palestine where the Zionists were moving to outright rebellion against British rule, and where the communities were sliding towards full-scale war against each other. In 1947, Britain handed over the task of finding a solution to the Palestine problem to the newly-formed United Nations, successor to the defunct League of Nations: in effect, it abandoned its mandate responsibilities. When the United Nations took over the task of trying to resolve the Palestine question, the Zionists were able to benefit, not only from international sympathy over the Holocaust, but also from the fact that the two post-war super-powers – the United States and the Soviet Union – both, at this pre-Cold War juncture, supported the Zionist cause: the United States, for reasons that have already been cited; the Soviet Union, because of their perception at this time that the Zionist leadership was anti-colonial and socialist in orientation. In November 1947, the United Nations General Assembly voted for a new partition plan that would create separate independent Arab and Jewish states in Palestine. In effect, international sanction had now been given to the creation of a Jewish state.

The future of Palestine would now be decided by events on the ground. The Palestinian Arabs rejected the United Nations partition plan, and a full-scale war therefore ensued in 1947-1948 between the Arabs and Jews of Palestine. In May 1948, as soon as the British had finally limped out of Palestine, the State of Israel was proclaimed, while the neighbouring Arab states came to the aid of their brother Arabs in Palestine. By the end of 1948, the new State of Israel had beaten off the Arab states and established an enlarged Israeli state, leaving only a rump of Palestinian Arab territory in Gaza and on the West Bank of the Jordan (see document 4 at the end of this chapter). The security of this new state was ensured, not only by military victory, but also by the flight or forcible removal – the modern description would be 'ethnic cleansing' – of some 700,000 Palestinian Arabs from the Jewish/Israeli-held areas. These Palestinian Arabs became refugees in neighbouring Arab states. In 1950, a Law of Return passed by the State of Israel facilitated unhindered Jewish immigration into Israel.

The history of Zionism illustrates graphically the fraught relationship between race, nation and colonialism. Racial conceptions of national identity in Europe excluded the Jews as 'outsiders'. This provided a crucial stimulus for the development of the Jewish national idea, or Zionism. The assertion of Zionism in its turn tended to intensify antisemitism, since Zionism appeared to confirm the antisemitic view that Jews did not 'belong' in Europe. Paradoxically, however, the Zionist movement used the classic language of European nationalism; moreover, in its search for a 'national home', Zionism also transformed itself into a typical European colonial project of the nineteenth century.

Documents

(Nb: in all the following extracts, editorial comments at the beginning of texts, or amendments and explanations in the texts themselves, will be placed in square brackets. Headings and subdivisions will be put in italics.)

1 – Leo Pinsker and the need for Jewish 'auto-emancipation'

[Theodor Herzl's *Der Judenstaat* (*The Jewish State*), first published in 1896, is regarded as the key text outlining the Zionist plan. However, Leo Pinsker's pamphlet, *Auto-Emancipation*, published anonymously in 1882, is in many ways a clearer statement of the dilemma facing the Jews of Europe at the end of the nineteenth century. Pinsker does not deal with the details of any projected Jewish state; rather, he outlines the reasons why the Jewish community in Europe had no alternative other than to develop a national consciousness, with a view to creating a Jewish homeland. In the passage below, Pinsker emphasises the psychological obstacles that the Jews would have to overcome – particularly the tendency to religious fatalism – if they were to retrieve their national status and dignity.]

The Jews must become a nation again

Long will the world have to await universal peace; but in the interim the relations of the nations to one another may be adjusted fairly well by explicit understandings, by arrangements based upon international law, treaties, and especially upon a certain equality in rank and mutually admitted rights, as well as upon mutual regard.

No such equality in rank appears in the intercourse of the nations with the Jews. In the latter case the basis is lacking for that mutual regard which is generally regulated and secured by international law or by treaties. Only when this basis is established, when the equality of the Jews with other nations becomes a fact, can the problem presented by the Jewish question be considered solved. Unfortunately, although such equality indeed existed in a long forgotten past, we can hope to see it restored only in the very remote future, for under present conditions any dream of the admission of the Jewish people into the ranks of the other nations seems illusory. It lacks most of those attributes which are the hallmark of a nation. It lacks that characteristic national life which is inconceivable without a common language, common customs, and a common land. The Jewish people has no fatherland of its own, though many motherlands; it has no rallying point, no center of gravity, no government of its own, no accredited representatives. It is everywhere a guest, and nowhere *at home*.

The nations *never* have to deal with a Jewish *nation* but always with mere *Jews*. The Jews are not a nation because they lack a certain distinctive national character, possessed by every other nation, a character which is determined by living together in one country, under one rule. It was clearly impossible for this national character to be developed in the Diaspora; the Jews seem rather to have lost all remembrance of their former home. Thanks to their ready adaptability, they have all the more easily acquired the alien traits of the peoples among whom they have been cast by fate. Moreover, to please their protectors, they often divested themselves of their traditional individuality. They acquired, or persuaded themselves that they had acquired, certain cosmopolitan tendencies which could no more appeal to others than they could bring satisfaction to the Jews themselves.

In seeking to fuse with other peoples, they deliberately renounced, to a certain extent, their own nationality. Nowhere, however, did they succeed in obtaining recognition from their neighbours as native-born citizens of equal rank.

The strongest factor, however, operating to prevent the Jews from striving after an independent national existence is the fact that they do not feel the need for such an existence. Not only do they feel no need for it, but they go so far as to deny the reasonableness of such a need.

In a sick man, the absence of desire for food and drink is a very serious symptom. It is not always possible to cure him of this ominous loss of appetite. And even if his appetite can be restored, it is still a question whether he will be able to digest food, even though he desires it.

The Jews are in the unhappy condition of such a patient. We must discuss this most important point with all possible precision. We must prove that the misfortunes of the Jews are due, above all, to their lack of desire for national independence; and that this desire must be aroused and maintained in them if they do not wish to exist forever in a disgraceful state – in a word, we must prove that *they must become a nation*.

This one apparently insignificant fact, that the Jews are not considered a separate nation by the other nations is, to a great extent, the hidden cause of their anomalous position and of their endless misery. The mere fact of belonging to this people is a mark of Cain on one's forehead, an indelible stigma which repels non-Jews and is painful to the Jews themselves. Nevertheless, for all its strangeness, this phenomenon has deep roots in human nature.

Antisemitism is stimulated by the Jews' lack of national, as opposed to religious status

Among the living nations of the earth the Jews occupy the position of a nation long since dead. With the loss of their fatherland, the Jews lost their independence and fell into a state of decay which is incompatible with the existence of a whole and vital organism. The state was crushed by the Roman conquerors and vanished from the world's view. But after the Jewish people had yielded up its existence as an actual state, as a political entity, it could nevertheless not submit to total destruction – it did not cease to exist as a spiritual nation. Thus, the world saw in this people the frightening form of one of the dead walking among the living. This ghostlike apparition of a people without unity or organisation, without land or other bond of union, no longer alive, and yet moving about among the living – this eerie form scarcely paralleled in history, unlike anything that preceded or followed it, could not fail to make a strange and peculiar impression upon the imagination of the nations. And if the fear of ghosts is something inborn, and has a certain justification in the psychic life of humanity, is it any wonder that it asserted itself powerfully at the sight of this dead and yet living nation?

Fear of the Jewish ghost has been handed down and strengthened for generations and centuries. It led to a prejudice which, in its turn, in connection with other forces to be discussed later, paved the way for Judaeophobia.

Along with a number of other subconscious and superstitious ideas, instincts and idiosyncracies, Judaeophobia, too, has become rooted and naturalised among all the peoples of the earth with whom the Jews have had intercourse. Judaeophobia is a form of demonopathy, with the distinction that the Jewish ghost has become known to the whole race of mankind, not merely to certain races, and that it is not disembodied, like other ghosts, but is a being of flesh and blood, and suffers the most excruciating pain from the wounds inflicted upon it by the fearful mob who imagines it threatens them.

[Antisemitism or 'Judeophobia' has also been sustained by the Jewish religion, or Judaism, which is seen as an alien and hostile cult.]

... Thus have Judaism and anti-Semitism passed for centuries through history as inseparable companions. Like the Jewish people, it seems, the real 'wandering Jew,' anti-Semitism, too, can never die. He must be blind indeed who will assert that the Jews are not *the chosen people*, the people chosen for universal hatred. No matter how much the nations are at variance with one another, no matter how diverse in their instincts and aims, they join hands in their hatred of the Jews; on this one matter all are agreed. The extent and the manner in which this antipathy is shown depends, of course, upon the cultural level of each people. The antipathy as such, however, exists in all places and at all times, no matter whether it appears in the form of deeds of violence, an envious jealousy, or under the guise of tolerance and protection. To be robbed as a Jew or to require protection as a Jew is equally humiliating, equally hurtful to the self-respect of the Jews.

Having analysed Judeophobia as an hereditary form of demonopathy, peculiar to the human race, and having represented anti-Semitism as based upon an inherited aberration of the human mind, we must draw the important conclusion: the fight against this hatred, like any fight against inherited predispositions, can only be in vain. This view is all the more important because it shows that we should at last abstain from polemics as a waste of time and energy, for against superstition even the gods fight vainly. Prejudice or instinctive ill will can be satisfied by no reasoning, however forceful and clear. These sinister powers must either be kept within bounds by material coercion, like every other blind natural force, or simply ignored.

The Jew as the eternal alien

In the psychology of the peoples, then, we find the basis of the prejudice against the Jewish nation; but we must also consider other, no less important factors, which render impossible the fusion or equalisation of the Jews with the other peoples.

No people, generally speaking, has any predilection for foreigners. This fact has its ethnological basis and cannot be brought as a reproach against any people. Now, is the Jew subject to *this* general law only to the same extent as the other nationalities? Not at all! The aversion which meets the foreigner in a strange land can be repaid in equal coin in his home country. The non-Jew pursues his own interest in a foreign country openly and without giving offence. It is everywhere considered natural that he should fight for these interests, alone or in conjunction with others. The foreigner has no need to *be*, or to *seem to be*, a patriot. But as for the Jew, he is not a native in his own home country, but he is also not a foreigner; he is, in very truth, the stranger *par excellence*. He is regarded as neither friend nor foe, but as an alien, of whom the only thing known is that he has no home. People do not care to *confide* in the foreigner, or to *trust* the Jew. The foreigner claims hospitality, which he can repay in the same coin in his own country. The Jew can make no such return; consequently he can make no claim to hospitality. He is not a guest, much less a welcome guest. He is more like a beggar; and what beggar is welcome? He is rather a refugee; and where is the refugee to whom a refuge may not be refused? The Jews are aliens who can have no representatives because they have no fatherland.

Since the Jew is nowhere at home, nowhere regarded as a native, he remains an alien everywhere. That he himself and his forefathers as well were born in the country does not alter this fact in the least. Generally, he is treated as an adopted child whose rights may be questioned; never is he considered a legitimate child of the fatherland. The German, proud of his Teutonic character, the Slav, the Celt – not one of them admits that the Semitic Jew is his equal by birth; and even if he be ready, as a man of culture, to admit him to all civil rights, he will never go as far as to forget the Jew in this, his fellow citizen. The *legal emancipation* of the Jews is the crowning achievement of our century. But *legal emancipation* is not *social emancipation*, and with the proclamation of the former the Jews are still far from being emancipated from their exceptional *social position*...

... To sum up what has been said: For the living, the Jew is a dead man; for the natives, an alien and a vagrant; for the property holders, a beggar; for the poor, an exploiter and a millionaire; for patriots, a man without a country; for all classes, a hated rival.

The need to develop a Jewish national consciousness

... If all the peoples of the earth were not able to blot out our existence, they were nevertheless able to destroy in us the feeling of our national independence. And as for ourselves, we look on with fatalistic indifference when in many a land we are refused a recognition which would not lightly be denied to Zulus. In the dispersion we have maintained our individual life, and proved our power of resistance, but we have lost the common bond of our national consciousness. Seeking to maintain our material existence, we were constrained only too often to forget our moral dignity. We did not see that on account of tactics unworthy of us, which we were forced to adopt, we sank still lower in the eyes of our opponents, that we were only the more exposed to humiliating contempt and outlawry, which have finally become our baleful heritage. In the wide, wide world there was no place for us. We prayed only for a little place anywhere to lay our weary heads to rest; and so, by lessening our claims, we gradually lessened our dignity as well, which was diminished in our own and others' eyes until it became unrecognisable. We were the ball which the peoples tossed in turn to one another. The cruel game was equally amusing whether we were caught or thrown, and was enjoyed all the more, the more elastic and yielding our national respect became in the hands of the peoples. Under such circumstances, how could there be any question of national self-determination, of a free, active development of our national force or of our national genius?

But recent persecution has raised Jewish national consciousness

... Happily, affairs are now in a somewhat different state. The events of the last few years in *enlightened* Germany, in Romania, in Hungary, and especially in Russia have effected what the far bloodier persecutions of the Middle Ages could not effect. The national consciousness, which until then had existed only in the latent state of sterile martyrdom, burst forth before our eyes among the masses of the Russian and Romanian Jews in the form of an irresistible movement toward Palestine. Though this movement has been poor in practical results, its existence attests, nevertheless, to the correct instinct of the people, to whom it became manifest that it needed a home. The severe tests which the Jews have endured have now produced a reaction which points to something other than a fatalistic submission to a punishment inflicted by the hand of God...

Nowadays, when in a small part of the earth our brethren have caught their breath and can feel more deeply for the sufferings of their brothers; nowadays, when a number of other dependent and oppressed nationalities have been allowed to regain their independence – we, too, must not sit even one moment longer with folded hands; we must not admit that we are doomed to play on in the future the hopeless role of the 'wandering Jew'...

... It is our bounden duty to devote all our remaining moral force to re-establishing ourselves as a living nation, so that we may finally assume a more fitting and dignified role.

The assertion of national identity, not religious identity, is the key to the survival of the Jewish people

We must seek our honour and our salvation not in illusory self-deceptions, but in the restoration of a national bond of union. Hitherto the world has not considered us as an enterprise of standing, and consequently we have enjoyed no decent credit.

If the nationalistic endeavours of the various people who have risen to life before our eyes bore their own justification, can it still be questioned whether similar aspirations on the part of the Jews would not be justified? They play a more important part than those peoples in the life of the civilised nations, and they have deserved more from humanity; they have a past, a history, a common, unmixed descent, and an undestructible vigour, an unshakeable faith, and an unexampled history of suffering to show; the peoples have sinned against them more grievously than against any other nation. Is not that enough to make them capable and worthy of possessing a fatherland?

The struggle of the Jews for unity and independence as an organised nation not only possesses the inherent justification that belongs to the struggle of every oppressed people, but it is also calculated to attract the sympathy of the people to whom we are rightly or wrongly obnoxious. This struggle must be entered upon in such a spirit as to exert an irresistible pressure upon the international politics of the present, and the future will assuredly bear witness to its results.

At the very outset we must be prepared for a great outcry. The first stirrings of this struggle will doubtless be ascribed by most of the Jews, who have, with reason, become timorous and skeptical, to the unconscious convulsions of an organism dangerously ill; and certainly the attainment and realisation of the object of such endeavours will be fraught with the greatest difficulties, will perhaps be possible only after superhuman efforts. But consider that the Jews have no other way out of their desperate position, and that it would be cowardly not to take that way merely because it offers only slim chances of success. 'Faint heart never won fair lady' – and, indeed, what have we to lose? At the worst, we shall continue to be in the future what we have been in the past, what we are too cowardly to resolve that we will be no longer: *eternally despised Jews*.

The Jews need a nation, not a 'Holy Land'

[In practical terms, Pinsker argued that the key was to find a home for the 'surplus' Jews of Europe, the 'unassimilable residue'. From this, the basis of a national home could be built. It is noticeable that Pinsker was anxious to break free from the religious notion that Palestine was the only possible home for the Jewish people. Although he did acknowledge that Palestine was a natural goal for Jewish national hopes, he wanted Jewish national identity to be based on the secular principles of modern nationalism, not on the religious principles of the 'redemption' of a 'chosen people'.]

... If we would have a secure home, so that we may give up our endless life of wandering and rehabilitate our nation in our own eyes and in the eyes of the world, we must above all not dream of restoring ancient Judaea. We must not attach ourselves to the place where our political life was once violently interrupted and destroyed. The goal of our present endeavors must not be the 'Holy Land', but a land of our own. We need nothing but a large piece of land for our poor brothers; a piece of land which shall remain our property, from which no foreign master can expel us. Thither we shall take with us the most sacred possessions which we have saved from the shipwreck of our former fatherland, the *God-idea* and the *Bible*. It is only these which have made our old fatherland the Holy Land, and not Jerusalem of the Jordan. Perhaps the Holy Land will again become ours. If so, all the better, but *first of all*, we must determine – and this is the crucial point – what country is accessible to us, and at the same time adapted to offer the Jews of all lands who must leave their homes a secure and unquestioned refuge which is capable of being made productive.

[From Arthur Hertzberg (ed.), *The Zionist Idea* (New York, Harper and Row Publishers, 1966), pp 180-192, 194
From B. Netanyahu (ed.), *The Road to Freedom* (New York, 1944), translated by David Blondheim, pp 74-95, 105-6]

2 – The Balfour Declaration of 1917 and the terms of the British Mandate

[As has been seen in the introduction to this chapter, the British Government in November 1917 made a promise to the Zionist leadership in Britain that, in the event of a British victory in the Middle East, the Jewish people would be granted a 'national home' in Palestine. This undertaking was taken up by the League of Nations after the war, and the terms on which Britain was granted a mandate over Palestine included the undertaking to implement the Balfour Declaration.]

The Balfour Declaration, 2 November 1917

His Majesty's Government view with favour the establishment in Palestine of a national home for the Jewish people, and will use their best endeavours to facilitate the achievement of this object, it being clearly understood that nothing shall be done which may prejudice the civil and religious rights of existing non-Jewish communities in Palestine, or the rights and political status enjoyed by Jews in any other country.[6]

The terms of the British Mandate for Palestine agreed by the Council of the League of Nations in 1922, and put into operation in 1923

[The preamble to the League of Nations mandate agreement for Palestine contained the following stipulations.]

... The Principal Allied Powers have... agreed that the Mandatory should be responsible for putting into effect the declaration originally made on November 2nd, 1917, by the Government of His Britannic Majesty, and adopted by the said Powers, in favour of the establishment in Palestine of a national home for the Jewish people, it being clearly understood that nothing should be done which might prejudice the civil and religious rights of existing non-Jewish communities in Palestine, or the rights and political status enjoyed by Jews in any other country; and
    ... Recognition has thereby been given to the historical connexion of the Jewish people with Palestine and to the grounds for reconstituting their national home in that country; and
    ... The Principal Allied Powers have selected His Britannic Majesty as the Mandatory for Palestine.

[In the Mandate agreement itself, the following are the most important articles relating to the Zionist movement. The following articles also point to the contradictions inherent in Britain's mandate obligations.]

Article 2
The Mandatory shall be responsible for placing the country under such political, administrative and economic conditions as will secure the establishment of the Jewish national home, as laid down in the preamble, and the development of self-governing institutions, and also for safeguarding the civil and religious rights of all the inhabitants of Palestine, irrespective of race and religion.

Article 3
The Mandatory shall, so far as circumstances permit, encourage local autonomy.

Article 4
An appropriate Jewish agency shall be recognised as a public body for the purpose of advising and cooperating with the Administration of Palestine in such economic, social and other matters as may affect the establishment of the Jewish national home and the interests of the Jewish population in Palestine, and, subject always to the control of the Administration, to assist and take part in the development of the country.

The Zionist organisation, as long as its organisation and constitution are in the opinion of the Mandatory appropriate, shall be recognised as such agency. It shall take steps in consultation with His Britannic Majesty's Government to secure the cooperation of all Jews who are willing to assist in the establishment of the Jewish national home...

Article 7
The Administration of Palestine shall be responsible for enacting a nationality law. There shall be included in this law provisions framed so as to facilitate the acquisition of Palestinian citizenship by Jews who take up their permanent residence in Palestine...

Article 15
The Mandatory shall see that complete freedom of conscience and the free exercise of all forms of worship, subject only to the maintenance of public order and morals, are ensured to all. No discrimination of any kind shall be

made between the inhabitants of Palestine on the ground of race, religion or
language. No person shall be excluded from Palestine on the sole ground of
his religious belief.

The right of each community to maintain its own schools for the education of its own members in its own language, while conforming to such
educational requirements of a general nature as the Administration may
impose, shall not be denied or impaired...

Article 22
English, Arabic and Hebrew shall be the official languages of Palestine. Any
statement or inscription in Arabic on stamps or money shall be repeated in
Hebrew and any statement or inscription in Hebrew shall be repeated
in Arabic.

[From League of Nations, 'Mandate for Palestine', Cmd 1785 (Dec. 1922)
in *State Papers* (GB), Accounts and Papers (13) Vol. XXV (London, HMSO,
1923)]

3 – The Partition of Palestine: recommendation of the Peel Commission, 1937

[Following on the Arab uprising of 1936, the Peel Commission recommended
in 1937 that Palestine be separated into two self-governing states, and that
the Arab section of Palestine be joined to Transjordan to form a larger Arab
state. The reasons for recommending this were summarized in the conclusions of the Peel Report.]

The need for partition: conclusions of the Peel Report

The problem of Palestine is briefly restated.

Under the stress of the World War the British Government made promises
to the Arabs and Jews in order to obtain their support. On the strength of
those promises both parties formed certain expectations.

The application to Palestine of the Mandate System in general and of the
specific Mandate in particular implied the belief that the obligations thus
undertaken towards the Arabs and the Jews respectively would prove in the

course of time to be mutually compatible owing to the conciliatory effect on the Palestinian Arabs of the material prosperity which Jewish immigration would bring to Palestine as a whole. That belief has not been justified, and there seems to be no hope of its being justified in the future.

But the British cannot on that account repudiate their obligations, and, apart from obligations, the existing circumstances in Palestine would still require the most strenuous efforts on the part of the Government which is responsible for the welfare of the country.

The existing circumstances are summarised as follows.

An irrepressible conflict has arisen between two national communities within the narrow bounds of one small country. There is no common ground between them. Their national aspirations are incompatible. The Arabs desire to revive the traditions of the Arab golden age. The Jews desire to show what they can achieve when restored to the land in which the Jewish nation was born. Neither of the two national ideas permits of combination in the service of a single State.

The conflict has grown steadily more bitter since 1920 and the process will continue. Conditions inside Palestine, especially the systems of education, are strengthening the national sentiment of the two peoples. The bigger and more prosperous they grow the greater will be their political ambitions, and the conflict is aggravated by the uncertainty of the future. 'Who in the end will govern Palestine?' it is asked. Meanwhile, the 'external factors' will continue to operate with increasing force. On the one hand in less than three years' time Syria and the Lebanon will attain their national sovereignty, and the claim of the Palestinian Arabs to share in the freedom of all Asiatic Arabia will thus be fortified. On the other hand the hardships and anxieties of the Jews in Europe are not likely to grow less and the appeal to the good faith and humanity of the British people will lose none of its force.

Meanwhile, the Government of Palestine, which is at present an unsuitable form for governing educated Arabs and democratic Jews, cannot develop into a system of self-government as it has elsewhere, because there is no such system which could ensure justice both to the Arabs and the Jews. Government therefore remains unrepresentative and unable to dispel the conflicting grievances of the two dissatisfied and irresponsible communities it governs.

In these circumstances peace can only be maintained in Palestine under the Mandate by repression. This means the maintenance of security services at so high a cost that the services directed to 'the well-being and development' of the population cannot be expanded and may even have to be curtailed. The moral objections to repression are self-evident. Nor need the undesirable reactions of it on opinion outside Palestine be emphasised. Moreover, repression will not solve the problem. It will exacerbate the quarrel. It will not help towards the establishment of a single self-governing Palestine. It is not easy to pursue the dark path of repression without seeing daylight at the end of it.

The British people will not flinch from the task of continuing to govern Palestine under the Mandate if they are in honour bound to do so, but they would be justified in asking if there is no other way in which their duty can be done.

Nor would Britain wish to repudiate her obligations. The trouble is that they have proved irreconcilable, and this conflict is the more unfortunate because each of the obligations taken separately accords with British sentiment and British interest. The development of self-government in the Arab world on the one hand is in accordance with British principles, and British public opinion is wholly sympathetic with Arab aspirations towards a new age of unity and prosperity in the Arab world. British interest similarly has always been bound up with the peace of the Middle East and British statesmanship can show an almost unbroken record of friendship with the Arabs. There is a strong British tradition, on the other hand, of friendship with the Jewish people, and it is in the British interest to retain as far as may be possible the confidence of the Jewish people.

The continuance of the present system means the gradual alienation of two peoples who are traditionally the friends of Britain.

The problem cannot be solved by giving either the Arabs or the Jews all they want. The answer to the question which of them in the end will govern Palestine must be 'Neither'. No fair-minded statesman can think it right either that 400,000 Jews, whose entry into Palestine has been facilitated by the British Government and approved by the League of Nations, should be handed over to Arab rule, or that, if the Jews should become a majority, a million Arabs should be handed over to their rule. But while neither race can fairly rule all Palestine, each race might justly rule part of it.

The idea of Partition has doubtless been thought of before as a solution to the problem, but it has probably been discarded as being impracticable. The difficulties are certainly very great, but when they are closely examined they do not seem so insuperable as the difficulties inherent in the continuance of the Mandate or in any other alternative arrangement. Partition offers a chance of ultimate peace. No other plan does.

The basic plan of partition

While the Commission would not be expected to embark on the further pro-
tracted enquiry which would be needed for working out a scheme of Partition
in full detail, it would be idle to put forward the principle of Partition and
not to give it any concrete shape. Clearly it must be shown that an actual plan
can be devised which meets the main requirements of the case.

... Treaties of alliance should be negotiated by the Mandatory with the
Government of Trans-Jordan and representatives of the Arabs of Palestine on
the one hand and with the Zionist Organisation on the other. These Treaties
would declare that, within as short a period as may be convenient, two
sovereign independent States would be established – the one an Arab State,
consisting of Trans-Jordan united with that part of Palestine which lies to the
east and south of a frontier such as we suggest in Section 3 below; the other
a Jewish State consisting of that part of Palestine which lies to the north and
west of that frontier. [See map below.]

Summary of the advantages of partition

Considering the attitude which both the Arab and the Jewish representatives
adopted in giving evidence, the Commission think it improbable that either
party will be satisfied at first sight with the proposals submitted for the
adjustment of their rival claims. For Partition means that neither will get all
it wants. It means that the Arabs must acquiesce in the exclusion from their
sovereignty of a piece of territory, long occupied and once ruled by them.
It means that the Jews must be content with less than the Land of Israel
they once ruled and have hoped to rule again. But it seems possible that on
reflection both parties will come to realise that the drawbacks of Partition are
outweighed by its advantages. For, if it offers neither party all it wants, it
offers each what it wants most, namely freedom and security.

The advantages to the Arabs of Palestine of Partition on the lines we have
proposed may be summarised as follows:

1 They obtain their national independence and can co-operate on an equal
   footing with the Arabs of the neighbouring countries in the cause of Arab
   unity and progress.
2 They are finally delivered from the fear of being 'swamped' by the Jews,
   and from the possibility of ultimate subjection to Jewish rule.

3   In particular, the final limitation of the Jewish National Home within a
    fixed frontier and the enactment of a new Mandate for the protection of
    the Holy Places, solemnly guaranteed by the League of Nations, removes
    all anxiety lest the Holy Places should ever come under Jewish control.
5   As a set-off to the loss of territory the Arabs regard as theirs, the Arab State
    will receive a subvention from the Jewish State. It will also, in view of the
    backwardness of Trans-Jordan, obtain a grant of £2,000,000 from the Bri-
    tish Treasury; and, if an agreement can be reached as to the exchange of
    land and population, a further grant will be made for the conversion, as
    far as may prove possible, of uncultivable land in the Arab State into
    productive land from which the cultivators and the State alike will profit.

The advantages of Partition to the Jews may be summarised as follows:

1   Partition secures the establishment of the Jewish National Home and
    relieves it from the possibility of its being subjected in the future to
    Arab rule.
2   Partition enables the Jews in the fullest sense to call their National Home
    their own; for it converts it into a Jewish State. Its citizens will be able to
    admit as many Jews into it as they themselves believe can be absorbed.
    They will attain the primary objective of Zionism – a Jewish nation,
    planted in Palestine, giving its nationals a same status in the world as
    other nations give theirs. They will cease at last to live a 'minority life'.

To both Arabs and Jews Partition offers a prospect – and there is none in any
other policy – of obtaining the inestimable boon of peace. It is surely worth
some sacrifice on both sides if the quarrel which the Mandate started could
be ended with its termination. It is not a natural or old-standing feud. The
Arabs throughout their history have not only been free from anti-Jewish
sentiment but have also shown that the spirit of compromise is deeply rooted
in their life. Considering what the possibility of finding a refuge in Palestine
means to many thousands of suffering Jews, is the loss occasioned by
Partition, great as it would be, more than Arab generosity can bear? In this,
as in so much else connected with Palestine, it is not only the peoples of that
country who have to be considered. The Jewish Problem is not the least of
the many problems which are disturbing international relations at this crucial
time and obstructing the path to peace and prosperity. If the Arabs at some
sacrifice could help to solve that problem, they would earn the gratitude not
of the Jews alone but of all the Western World.

As to the British people, they are bound to honour to the utmost of their power the obligations they undertook in the exigencies of war towards the Arabs and the Jews. When those obligations were incorporated in the Mandate, they did not fully realise the difficulties of the task it laid on them. They have tried to overcome them, not always with success. The difficulties have steadily become greater till now they seem almost insuperable. Partition offers a possibility of finding a way through them, a possibility of obtaining a final solution of the problem which does justice to the rights and aspirations of both the Arabs and the Jews and discharges the obligations undertaken towards them twenty years ago to the fullest extent that is practicable in the circumstances of the present time.

[From Colonial Office, *Palestine Royal Commission: Summary of Report* (London, HMSO, 1937), Colonial No. 135, pp 24-27, 35-37]

4 – Maps

Map 7   Palestine: proposed partition   Map 8   Israel and Palestine after
         scheme of 1937   the 1948-1949 War

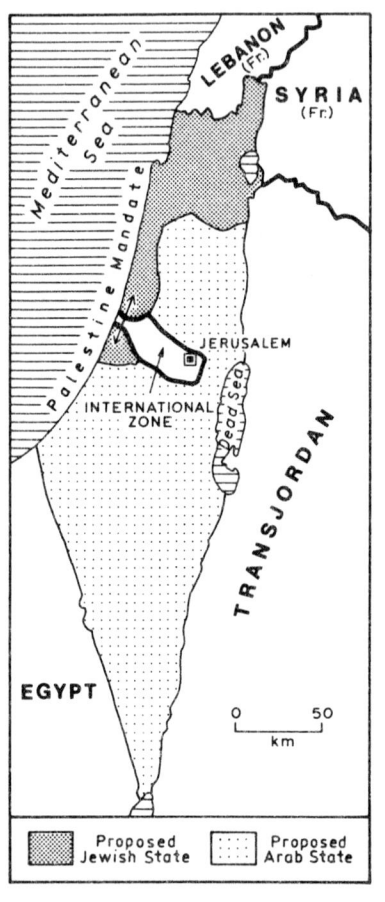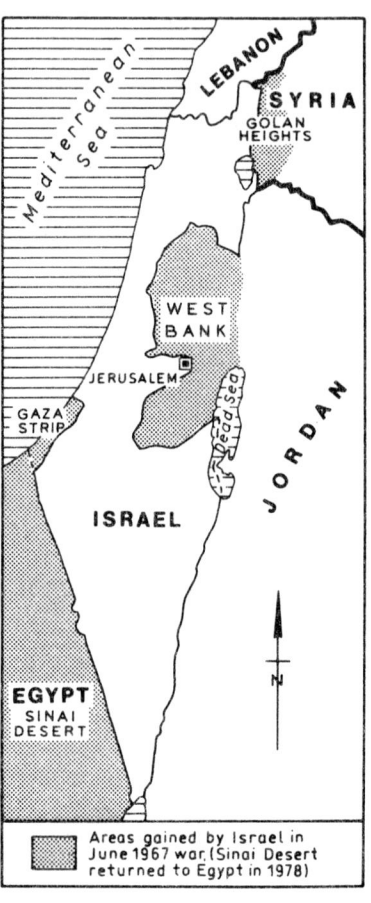

5 – Map

Map 9   The 'Mandates' in the Middle East between World War I and
World War II

(The Kurdish people were not given their own state: the Kurdish area is
indicated.)

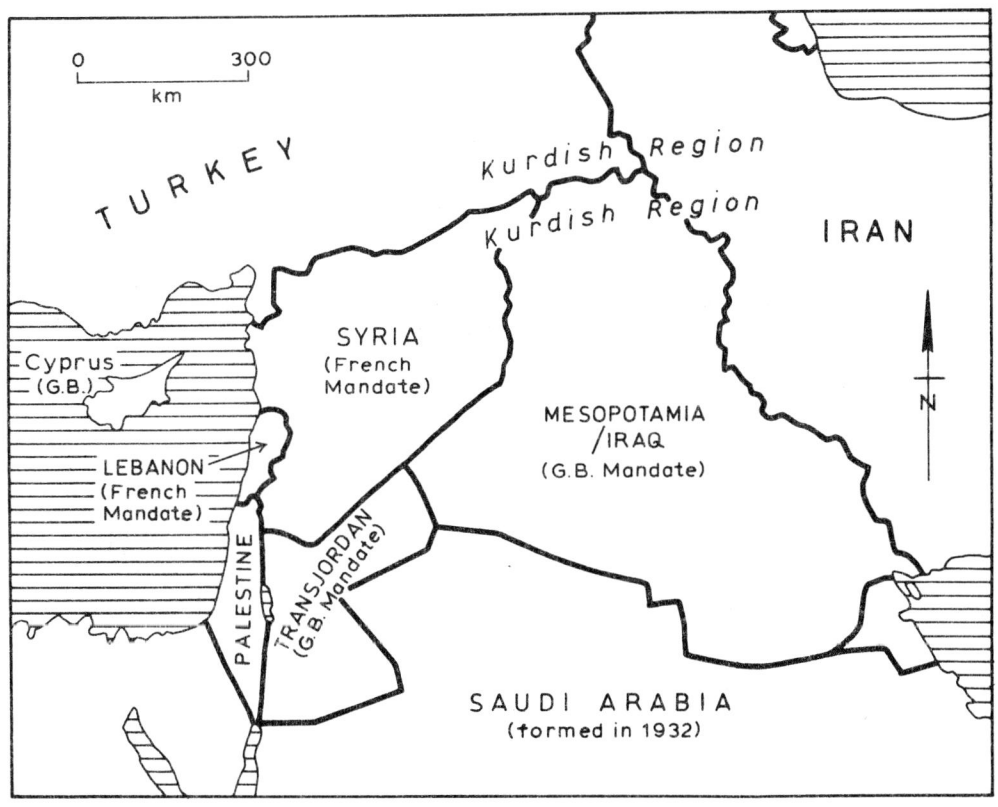

NOTES ON CHAPTER 8

1   See section on Chaim Zhitlovsky (1865-1943), especially pages 170-175, in Sol Liptzin (ed.), *The Flowering of Yiddish Literature* (New York, Thomas Yoseloff).

2   See J.V. Stalin's 'Marxism and the National Question' (1913), in *Marxism and the National and Colonial Question* (London, Lawrence and Wishart Ltd, 1947), pp 42, 56-57, 61.

3   Shlomo Avineri, *The Making of Modern Zionism: The Intellectual Origins of the Jewish State* (London, Weidenfeld and Nicolson, 1981), pp 178-182.

4   See 'Introduction' to Theodor Herzl, *The Jewish State* (New York, Dover Publications, 1988); first published in 1896.

5   Walter Laqueur and Barry Rubin (eds), *The Israel-Arab Reader: A Documentary History of the Middle East Conflict* (London, Penguin Books, 1987), pp 11-12.

6   This last phrase is explained by the fact that some eminent British Jews opposed the Balfour Declaration, and, indeed, the objectives of Zionism itself, on the grounds that such a declaration would confirm the views of antisemites that Jews were not loyal to the countries in which they presently lived. The Balfour Declaration, it was feared, would stimulate increased antisemitic feeling, and be used to justify demands for the removal of all European Jews to 'their' Jewish homeland.

Chapter 9

Colonialism and Arab Nationalism

> Hold on firmly together to the rope of God, and do not
> be divided among yourselves.
>
> Qur'an, chapter 3, from verse 103

The foundations of Arab identity and the colonial experience

Three factors have played a key role in Arab identity: language, religion and
land. To a great extent, the core of Arab identity has been the language,
Arabic. Because Arabic was the language of the religion of Islam, Arab
identity was interlinked with the fortunes of Islam; if Arabic gave Islam its
language, Islam gave the Arabic-speaking people a foundation for their civilisation. Furthermore, the expansion of Islam spread this Arabic-speaking
civilisation from Baghdad in West Asia to Morocco in north-west Africa. On
the other hand, the relationship between 'Arab-ness', Islam and territory was
never symmetrical. Despite its Arabic-language foundations, Islam was a
religion for all mankind, not just for the Arab people. The vast majority of
the world's Muslims are not Arabs, and all races have an equal status in Islam.
Conversely, not all Arabs are Muslims: there are significant ancient Christian
Arab communities – amounting to some 7 per cent of the whole Arab world
– in Egypt, Palestine, Syria, Lebanon and Iraq in particular. Islam, therefore,
is wider than the Arab world, and to some extent divides the Arab world.
Moreover, the area of Arab civilisation created by the expansion of the first
Islamic Empire – sprawling as it does from the Atlantic to the Persian gulf,
and from the Mediterranean to central Africa – is far too widespread to
provide a basis for sustained political unity. There has always, therefore, been
a tension between the assertion of Arab unity on the one side, and the local
Arab identities on the other – Syrian, Egyptian, etc – that have emerged and
taken root over time.

The development and indeed the shape of Arab nationalism was greatly affected by the world-wide phenomenon of European colonialism. In this sense, the origins of modern Arab nationalism were very similar to the other nationalist movements of Asia and Africa, which were at roughly the same time shaped by the boundaries of the states that were created by the colonial powers; influenced by the ideology of nationalism that emerged in nineteenth- and twentieth-century Europe; and stimulated by the need to give some coherence to the natural instinct for resistance to alien colonial rule. It was not pre-ordained that resistance to colonial rule – anti-colonialism – should take a nationalist form. But, in the course of the early twentieth century, and particularly after the First World War, the anticolonial struggle defined itself in nationalist terms; primarily because the post-First World War settlement had made the nation-state the basic legitimate unit of the international system, and because the language of nationalism was a language that the European colonial powers understood. Once again, the pivotal importance of the immediate post- First World War period needs to be emphasised.

Arab unity, religion, ideology and national identity

In linguistic terms, the Arabic language is part of the Semitic language family that includes Hebrew; the two languages are very similar in terms of basic structure, grammar and vocabulary. Both the Arabs and Jews claim a common ancestor, the nomadic chieftain Abraham ('Ibrahim' in Arabic), and the ancestral 'cradle' of Arab civilisation is the southern and central part of what is now called the Arabian peninsula. Though there was a rich pre-Islamic Arab culture, Arab identity has been primarily defined by the influence of the Prophet Muhammad (571-631AD), who began his religious mission in Mecca and founded a religio-political community in Medina that, under Muhammad and his successors ('Caliphs'), became a gigantic Islamic Empire stretching from Spain to Afghanistan. The central texts of Islam are the Qur'an, regarded by Muslims as the word of God transmitted to Muhammad, and the Hadiths, a collected record of the sayings and deeds of the prophet. These are written in the Arabic language, and have not just formed the basis for Islam, but have fundamentally affected every aspect of Arab civilisation – its customs, culture and literature, law, and politics. The expansion of the Islamic Empire also expanded this Arabic-speaking civili- sation; and, through this process, many indigenous groups were subsumed into a wider Arab identity. Although the Islamic Empire gradually broke up after the seventh century AD, Arabic-Islamic civilisation took permanent root - albeit in separate kingdoms – through the whole of coastal North Africa, Arabia and West Asia up to the Persian frontier.

From the twelfth to the sixteenth centuries, the Arab world delineated above was divided between competing dynasties. In the course of the sixteenth century, however, large areas of the Arab world were absorbed into the empire of the Ottoman Turks, themselves Muslims, but completely distinct in ethnic and linguistic terms from the Arabs. This Ottoman Empire was a perfect example of a pre-nation state: although an ethnic-Turkish stratum dominated the empire, it was essentially an Islamic Empire, where the Sultan (political leader) of the empire also saw himself as the Caliph (essentially, religious leader) of the Islamic world as a whole. Distinctions of status within this truly 'multi-cultural' empire were made by religious affiliation as well as ethnic grouping: as such, the Muslim Arabs had a privileged position. Nevertheless, their status as lieutenants to a Turkish Ottoman leadership was a decline from the glorious early centuries of Islam.

From the nineteenth century, the whole of Islam, as well as the Ottoman Empire itself, came under threat from the expansion of the European empires. One of the earliest objectives of the new European maritime empires was to by-pass the Ottoman stranglehold over the eastern Mediterranean; and, step-by-step, Portugal, the Netherlands, France and Britain gained control – from roughly the seventeenth to the early nineteenth centuries – of huge sections of the Islamic world, particularly in the East Indies and the Indian sub-continent. By the early nineteenth century, Britain and France began to threaten the Ottoman Empire itself, particularly at the edges of the Arab area. In subsequent decades, Britain established a colony in Aden (1839) and protectorates over the southern and eastern coast of Arabia. From 1830 on, France gained a foothold in North Africa, particularly in Algeria, and a full-scale European settlement project was initiated with the ultimate objective of turning Algeria into an 'Overseas France'. This policy of encouraging European settlement was later followed by France in Tunisia, and by Italy from 1911 onwards in Libya. From 1882, Britain took over the government of Egypt 'on behalf of' the Ottoman Sultan, and subsequently expanded British control southwards to Sudan. Gradually, directly or indirectly, the Arab world was being subsumed into the networks of European global dominance.

The Arabs reacted in a number of ways to this threat of European domination and – in North Africa at least – settlement. In the nineteenth century, there were significant outbreaks of resistance against the French

colonisation of North Africa, and against the imposition of British rule in
Egypt. If we consider the general character of Arab resistance to European
control in the period before the First World War, it is clear that it was mainly
focused against the 'kafir' (unbeliever) threat to the religion and civilisation
of Islam. The widespread undercurrent of resistance throughout the Arab
world to European rule and influence was largely headed by local religious
teachers.[1] In the case of the rebellion of the 'Mahdi' ('directed by God') in
Sudan in the 1880s, Islamic resistance took the form of a messianic movement designed to restore the purity of the original Islamic state.

However, the main concern of educated and, to a degree, 'westernised'
Muslims was the apparent backwardness of Islamic civilisation, and the need
therefore, not merely to defend, but to reform Islam if it was to respond
effectively to the seemingly irresistible dynamism of European civilisation.
The Islamic Reform movement of the late nineteenth and early twentieth
centuries contained many diverse views. But its basic notion was that the
essence of Islamic doctrine had to be liberated from the fossilised body of
accumulated custom and tradition that surrounded it, and that its enlightened
universal principles should form the basis for a revitalised Islamic world. The
modern findings of science, technology, political reform and social studies
should, therefore, be absorbed into the thinking of Islam and at the same
time be 'Islamicised'. The Islamic Reform movement was essentially an
Islamic version of the broad 'cultural revolution' that swept the colonised
world in the decades before the First World War; an educational revolution
driven by the belief that the colonised world had to revitalise and modernise
its own civilisations before it could effectively challenge European global
dominance.

It is one of the paradoxes of the era of European global control that the
dissemination of European cultural, educational and political ideas inevitably
also spread those ideas – particularly nationalism, democracy ('self-determination') and socialism – that would help give a focus and justification for the
anti-colonial resistance that would eventually destroy the European empires.
In parallel with the Islamic Reform movement, the years before the First
World War also saw the development of Arab movements for educational
reform and for the resuscitation of an Arab – rather than specifically Islamic
– cultural and national identity. This reassertion of 'Arab-ness' was not only
a reaction to the growing European presence, but also to the fact that the
Ottoman Empire was increasingly being identified, not as an Islamic, but as
a Turkish Empire. The growth of Turkish nationalism – another phenomenon
of this era – and the fact that the Turks dominated the Ottoman Empire,

emphasised the subordinate role of the Arabs within the empire, and itself helped to stimulate a reactive Arab national consciousness.

The First World War had a crucial effect on Arab nationalism. As has been seen in the previous chapter, the British, with their headquarters in Egypt, tried to exploit Arab resentment against Turkish rule by promising in 1915 a vaguely-defined independence for the Arabs in return for Arab support in defeating the Ottoman Empire. The British promise was hedged about by qualifications which made it clear that Britain and France were determined to subordinate this Arab 'independence' to overall Franco-British strategic control of the region. This became horribly clear in 1920, when the League of Nations denied the right of immediate self-determination to the Arab regions of the former Ottoman Empire, but rather 'mandated' Britain and France to exercise temporary political authority in these areas. As has been seen, Britain was granted mandate authority in Palestine, Jordan and Iraq. For her part, France bludgeoned aside the independent Arab state that had been declared in Damascus by the leaders of the Arab revolt (1916-1918) against the Turks, and established mandates in Lebanon and Syria. An even deadlier blow to Arab national susceptibilities was delivered by the Balfour Declaration of 1917, which opened Arab Palestine to Jewish colonial settlement.

During the period 1920-1950, however, Britain saw a partnership with the Arab world as the key to the maintenance of its influence in a region that was of vital strategic importance – the Suez Canal, for example – and of vital economic importance because of its oil reserves. By 1939, it had abandoned its 'Balfour' obligation to create a 'Jewish homeland' in Palestine. By 1950, Britain had presided over the creation of a network of independent and semi-independent Arab states, dominated on the whole by traditional dynasties and élites that were prepared to work within an overall framework of British and, to a lesser extent, French patronage. It was in this regional context that a large number of the Arab states – Iraq, Syria, Lebanon, Jordan, Egypt and Libya – moved to independence during this period. The main areas that were by 1950 still under some form of colonial control were the kingdoms of eastern Arabia, Aden and South Yemen, and French North Africa. European control was most firmly implanted in Algeria, where over a million European settlers were determined to maintain an umbilical link with France.

It was precisely during this period, and particularly during the decades of the 1930s, 1940s and 1950s, that a new more radical form of nationalism emerged in the Arab world: a nationalism that regarded Britain, not as the Arab world's patron and ally, but as its principal oppressor and adversary.

This radical nationalism emerged among the younger, well-educated urban stratum of the Arab world, a stratum that had been politicised by the disappointments of the First World War; by the subsequent imposition of French and British control throughout the Arab world; by the failure of the various political élites to assert the right to full Arab self-determination; and by the relentless growth of Zionist settlement in Palestine, culminating in the creation of the State of Israel in 1948.

Though there were, of course, many variations of programme, it is possible to identify the main ingredients of the ideology of radical Arab nationalism. In the first place, it is important to note that Islam did not play a central role: insofar as Islam had a place in radical Arab nationalism, it was seen as a fundamental basis of Arab identity rather than as an autonomous spiritual force. Radical Arab nationalism was crucially influenced – as were the other nationalist movements of the colonised world at that time – by the communist (or 'Marxist-Leninist') ideology of the Russian Revolution: particularly the notion that capitalism and colonialism were interdependent. The Arab nationalists were, however, acutely conscious that the Arab 'masses' – who were deeply influenced by Islam in their everyday life – would never accept the atheist philosophy of communism; and the nationalists themselves tended to reject the communist notion of the 'class struggle', an idea that would divide rather than unite the Arab world. A specific form of 'Arab socialism' was therefore promoted, that was designed to ward off the combined forces of European colonialism and capitalism. Arab nationalism and Arab socialism were seen as interlinked: socialism would help mobilise the Arab 'masses' in a common national endeavour to liberate Arab economies from foreign control, and would subsequently enable the people as a whole to benefit from a new 'nationalised' economic system with an underpinning of state planning and state control of the key sectors of industry.

The specific objectives of Arab nationalism were, first, the removal of the conservative Arab regimes – mainly monarchies – that worked within the British-dominated Middle East. The ultimate objective, of course, was the liberation of the Arab world from foreign – colonial, or, in the case of the growing economic power of the United States, 'neo-colonial' – political and economic control. There was also a fundamental common determination to undo the humiliation of 1948 and assert Palestinian Arab rights against what was seen as the alien and illegitimate colonial implantation of the State of Israel. Above all, the ultimate dream of this new radical Arab nationalism was the creation of some form of Arab unity that would – in a manner that was difficult to define in detail – transcend the political boundaries of the separate Arab states.

The period 1948-1967 was the high point of radical Arab nationalism. The starting-point of this new era was probably the withdrawal of Britain from Palestine – the first unmistakable sign that the era of British dominance was coming to an end – and the subsequent failure of the traditional Arab leadership to prevent the establishment of the State of Israel. In 1952, the Egyptian monarchy was removed: a few years later, Gamal Abdul Nasser (or, more correctly, Jamal 'Abd al-Nasir) became undisputed leader of the new Egyptian regime. Thereafter, the ideas and the example of Nasser became embodied in a term – 'Nasserism' – that exercised an incalculable influence on the Arab world, particularly its increasingly politicised youth (see document 1 at the end of the chapter).

Thereafter, the pace of change in the Arab world rapidly accelerated. In 1954, the Algerian Revolution against French rule began, headed by a Front de Libération Nationale (FLN), whose ideology was a classic radical compound of nationalism and socialism. In 1956, Nasser nationalised the British and French-owned and run Suez Canal, and eventually forced these two powers to accept this humiliating *fait accompli*. In Syria and Iraq in particular, the Ba'th ('Resurrection') movement, formed by the Christian Arab Michel Aflaq in 1940, gained increasing influence: the main ideological ingredients of Ba'th combined nationalism and Arab socialism, coupled with a commitment to the ideal of Arab unity. In 1958, the pro-Western Iraqi monarchy was overthrown. In 1962, the French at last evacuated Algeria – along with most of its White settlers – and an FLN regime was established. In the same year, a rebellion broke out in North Yemen directed against the highly conservative monarchy there. In 1969, the pro-Western monarchy of Libya was overthrown and replaced by a regime headed by a fervent Nasserist, Muammar al-Qadhafi (Gaddafi). Additionally, Ba'th-dominated regimes were established in Syria and Iraq in the course of the 1960s.

The mid-1960 period saw the high tide of radical Arab nationalism. The turning-point was undoubtedly the June 1967 war, when the Arab armies of Egypt, Jordan and Syria were humiliatingly defeated, and these countries were forced to cede large chunks of territory to Israel. Ever since 1948, a *de facto* state of war had existed between Israel and the Arab states, and the years after 1948 were marked by continual tension on the borders of Israel. This tension exploded into outright war in 1956, a war that was eventually halted by United Nations intervention. By the mid-1960s, a combination of factors – the general climate of radical Arab nationalism, the growth of Palestinian

Arab militancy, Israeli determination to achieve strategic security, and the instability of the international situation – led inexorably to a new confrontation. On the morning of 6 June 1967, Israel launched a devastating 'pre-emptive' assault that culminated in the occupation of the Golan Heights of Syria, the West Bank of Palestine (at the time part of the kingdom of Jordan), the Gaza Strip and Egypt's Sinai Desert (see map at the end of chapter 8). The blow these events inflicted on the self-confidence of the Arab world and its nationalist regimes can hardly be over-estimated.

There were other signs, however, that radical Arab nationalism was essentially a phenomenon of the anti-colonial era that would not survive in the post-colonial world. During the late 1950s and 1960s, attempts to build the basis for a genuine Arab unity failed: the separate Arab regimes were too jealous of their interests. 'Arab socialism' did not deliver the expected economic strength and social welfare, but rather corruption, 'clientalism' and stagnation. Moreover, the Ba'thist regimes of Syria and Iraq rapidly degenerated into grim tyrannies whose sole *raison d'être* became 'regime survival' at any cost. The massive funeral of Nasser in 1970 symbolised the end of an era.

The aftermath of the Arab nationalist era has seen diverse trends in the Arab region. Firstly, American anxiety to ensure that its main interests in the region – the security of the West's oil supplies; the prevention during the Cold War of Soviet penetration of the Arab world; and the survival of Israel – forced the United States to intervene more directly, particularly after yet another Arab-Israeli war in 1973. As a consequence, the United States has built up a network of pro-Western states, particularly among the monarchies of the Arabian peninsula that had been able to survive the nationalist era. Secondly, the states of the region – although they have always respected the sentiment towards Arab unity – have tended more and more to emphasise their own distinct national identities, and pursue their own separate national interests. This trend was perhaps illustrated most vividly by the visit of Egypt's Anwar Sadat – the successor to Nasser himself – to Jerusalem in 1977, and his separate negotiations with Israel for the return of the Sinai Desert to Egypt.

An immediate judgement might be that the radical Arab nationalism represented by Nasser was to an extent created and defined by the phenomenon of European colonialism. In the aftermath of this unifying threat, the natural diversity of the Arab world re-emerged. What must be born in mind, however, is the point made at the beginning of this chapter: the constant tension between an overall Arab identity, an Islamic identity, and local state identities. In the decades since the 1960s, the aspiration for some form of unity that transcends the nation-states of the region remains a potent force. With the apparent failure of Arab nationalism to achieve its more ambitious goals, however, this yearning for unity has been increasingly expressed in Islamic, not national terms. The dream of renewing and reforming the Arab world through the spiritual force of Islam is especially appealing to newly urbanised societies only recently uprooted from the traditional life of the countryside. Islam and the aspiration to Arab unity remain forces beneath the surface that no Arab regime can afford to ignore.

Documents

(Nb: in all the following extracts, editorial comments at the beginning of texts, or amendments and explanations in the texts themselves, will be placed in square brackets. Headings and subdivisions will be put in italics.)

1 – 'Nasserism' and the Arab Revolution

[By far the most important figure in the 'Arab Revolution' of the post-1945 period was Gamal Abdul Nasser (1918-1970), an army officer who partici-pated in the *coup d'état* of July 1952 which removed the Egyptian monarchy and *ancien régime*, and soon gained a predominant position in the Revolution Command Council that took over power. In the following extracts from his book, *Egypt's Liberation: The Philosophy of the Revolution*, published in 1955, the main themes of Arab nationalism are addressed, particularly the issues of Arab unity, decolonisation, the threat posed by Israel, and the need to create a new post-colonial society that would give a better future for the people of the Arab world.]

The national revolution versus the social revolution

I can now state that we are going through two revolutions, not one revolution. Every people on earth goes through two revolutions: a political revolution by which it wrests the right to govern itself from the hand of tyranny, or from an army stationed upon its soil against its will; and a social revolution, involving the conflict of classes, which settles down when justice is secured for the citizens of the united nation.

Peoples preceding us on the path of human progress have passed through two revolutions, but they have not had to face both simultaneously; their revolutions, in fact, were centuries apart in time. For us, the terrible experience through which our people are going is that we are having both revolutions at the same time.

This terrible experience stems from the fact that both revolutions have attendant factors which clash and contradict violently. To be successful, the political revolution must unite all elements of the nation, build them solidly together and instil in them the spirit of self-sacrifice for the sake of the whole country. But one of the primary features of social revolution is that it shakes values and loosens principles, and sets the citizenry, as individuals and classes, to fighting each other. It gives free rein to corruption, doubt, hatred and egoism.

We are caught between the millstones of the two revolutions we are fated now to be going through. One revolution makes it obligatory that we unite and love one another, fighting side by side to achieve our ends; the other brings dissension upon us against our desires, causing us to hate each other and think only of ourselves...

But what is it we want to do? And how is it to be done?

Defining Egyptian identity: the need to overcome the national 'inferiority complex' and 'colonized' mentality of the Egyptian and Arab people

...There can be no doubt that all of us dream of an Egypt free and strong. That is something about which there is no dispute between one Egyptian and another. But as for the way to achieve freedom and strength, that is our Gordian knot.

It fell to Egypt that she should be the geographical crossroads of the world. So often were we a channel for the invader! So often were we the prize of covetous adventurers! It is impossible to account for the many factors involved in the psychology of our people unless we carefully analyse the many circumstances that have historically beset us.

To my mind, it is not possible to disregard the Pharaonic history of Egypt, or the interaction of Greek culture and our own. Then there came the Roman invasion and the Islamic conquest, together with succeeding Arab waves of immigration.

I believe that we must also dwell at length on our history through the Middle Ages, since it was the vicissitudes of that period which contributed so much to what we think and how we act today.

If the Crusades were the beginning of the Renaissance of Europe, they were the beginning of the dark ages in our country. Our people alone bore most of the sufferings of the Crusades, out of which they emerged poor, destitute and exhausted. In their exhaustion they were simultaneously destined by circumstances to submit to and suffer further indignity under the hoofs of the Mongol and Caucasian tyrants. They came to Egypt as slaves, murdered their masters and became masters themselves. They were driven into Egypt as Mamelukes (ie, owned) but shortly they became kings in our good and peaceful land. [The Mameluke sultanate originated from slave-mercenaries, mainly from the Turkish area, who had been recruited by the previous dynasty, and who seized power and dominated Egypt and Syria between 1250 and 1517.]

Tyranny, oppression and ruin characterised their rule in Egypt, which continued for many centuries. During that period, our country was transformed into a jungle ruled by wild beasts. The Mamelukes considered it an easy prey, and they struggled ferociously among themselves about the sharing of the booty. The booty was our souls, our minds, our wealth and our land.

Sometimes when I re-read the pages of our history, I feel a tearing grief because of that period – a period during which we were the victims of a tyrannous feudalism which did nothing for us except suck the life-blood from our veins. Nay, even worse – it robbed us of all sense of strength and honor. It left in the depths of our souls a complex which we will have to fight for a long time to overcome.

In fact, it is that complex, in my estimation, that is responsible for certain aspects in our political life. Many people, for example, stood to one side as mere spectators, observing our revolution [of 1952], as though they had nothing to do with it. They only waited for the result of a struggle between two opposing forces, neither of which concerned them.

Sometimes I resent this. Sometimes I demand of myself and my comrades: why don't these people come forward? Why don't they come out of their hiding places to speak up and to act? This is only to be accounted for, in my opinion, by the numbing effects of the Mameluke rule. The Mameluke rulers had fought each other, and their warriors had met in fierce battles on the streets, while the people would stampede to their houses, locking themselves in, and thus avoiding a struggle which was not their concern.

It sometimes appears to me that we content ourselves overmuch by wishful thinking. In flights of fancy we fulfil our desires and enjoy in imagination things which we never bestir ourselves to realise. Some of us are still susceptible to such daydreams. Such people have not yet fully realised that the land is actually theirs, and that they, and none other, are their own masters...

New influences, new subjection for the Arab world: the impact of European colonialism

And then what happened to us after the Mamelukes? The French expedition came [1798-1799] and smashed the iron curtain which the Mongols had erected around us. New ideas flowed in, and new horizons opened up before us, of which we had been unaware...

As I see it, we were like a sick man who had been shut up in a closed room for a long time. The temperature of the closed room rose high until he was almost choked. All of a sudden a storm blew and shattered the door and the windows. The currents of cold air rushed in and the perspiring sick body shivered with chill. The sick man was, to be sure, in need of a breath of air, but it was a powerful gale that blew over him. The frail and exhausted body succumbed to fever.

This was exactly what happened to our society. For us, it was a perilous experience, whereas the Europeans had evolved by an orderly process, gradually bridging the gap between the Renaissance which followed the Middle Ages and the nineteenth century. The stages of evolution there came naturally.

But with us everything came as new and strange. We had been living in isolation, cut off from the rest of the world, especially after the trade with the East had changed routes and travelled via the Cape of Good Hope. Then, suddenly [after the building of the Suez Canal in 1869] we were coveted by the countries of Europe, since we became for them the bridge to be crossed for their colonies in the east and the south.

Waves of thoughts and ideas came over us while we were not yet developed enough to evaluate them. We were still living mentally in the captivity of the thirteenth century, in spite of a few manifestations of the nineteenth, and afterwards of the twentieth century. Our minds tried to catch up with the caravan of human progress, although we were five centuries or more behind. The pace was fearful and the journey was exhausting.

There is no doubt that this situation is responsible for the lack of a strong and united public opinion in our country. The differences between individuals are great, and between generations they are still greater.

I used to complain that the people did not know what they wanted and could not agree on any program to be followed. Then I realised that I was demanding the impossible and that I had disregarded the circumstances of our society.

We live in a society that has not yet taken form. It is still fluid and agitated and has not yet settled down or taken a stabilised shape. It is in the process of an evolution, striving to catch up with those other nations that have preceded us on the road.

With no intention of flattering, I believe that our people have nonetheless achieved a miracle. It is quite possible that any other nation, under the same conditions, would have faded away, drowned by such currents as have [all] but submerged us. But we have stood firm against the violent flood. It is true we have almost lost our balance on certain occasions, but it is our destiny never to have fallen but that we rose again.

Sometimes I examine the conditions of an average Egyptian family among the thousands of families living in Cairo. It may be the father is a turbaned farmer who has been born outside the city, in the heart of the countryside. The mother is a descendant of a Turkish family. The sons are being educated at an English-style school, while the daughters attend schools run on the methods of the French. And all this is being backgrounded by a curious mixture of thirteenth and twentieth-century ways of life...

Egypt's identity and place in the world: the Arab, African and Islamic 'circles' of identity that surround Egypt

Sometimes I sit in my study reflecting on the subject, asking myself: What is our positive role in this troubled world, and where is the place in which we should fulfil that role?

I review our circumstances and discover a number of circles within which our activities inescapably must be confined and in which we must try to move.

Fate does not jest and events are not a matter of chance – there is no existence out of nothing. We cannot look at the map of the world without seeing our own place upon it, and that our role is dictated by that place.

Can we fail to see that there is an *Arab* circle surrounding us – that this circle is a part of us, and we are a part of it, our history being inextricably part of its history.

These are facts and no mere idle talk. Can we possibly ignore the fact that there is an *African* continent which Fate decreed us to be a part of, and that it is also decreed that a terrible struggle exists for its future – a struggle whose results will be either for us or against us, with or without our will? Can we further ignore, the existence of an *Islamic* world, with which we are united by bonds created not only by religious belief, but also reinforced by historic realities?...

The need for leadership in the Arab world: Egypt's role

I do not know why I recall, whenever I reach this point in my recollections as I meditate alone in my room, a famous tale by a great Italian poet, Luigi Pirandello – *Six Characters in Search of an Author*. The pages of history are full of heroes who created for themselves roles of glorious valor which they played at decisive moments. Likewise the pages of history are also full of heroic and glorious roles which never found heroes to perform them. For some reason it seems to me that within the Arab circle there is a role, wandering in search of a hero. And I do not know why it seems to me that this role, exhausted by its wanderings, has at last settled down, tired and weary, near the border of our country and is beckoning to us to move, to take up its lines, to put on its costume, since no-one else is qualified to play it.

Here, let me hasten to say that this role is not one of leadership. It is rather a role of interaction with, and responsibility to all the above-mentioned factors. It is a role such as to spark this tremendous power latent in the area surrounding us; a role tantamount to an experiment, with the aim of creating a great strength which will then undertake a positive part in the building of the future of mankind.

There is no doubt that the Arab circle is the most important, and the one with which we are most closely linked. For its peoples are intertwined with us by history. We have suffered together, we have gone through the same crises, and when we fell beneath the hooves of the invaders' steeds, they were with us under the same hooves.

We are also bound in this circle by a common religion.

The centre of Islamic learning has always moved within the orbit of its [the Arab world's] several capital cities – first Mecca, then shifting to Kufa, then to Damascus, next to Baghdad, and finally to Cairo.

Lastly, the fact that the Arab states are contiguous has joined them together in a geographical framework made solid by all these historical, material and spiritual factors.

The key role of Palestine in defining Arab national consciousness

So far as I can recall, the first glimmers of Arab consciousness began to steal into my consciousness when I was a student in secondary school. I used to go out on a general strike with my comrades every year on the second of November to protest [against] the Balfour Declaration, which Britain had made on behalf of the Jews, giving them a national home in Palestine, thus tyrannously wresting it from its rightful owners. And at that time, when I asked myself why I went on strike with such zeal, and why I was angry about this act [concerning] a country I had never seen, I could find no answer except in the echoes of sympathetic emotion.

Then a kind of understanding began to develop when I became a student in the Military Academy, where I studied in particular the history of all past military campaigns in Palestine and in general the history of the area and its conditions which have made of it during the past hundred years an easy prey for the fangs of hungry beasts...

The result was that when the Palestine crisis [1948] began, I was utterly convinced that the fighting there was not taking place on foreign soil, nor was our part in it a matter of sentiment. It was a duty necessitated by self-defence...

For the present, I do not wish to dwell upon the details of that war. It is a subject about which accounts differ. What concerns me is the important lesson it teaches.

The Arabs entered Palestine [to help the Palestinians in 1948] in a single wave of enthusiasm. They did so on the basis of common knowledge and a common estimate shared by all as to the outer borders of their security. The Arab states emerged from Palestine with a common bitterness and disappointment; then, each in its own internal affairs encountered the same factors, the same ruling forces that had brought about their defeat, and forced them to bow their heads in humiliation and shame...

When the struggle was over in Palestine and the siege lifted, and I had returned to Egypt, the Arab circle in my eyes had become a single entity. The events that have taken place since have confirmed by belief. I have followed developments in the Arab countries, and I find they match, point for point. What happened in Cairo had its counterpart in Damascus the next day, and in Beirut, in Amman, in Baghdad and elsewhere. This all fitted in with the picture drawn by long experience. It is a single region. The same circumstances, even the same forces, united against all of it.

Arab nationalism and the anti-imperialist struggle

And it was clear that the foremost of these forces was imperialism.

Even Israel itself is but a result of imperialism. For if Palestine had not fallen under the British mandate, Zionism would never had been able to muster enough support to realise a national home in Palestine. The idea would have remained a mad hopeless dream…

When all these truths had impressed themselves upon me, I began to realise the need for a common struggle. I said to myself that so long as the region is one region, sharing the same conditions and problems, and the same future (and, however he tries to change his disguise, the same enemy) – so long as this is true, why do we scatter our efforts?

The experiences which followed the July 23 [1952] revolution [in Egypt] have increased my conviction of the necessity for a common struggle. And now, the hidden parts of the long developing picture began to be disclosed, the obscuring shadows began to disappear.

I admit that in the process, I also began to see the great obstacles which block the path to the common struggle, but I began to believe that these obstacles, being the creation of the common enemy, had to be removed.

Finally, I began to make political contacts for the sake of unifying the struggle by whatever means. After a month of such contacts, I came to the important conclusion that the first obstacle in our path is doubt. It was clear that the roots of this doubt were planted in us by our old common enemy in order to prevent us from embarking upon unified action…

I do not want to minimise the obstacles to unity in the common struggle. There is no doubt that these obstacles have their roots in the nature of the situation and in the historical and geographical circumstances of our people. But it is also certain that with a little flexibility, based on foresight, not on neglect, it will be possible to call into being a plan upon which everyone will be able to agree without reservation – a plan for carrying out the common struggle.

I do not doubt for a moment that our common effort will achieve for us and our peoples everything we desire. For I shall always maintain that we are strong. The only trouble is that we do not realise just how strong we are…

… And now I go back to that wandering mission in search of a hero to play it. Here is the role. Here are the lines, and here is the stage. We [Egyptians] alone, by virtue of our place, can perform the role.

[From Gamal Abdul Nasser, *Egypt's Liberation: The Philosophy of Revolution* (Washington DC, Public Affairs Press, 1956), pp 39-41, 61-69, 85-91, 94-95, 98-99, 103-105, 114]

2 – The Arab world and the question of Palestine

[It will be apparent from Nasser's writings that the fate of Palestine played a
key role in stimulating a sense of Arab unity after the Second World War.
Arab unity was to a degree built up around the issue of Palestine after the
humiliating defeats of 1948 and 1949. Arab nationalism was, however, dealt
a stunning blow in June 1967 when Israel – in the course of the so-called Six
Day War – seized control of Egypt's Sinai desert, the Gaza strip, the West
Bank of Palestine (which had been under Jordanian control), and the Golan
heights in Syria (see map at the end of the previous chapter). Most important of all, perhaps, was the fact that a new wave of refugees left Palestine.

The deepening plight of the Palestinian people, and the inability of the
united Arab world to assert its will against Israel, stimulated a new and profound crisis of confidence within the Arab world. In the following article,
published in *The Observer* newspaper in 3 September 1967 by Albert
Hourani, a Christian Arab and one of the most eminent modern academics
to come to the West from the Arab world, explains the importance of
Palestine for the Arabs, and tries to illuminate to an apparently uncaring
West the Arab Palestinian case.]

At the heart of the Middle Eastern problem lies the problem of Palestine: the
struggle of Palestinian Arabs and Jewish settlers for possession and
mastery of the land. Now [1967] that the Powers have been drawn in and
a local crisis has become a world-wide one, it is easy to forget the local
causes of it; but this is dangerous, for unless they are treated the crisis may
return.

The struggle of the Arabs and Jews for Palestine cannot be explained by
ancient religious hostility. Jews (and Christians) had always lived among the
mainly Arab Muslim population of Palestine, and relations between them
had usually been correct. But in the 1880s a new type of Jewish immigration
began, mainly from Eastern Europe, inspired by the Zionist idea of a Jewish
national home: this soon aroused the hostility of Ottoman officials and part
of the population.

During its 30 years of rule, 1917-1947, Britain bound itself by the
Balfour Declaration and the Mandate to encourage the Jewish national
home, subject to the rights of the existing population; immigration increased,
particularly after the rise of Hitler, and Arab opposition became almost universal and drew in the surrounding Arab States.

This hostility sprang from the attempt to implant a new society in a land already occupied by an old one. When the settlers came they found a complete society already there: farmers, craftsmen and merchants, ancient towns and villages, religious institutions, a culture expressed in Arabic, a leadership which formed part of the Arab Ottoman élite. The aim of the newcomers was not to be absorbed into it but to create their own society with its farms and cities, institutions, Hebrew culture and political leaders.

In the age of European expansion, other such attempts were made to plant new societies amidst old ones. They always caused strain, but Zionist settlement in Palestine had special features. The new Jewish society, by the nature of the Zionist idea, was to be a complete and exclusive one. Its aim was to create a wholly Jewish economy: land bought by the Jewish National Fund became the inalienable property of the Jewish people and no non-Jew could ever be employed on it.

The Zionist idea

It is true, the Zionists bought their land. But in the Middle East political power and ownership of land have always gone together, and the Arabs were convinced that if the Jews had power they would seize the greater part of the land. That the Jews *would* take power became first a danger, then a certainty, as the Jewish population grew. Because of the nature of the Zionist idea, the new Jewish society was an expanding society, open to all who wished to come in. In 1922 Jews formed 13 per cent of the population in Palestine; in 1935, 28 per cent; in 1947, 33 per cent.

As numbers grew, the idea of a Jewish national home turned into that of a Jewish state, and this was unacceptable to the Arabs, not only because by the 1930s most of them were moved by the idea of an Arab state of which Palestine would be a part, but because in a Jewish state they would have no choice (whatever guarantee the mandate might contain) except between being a powerless minority and leaving their country.

Some Zionist leaders did indeed talk of a 'bi-national state' [one state, with two nations in it], but attempts at political agreement broke on the question of immigration. The Arabs wanted to preserve the Arab character of Palestine, and so wanted little or no Jewish immigration. The Zionists wanted to keep the doors of Palestine open, no matter what the form of government.

Here lay the dilemma of their policy; they wanted agreement with the Arabs and they wanted unlimited immigration, but they could not have both, and if forced to choose most of them would choose immigration.

The British, who were politically responsible, had no clear or stable policy on this matter. They had obligations to the Arabs and so opposed the idea of a Jewish state: they had obligations to the Zionists and so permitted immigration, not as much as the Jews wanted but enough to make a Jewish state possible. In 1948, unable to reach agreement with the two parties, they withdrew in circumstances which made fighting inevitable, and there happened what the Arabs had feared for so long.

The dynamic, exclusive, alien society which had grown up among them [the Jews] seized power in the greater part of Palestine, with encouragement and help from some Western states, secured control of the land and brought in immigrants on a large scale; and two-thirds of the Arab inhabitants lost their lands and homes.

All wars create refugees, and after the armies have departed the peasants and merchants return to take up their lives again. Civilised governments accept that they have a responsibility for those who live in the land they rule. But after the armistice agreements of 1949 Israel refused – with limited exceptions – to allow the Arab refugees to return. In a situation like this everything becomes political, and the Israelis made political use of the refugees.

Conquered land

By refusing to consider the refugee problem except in the framework of a peace settlement with the surrounding Arab states, they linked together two matters which had no moral connection; for the return of the refugees was an obligation which they owed not to the surrounding Arab states but to the Palestinian Arabs themselves, as inhabitants of the land they had conquered. To make such a connection was the more tempting because Israel did not really wish the refugees to return. Even at a peace settlement it would only have offered to take back a small number; for what it wanted was to have the land without its inhabitants, so as to settle its own immigrants.

(This policy was made morally acceptable to Israelis and the outside world by the 'myth' that the Arabs left willingly under orders from their leaders. No more than the most tenuous evidence was produced for this, and, in fact, the flight of the Arabs presents no mystery. Some left for reasons of prudence, some from panic during the fighting, some were forced to go by the Israeli Army. What has happened this year [1967] throws some light on this. It is clear that no Arab Government ordered the Palestinians to leave this year, but a quarter of the inhabitants of the West Bank left in two months – and for the same reasons.)

Nothing could show more clearly that the basic dilemma of Zionist policy was still there. If it wanted land for immigrants, it was sensible to stop the return of the refugees. But if it wanted peace with the Arabs, then it was fatal.

After 1948, the first step to peace was that Israel should recognise its responsibility to the Arabs who lived in its territory but had been displaced by the fighting. Only this could have set in motion a train of events leading towards peace; and only Israel, as victor and beneficiary of the war, could have taken the step. Israel never did so, and its attitude was accepted by the Western Powers. Every year the United Nations passed a resolution calling for the return or compensation of the refugees, but no one tried seriously to carry it out.

Shock of exile

The assumption which underlay the attitude of Israel and the Western Powers was that sooner or later the refugees would melt away, absorbed into the surrounding Arab peoples, and then the problem of Palestine would cease to exist. But this was a false assumption. It was not a mass of individuals who fled in 1948, it was the greater part of a society. A common land and language, a common political fate, and the shock of exile created a Palestine Arab nation. After 1948 it lived scattered.

Allowing for natural increase, by the beginning of this year [1967] there must have been rather more than two million Palestinian Arabs: almost 400,000 in the Gaza Strip, 300,000 in Israel, 1,300,000 in Jordan [including what is now known as the West Bank of Palestine], 150,000 each in Lebanon and Syria. About two-thirds of them were still registered refugees. Many of these had become wholly or partly self-supporting; if more had not, it was not (as is often said) because the host-countries did not wish them to be settled, but because the absorption of refugees depended on the pace of economic development, and this was bound to be slow in the early stages. In no country was their position satisfactory.

In Jordan they had full citizenship, but Palestinians and Tranjordanians had not yet been welded into a complete unity, and positions of real power remained in Transjordanian hands; an intelligent policy of development created an economy into which some of them were absorbed, but the refugees formed a third of the whole population, and a country with such limited resources could not absorb so large a number in 20 years.

In Israel, their position was tolerable: they had civil and political rights, but fewer opportunities of higher education and skilled employment than Jews, they lived under a strict military control (until a relaxation in recent months) and were virtually shut out of the political community.

Thus the Palestinian Arabs remained in being as a nation which had lost almost everything but was determined to continue to exist: that is to say, to live with one another, and to live in Palestine. After 1948 this was the heart of the 'Palestine problem'; the *de facto* existence of Israel was not in serious danger, but what remained to be assured was the existence of the Palestinian nation. Its attitude to Israel was shared by the other Arab nations, for many reasons. The individual losses of the refugees were felt throughout Jordan, Syria and Lebanon, which belonged to the same geographical and historical unit as Palestine, and where almost every family had Palestinian connections.

More widespread still was a sense of human indignity, a feeling that in the eyes of Israel and the West the Arabs were surplus human beings, to be removed and dumped elsewhere to redress a wrong not they but Europe had done to the Jews. It seemed to most Arabs that Western Governments talked in one way about the rights of the Jews and in another about those of the Arabs. They often said that Israel was here to stay; they never said that the Palestinian Arab nation was here to stay. They talked in language of high principles and threats about Israel's right to free navigation; they used a milder language about the rights of the refugees to return or compensation. Unwise statements by Arab spokesmen about throwing Israel into the sea were widely quoted and condemned; no-one seemed to care that Israel had, in fact, thrown a large number of Arabs into the desert.

Together with this went an almost universal fear. So long as Israel remained open to all Jews who wished to immigrate, so long as it could maintain Western standards of technology and hope for wide support in Europe and America, there would be a danger of its expanding into the territory of the surrounding states. Sooner or later, most Arabs believed, Israel would absorb the rest of Palestine, and perhaps parts of southern Syria and Lebanon as well; for a second time the Palestinians would have to move out, and would find themselves walking down the road to Jericho or scrambling across the Jordan bridges...

More refugees

The Israeli victory [of 1967] has changed many things in the Middle East, but it has not changed the problem of Palestine. The Palestinian Arab people are still there, still in ruin and exile, still determined to exist. Perhaps two-thirds of them are now under Israeli rule; many more refugees have been created, and it is not certain that Israel will allow most of them to return; many who are not refugees have been ruined by the occupation of [the West Bank of Palestine]; every individual Palestinian has now suffered or lost something because of Israel.

... In spite of Israeli hopes and efforts, there is no reason to believe that the attitude of Palestinian Arabs towards Israel has changed, except to be hardened by new losses. The Arab states have more and not less reason to think of Israel as an expansionist state which, with the help or acquiescence of the US, may dominate politically and economically the region lying between Nile and Euphrates.

It seems not impossible that the Arab states will be persuaded to make a declaration of non-belligerence and the Israelis to withdraw from the conquered lands. The basic dilemma of Israeli policy remains. The Palestinian Arabs are the estranged neighbours with whom Israel must be reconciled if it is to become 'like all nations'; and it remains true, as it has been since 1948, that the first step towards a stable *modus vivendi* is one which only Israel can take – to accept its responsibility towards the indigenous people of the land it controls, and to grant the refugees the right of return or compensation...

[From *The Observer*, 3 September 1967]

NOTES ON CHAPTER 9

1   Albert Hourani, *A History of the Arab Peoples* (Cambridge, Mass., The Belknap Press of Harvard University Press, 1991), pp 312-313.

Chapter 10

Conclusion
Race and Nation: Unity and Diversity in the Modern World

The survival of the nation-state

After the First World War, the nation-state – a state, that is, founded on the principle of nationality – became the standard political unit so far as Europe was concerned. After the Second World War, the disintegration of the European colonial empires led to the creation a global system of nation-states. If we look at the world today, it could be argued that the dominance of the nation-state is absolute. There are few states today – the Vatican State is one obvious example – that do not base their 'legitimacy' on the claim that they are the expression of a national identity. The last major non-national state was the Union of Soviet Socialist Republics (USSR, or Soviet Union), which claimed to be a socialist super-state constituting a federation of subordinate nation-states. In 1991, the Soviet Union broke up, and the constituent nation-states thereafter became sovereign independent nation-states. Even in an ambiguous case like the United Kingdom of Great Britain and Northern Ireland, there is generally understood to be some kind of British national identity that subsumes within it the separate constituent national identities of England, Wales, Scotland and Northern Ireland.

This assertion of the supremacy of the nation-state naturally raises the question of the future role of the regional free-trade and cooperation associations that have emerged since the Second World War. Most of these – for example the North American Free Trade Area (NAFTA) – do not pretend to be anything more than mutually beneficial cross-border arrangements between fully sovereign states. The European Union (EU), however, has evolved into something much more substantial that has the power in areas of law, taxation and the economy to curtail the sovereignty of its member states. The question then arises whether organisations like the EU presage the development of new 'super-states' that may eventually supersede the nation-state. Although the European Union has absorbed some sovereign rights normally held by nation-states, it is still manifestly weak in the areas of internal (law and order) and external (defence) security, and relations with the outside world (foreign policy). The European Union has no common foreign policy, no common defence policy and no common system of policing. More significantly, it would be very difficult to develop united policies in these areas in the foreseeable future. There may well be a gradual evolution towards greater European unity, but at the moment the rhetoric of European unity vastly outruns the reality.

Indeed, the inclination to move towards greater union and coordination in Europe is more than counterbalanced by continuing pressures for self-determination and the creation of new nation-states. The 1990s have seen the emergence of new independent states in the former Soviet Union, Yugoslavia, and former Czechoslovakia. There is pressure for – at the very least – greater autonomy for Scotland, Wales and Northern Ireland within the United Kingdom, and there are similar pressures within Spain and Belgium. The aspiration for national sovereignty remains alive and well.

Looking beyond Europe, the experience of the Kurdish peoples since the end of the First World War has demonstrated the possible fate of a people who do not gain their own nation-state in a world of nation-states. Swept over by waves of invasion throughout their history, and wedged between the Turkish, Arab and Persian regions, the Kurds (with a population of some eleven-to-twelve million) have suffered the penalty of their marginal position as a dispersed mountain people, their economic backwardness, and their lack of political influence, particularly during the crucial post-First World War period. They have, therefore, found themselves trapped in nation-states dominated by alien national groups. The Kurds, whose homelands are positioned at the edge of these states, have increasingly found their culture and language – their very identity – under threat. As a minority – a minority, moreover, whose size and cross-border links with Kurds in neighbouring countries have made them all the more suspect as a threat to national unity and security – they have been subjected to every possible variety of persecution, including, in Iraq, attempted genocide. But, precisely because the bulk of the Kurdish people are distributed between four nation-states – Turkey, Iraq, Iran and Syria – there is a firm regional consensus against the creation of Kurdish nation-state, or 'Kurdistan'. The fate of the Kurds is an object-lesson in the danger of being a minority everywhere and a majority nowhere (see map at the end of chapter 8).

The failure of 'joint-sovereignty' solutions also provides compelling evidence of the strength of the nation-state and the idea of national sovereignty. Where there is a sovereignty dispute between two nations over some territory – as in the case of Northern Ireland that has already been examined – some form of 'joint sovereignty' arrangement would often appear to provide a common-sense solution. There are, however, no cases where genuine joint sovereignty has been practised in the post-colonial world[1]; the whole weight of the concept of absolute nation-state sovereignty has worked against its implementation.

In the disputes between Britain and Spain over Gibraltar, and Britain and Argentina over the Falkland Islands – where Spain and Argentina respectively claim the territories concerned, while the inhabitants claim the right, according to the principles of self-determination, to adhere to Britain – joint sovereignty could satisfy the national claims of both sides. However, neither Spain nor Argentina have seen joint sovereignty agreements as anything more than transitional arrangements in a process that would ultimately transfer full sovereignty to themselves. The inhabitants of Gibraltar and the Falklands are, consequently, adamantly opposed to anything less than the security of complete British sovereignty. In the case of Northern Ireland, joint sovereignty would solve a slightly different problem: that, at present, the minority Catholic community is, in its own eyes, denied its national rights; and that, if the population balance should change in the future, a substantial Protestant minority community would, by the same token, be denied its national rights. Once again, however, there is very little evidence as yet to suggest that joint sovereignty is seen as a viable solution. Even if it were, it is likely that it would be seen only as a transitional mechanism leading to a 'transfer' of sovereignty. Nothing could reveal more clearly the dominance of the concept of national sovereignty in our age.

Nations and the international system

As has been seen in the first chapter, Dante Alighieri (1265-1321) in his *Monarchy* argued that a 'universal monarchy' was the best way of ensuring a global peace and stability that would enable humanity as a whole to achieve its inherent God-given potential. In the late eighteenth century, the German philosopher Immanuel Kant came up with a very different system in order to achieve the same end: global peace. He argued that an international system based on the unit of genuine 'republics' – states, that is, where responsible citizens as a whole controlled the political system – would put an end to the competition for territory between dynasties that was the major cause of war. Territories, in other words, would no longer be seen as the personal assets of monarchies, to be acquired or disposed of without reference to the wishes of their inhabitants. The creation of 'republics' controlled by their 'citizens' would therefore not only create a more just political system, but also greatly reduce the causes of war between states.[2]

This optimistic 'Enlightenment' view was an early version of Woodrow Wilson's plan for the establishment after the First World War of a European system based on the unit of the nation-state. Ideally, the legitimate nation-state was to be founded on the principle of 'self-determination'; and self-determination combined the principle of democracy with the principle that each self-defining nation should have the right to create its own state. Democracy, in other words, provided the means of achieving national goals. The expectation was that an international system based on such nation-states would be more stable, for the simple reason that the aspirations of these nation-states would naturally be limited to the protection of national rights and national territory. It was hoped, therefore, that, whereas dynastic states endlessly jostled for territorial advantage in order to enhance their relative power, territorial disputes in a nation-state system would be decided by the principle that the inhabitants of the disputed territories had the right – through 'self-determination' – to decide their own national destiny.

In the first instance, this principle was only applied to Europe, the Americas and small sections of the rest of the world. The history of Europe since 1919 shows that it did not bring stability or peace. The reasons for this failure are outlined in chapter 4. In the first place, attempts to apply the principle of self-determination had to confront the fact that there were large areas of Europe where ethnic groups competed for the same territory. Consequently, after 1919 there were endless disputes between neighbouring nation-states and within these nation-states. Disputes over territory, there-fore, were if anything more frequent and, indeed, more destructive, because they involved ethnic groups as a whole; unlike dynastic territorial disputes, which were often conducted over the heads of the population.

In the second place, the link between nationalism and democracy – the core of the Wilsonian view of self-determination – was frequently severed in most of Eastern and Central Europe after 1919.[3] Worse still, in those states where democracy did break down, the new authoritarian governments often sought to 'legitimise' their regimes and win mass support by pursuing aggressive nationalist policies. Nationalism, in fact, has proved to be an ideal means of mobilising the support of a population that has been denied the right of political participation. One can even see the outlines of the new political contract of the nationalist era: the population cedes its political rights in return for the government achieving ambitious national goals. It is certainly true, right up to the present day, that the success or even the survival of an authoritarian regime may depend on its ability to satisfy nationalist aspirations.[4]

After the end of the Second World War, a new international system was put in place, with the United Nations replacing the League of Nations, but still based on the unit of the nation-state. Almost from the outset, however, global stability was mainly ensured, particularly in Europe, by the Cold War confrontation between the 'West' and the 'Communist Bloc'; effectively between the two super-powers, the United States and the Soviet Union. Since this was a global confrontation, large areas of the world were locked into what could be called an 'antagonistic condominium', where the penalty for a resort to war, in Europe in particular, would have been general devastation by nuclear weapons. Even outside Europe, both sides had a mutual interest in ensuring that local conflicts did not get out of hand.[5] Both sides, too, had an interest in avoiding the unpredictable consequences if the existing nation-state structures were to collapse in the way that they had collapsed in Europe after 1938. These crucial factors helped to sustain what might otherwise have been a very vulnerable international system after 1945.

After the disintegration of the Soviet Union in 1991, the global discipline that had formerly been indirectly sustained by this 'balance of terror' came under threat. This is demonstrated in Europe by the break-up, not only of the Soviet Union, but also of Yugoslavia and Czechoslovakia. Discreetly or openly, however, the United States has continued to play a key mediating role globally, and particularly in the dangerous confrontations between Israel and the Arab states; Greece and Turkey; Pakistan and India; and North and South Korea. It has also mediated between Russia and the Ukraine over the vitally important issue of nuclear weapons, and has exercised a decisive influence in the nationalist squabbles between Croats, Serbs, Bosnians, Albanians and Macedonians.

Nations and the international system: the impact of decolonisation in the world beyond Europe

Whereas the nation-states of Europe have endured three phases of trauma and upheaval – the immediate post-First World War period; the Second World War period; and the aftermath of the collapse of communism in 1989-1991 – the nation-states that emerged from decolonisation in Asia and Africa have, on the whole, remained intact. Some colonial regions were partitioned in the process of gaining independence: Palestine/Israel, India/Pakistan, Korea and Vietnam are obvious examples, though Vietnam was reunified, after a twenty-year war, in 1975. Cyprus was partitioned by Turkish military action fourteen years after independence, but the partition has not been internationally recognised. Two other examples of the break-up of the nation-states that were created during decolonisation are the separation of East Pakistan (Bangladesh) from West Pakistan, and Eritrea's separation from Ethiopia. The most notorious violation of the post-colonial state system was the Indonesian annexation of East Timor in 1975.[6]

As has already been noted, there are substantial international pressures in favour of maintaining the unity of existing nation-states, not least because the process of the disintegration of nation-states can disturb the international system in unpredictable ways. There are, however, other reasons for the stability of the international nation-state system that evolved after the Second World War, and they can to an extent be explained by the dynamics of decolonisation itself.

On the face of it, the survival of the nation-state system of the decolonised world is all the more remarkable, in that many of these states are virtually colonial creations. In many cases – for example, India, Malaysia and Indonesia – indigenous pre-colonial states were lumped together to form a new colonial state. In other cases, colonial states were carved out of a region to suit the immediate strategic needs of the colonial powers: Iraq and Palestine are obvious examples. Virtually all the boundaries of the African and Asian states were delineated during the colonial period, and followed the logic of colonial expansion rather than that of any indigenous political evolution. Quite often, the result was that distinctive ethnic regions were divided, and have remained divided ever since. To take two examples from South-East Asia: the Lao people were divided between Siam (now Thailand) and French Indochina; and the Malay people were divided between Siam, British Malaya and the Dutch East Indies (now Indonesia). There are many other examples in Asia and Africa.

Paradoxically, the survival of nation-states formed in this arbitrary way, often without respect for the principles of ethnic coherence or historical evolution, has depended to a very great degree precisely on the instability of their origins. The early anti-colonialists – European-influenced and often European-educated – used the language of nationalism and self-determination in order to challenge colonialism. While, therefore, anti-colonial sentiments were real enough, a sense of nationhood often had to be virtually 'invented'; and this 'invented' national consciousness was inevitably defined by the state that the colonial power had created. In the 1920s, for example, young anti-colonialists 'created' an Indonesian national identity – with its national language, its flag and its national anthem – out of the sprawling territories known as the Dutch East Indies. In the course of the early twentieth century, a large number of similar 'non-historic' national identities were asserted, which were thereafter sustained by the dynamic relationship between anti-colonialism and nationalism. The fact that, in the course of the ensuing national struggle, the colonial powers would seek to exploit ethnic, historic and religious divisions in order to justify the continuation of colonial rule made it all the more important for the anti-colonial nationalists to assert the principle of national unity at all costs.

Many of the new nation-states that emerged to independence, therefore, had been defined by colonialism – certainly in terms of their borders – and their nationalist movements had been forged and held together by the anti-colonial struggle. To the degree, therefore, that national unity depended on resistance to the colonial presence, there was a danger that the removal of the colonial power would expose all the inherent divisions – particularly ethnic and religious diversity – of the post-colonial states. Many formerly colonised areas did, indeed, see the emergence of separatist movements in the years after independence, as various minorities found themselves at a disadvantage in the new post-colonial states and struggled to assert their own right to self-determination. Among the many examples are the separatist rebellions of the Ibo people in Nigeria; the non-Muslim Black Africans of southern Sudan; the Kurds of Turkey and Iraq; the Punjabi Sikhs and Muslim Kashmiris of India; the Tamils of Sri Lanka; the Karens of Burma; and the West Papuans of Indonesia.

It is precisely this general threat to the unity of the post-colonial nation-states that has helped to hold them together. Whatever their other differences, these states had a common interest in ensuring that separatist movements did not succeed. There was – and still is – a perception that, once the process of separatism began in a region it might lead to the unravelling of the whole nation-state structure that emerged in the post-Second World War period. For this reason, there is also a notable reluctance to sanction any arrangement that would lead to the partition of existing states, even in those cases – for example, Sudan (between the Muslim-Arab north and the Christian-African south) – where partition would appear to be the only feasible solution. There is a similar reluctance in the post-colonial world to highlight the issue of minority rights, or to allow international pressure – normally originating from the West – to interfere in these matters.

The only two cases of successful separatist movements that have created new post-colonial nation-states are in themselves instructive. The separation of East Pakistan – now Bangladesh – from West Pakistan was a recognition of an overwhelming geopolitical reality: the two 'Pakistans' were separated by the whole sub-continent of India. The separation of Eritrea from Ethiopia was not a rejection, but a reconfirmation of the boundaries created by colonialism. Eritrea had been an Italian colony, while Ethiopia had – until the ill-fated Italian invasion of 1936 – remained independent. After the Second World War, the two had been clumsily grafted together by the United Nations in 1950 – and the graft did not take.

The modern triumph of the ideology of nationalism demonstrates the extent to which the modern world has been shaped by the expansion of Europe. The nation-states of North and South America, and of Australia and New Zealand, are essentially European settler creations that asserted, or were granted, their independence in the nineteenth and early twentieth centuries. The nation-states of Asia and Africa were likewise formed by the patterns of European rule. The new Asian and African states that emerged after 1945, however, had learned from the bitter experiences of Europe that the ideology of nationalism could be a destructive as well as a constructive force. It is because of this that the nations of Asia and Africa have maintained their consensus against permitting the ideology of nationalism and self-determination to threaten – via separatist movements, partitions, concessions to minorities, or even the granting of substantial autonomous rights to regions – the cohesion of the states that were created by decolonisation.

Whether this consensus can be maintained, and the separatist pressures of Asia and Africa can be held in check in the long term, remains to be seen. It is at least possible that the very policies – which could be collectively characterised as a general determination not to make concessions to separatist aspirations, minority rights, or even demands for real regional autonomy – that have helped hold together the nation-states of post-colonial Asia and Africa up till now, may destabilise these regions in the future.

Nationalism and global forces

At the beginning of this book it was suggested that the history of Europe and the Mediterranean could be seen as a continual tension between concepts that emphasised the principle of global unity, and those that emphasised the essential diversity of humanity. Judaism, Christianity and Islam have all – albeit in different ways – asserted the principle that humanity is governed by a universal morality. Christianity, however, has tended to draw a distinction between the spiritual and the temporal realms, between 'church' and 'state'. To an extent, therefore – though not without considerable tension – the universal mission of Christian churches has been able to coexist with a world divided into nation-states. In the case of Judaism, the contest between the idea of Zionism as essentially a spiritual mission, or as the fulfilment of a national goal, has always been latent in the modern history of Zionism, and still divides opinion in the modern state of Israel. The religion that is least amenable to the national idea is Islam, with its ultimate mission to create a universal Islamic community without any differentiation between political, social and religious spheres. The tension between Islam and the nation-state is evident throughout the Islamic world. Governments in the Islamic world have tended to balance between a generous accommodation of 'moderate' Islam that is prepared to work within the boundaries of the nation-state, and harsh repression of 'radical' Muslims who disturb the political status quo, and agitate for Islamic unity at the expense of national loyalty.

The eighteenth-century Enlightenment saw the promotion of what might be called a secular version of a world-wide religious system: namely, the assertion of universally-valid 'rights of man', the origin of the modern concept of 'human rights', enshrined in the Charter of the United Nations of 1945, and in the Universal Declaration of Human Rights adopted by the United Nations General Assembly in 1948.[7] In its early stages, the doctrine of the 'rights of man' was not only connected to, but provided the stimulus for, the idea of the nation-state. As we have seen, in the American and French Revolutions, the declaration of these 'rights' as the foundation of government was seen as a necessary precondition for the existence of a legitimate nation-state. Through the course of the nineteenth century, however, the 'legitimacy' of the nation-state tended more and more to be defined by ethnicity, with the scope of fundamental 'rights' narrowed down to the right of each ethnic group to found its own state. Thereafter, the assertion of universal human rights more often conflicted than coincided with the ideology of nationalism. Both the League of Nations after 1919 and the United Nations after 1945 tried to balance the 'right' of nations to self-determination with the protection of the 'human rights' of individuals and minorities within these states. While nations have proved to be happy to highlight the poor 'human rights' record of other nations, they tend to regard any criticism of their own record as an impertinent infringement of national sovereignty. There is, in any case, no effective means of enforcing human rights. In this area, the sovereignty of the nation-state remains supreme.

The ideology of communism at one time offered a far more substantial 'global' challenge to nationalism and the nation-state. Karl Marx (1818-1883) argued that the processes of industrialisation and colonisation – powered by the relentless competition for profit – had created a truly global market in which the world's resources were being increasingly absorbed by an all-powerful 'capitalist' class. In this economic system, the nation-state was nothing more than an instrument of capitalism, a power-house that would defend the interests of the capitalist class against revolution from below and threats from outside, and at the same time force open and protect new markets. Marx, and after him Lenin, argued, however, that the real axis of global confrontation was not between nation and nation, but between the dispossessed of the world (the 'proletariat' of Europe and the oppressed populations of the colonies) and the 'possessors': that small but absolutely dominant capitalist class. The whole emphasis of the communist movement, founded by Marx and given teeth by the creation of a communist state in Russia in 1917, was on the need to overcome national differences, unite the dispossessed of the world, and initiate an international struggle against the capitalist system.[8]

In the 1980s, the international communist threat to the capitalist system collapsed, and the open global market system has subsequently established unchallenged economic supremacy. In the 1980s and 1990s, tariff barriers have been increasingly lowered by international negotiations, and hitherto closed markets have been opened. The doctrine of international free trade has come to be seen as a universal economic panacea. As a consequence, world-wide business enterprises (the so-called multinationals) straddle the world as never before, with the ability to shuffle between nations and regions their investments, their supply-sources, their markets, their plant and their labour-force. The influence that they can exert, both on the international economy as a whole, and on the decisions of individual nations, has led many to question whether the operation of this new global economic network is not a fundamental threat to national sovereignty and the hitherto unbreachable international system based on the sovereignty of the nation-state.

Furthermore, a global network of communications is increasingly capable of by-passing national communications, thereby posing a serious threat to national cultures, perhaps even national identities. This communications network projects to the world one dominant language – 'commercial' English – and one international culture, which might be described as a distillation of American popular culture as seen through the eyes of Hollywood. Nowadays, the most appropriate symbols of international unity are not the hammer-and-sickle of communism, nor the crescent of Islam, nor yet the somewhat pallid flag of the United Nations, but Mickey Mouse and the Coca-Cola bottle.[9]

If we were to follow Marx's line of thinking to its logical conclusion, perhaps we could argue that international capitalism, having created the nation-state in order to establish a global market, has now effectively super-seded its own creation. From a different perspective, the nation-state could be seen as the last effective bulwark against the dominance of an unregulated and unaccountable global market.

Race and nation

When considering the relationship between race and nation, it is important to reiterate the point that 'race' as a subject of scientific investigation should be distinguished from the concept of 'race' as it is used in political discourse. In general, the ideology of racism has primarily been used, not so much to define the nation, as to identify those who cannot belong to the nation. Hitler's racial philosophy, for example, was rather vague in defining what an 'Aryan' or even a German was; it was lethally precise, however, in identifying those ethnic communities – notably the Jews and the Gypsies – who did not belong, either in Germany or in Europe. The influence of the concept of race on nationalism and the nation has tended to have a divisive impact within nation-states by isolating those alien elements in the nation-state that are excluded from the national family. However, it also operates at a wider level than the nation-state by identifying and giving political significance to fundamental fault-lines between mutually alien cultures and civilisations.

Throughout the history of Europe, from Homer to the present-day, the sense of a fundamental gulf between Europe and alien civilisations to the south and east has persisted. For Hellenic Greece, it was the Persian Empire that was seen as an inherently alien threat; for the Romans, it was a con-frontation between the ordered Roman-Hellenic world and a jumble of 'Oriental' potentates beyond the empire; for mediaeval and early modern

Europe, an apocalyptic religious struggle between Christianity and Islam; and for Hitler, a new crusade of European civilisation against the degenerate forces of 'Judaeo-Bolshevism'.

In his famous book, *Orientalism* (1978), Edward Said examined the ways in which the literature of Europe both demonised and 'exoticised' that vague entity, the 'Orient'. The underlying objective of this body of literature, Said argued, was to create the sense of an alien, impenetrable, irrational 'other' world that was at the same time inferior to, and a threat to the 'rational' values of European civilisation; thus implicitly providing a justification for European colonial expansion and global dominance.[10]

While this hypothesis is convincing, it could be argued that the civilisations of Asia and Africa see Europe through as distorting a lens as Europe sees Asia and Africa. How often, for example, is European and American culture depicted in Asia and Africa as a morass of gross materialism, immorality and spiritual and social disintegration: an alien, 'other' civilisation that is an object of combined fear and contempt? The delineation of the fault-lines between mutually alien civilisations has often been a two-way process.

The sense of this ultimately 'racial' gulf between antagonistic civilisations – different in terms of culture, values, customs and dress – is not, even today, confined to the realms of rhetoric. It also has political ramifications. There is, for example, an underlying notion in Europe that the Islamic world in particular poses a threat to Western civilisation: a threat that is manifested in the mass immigration of peoples who have no affiliation with European values; terrorist activities in Europe; and the sometimes lurid anti-Western rhetoric both of marginal Islamic groups and of states such as Iran. Conversely, many in the Islamic world see a threat from the West, exemplified by the whole colonial experience; Western support for Israel, which is seen as a European outpost; the strange combination of Western support for non-democratic regimes, and at the same time criticism of human rights abuses in the Islamic world; and – above all, perhaps – the corrosive influence of 'degenerate' Western culture.

This sense of a deep-rooted cultural, religious and racial confrontation has real political consequences. It is surely significant that Muslim Turkey – a staunch NATO ally of the West – is somehow seen as inherently ineligible to join the European Union, while strenuous efforts are made to draw the erstwhile enemy Russia into pan-European organisations. Nor is it insignificant that the United States – for all the rhetoric about its new links with the 'Pacific Rim' nations – has assiduously built up an interlocking network of alliances and politico-military arrangements that bind together the United

States, Europe and Russia. At the very least, it is possible to see the outlines of a hemispheric 'racial' divide – not so much between Europe and the Orient, as between a 'white' north and a 'non-white' south.[11]

Race and Nation: national identity and minority rights

In the political rather than the scientific sphere, what is normally meant by 'racial' difference is a general sense of the 'alien-ness' or 'otherness' of communities or individuals that come from radically different cultures and religions, or whose appearance – in terms of skin-colour or even costume – is manifestly different. The ideology of racism exploits this deep-rooted sense of difference and builds, using the potent emotions of hatred and fear, a political programme on the apparent threat that is posed by such 'outsiders'.

After the Second World War, Europe was brought face-to-face with the terrible consequences of racist ideology. In this period, the issue of race became virtually a taboo subject. In 1946, the French philosopher Jean-Paul Sartre asserted that 'antisemitism is not in the category of thoughts protected by the right to freedom of opinion',[12] and this precept was extended in respectable discourse to the expression of racist opinions in general. In the realm of policy-making and the question of the treatment of minorities, the general ideal was that of a 'colour-blind' integration of all races within the national family. This 'integrationalist' ideal was perfectly expressed in 1946 in the constitution that colonial Britain framed for the new multi-racial nation of Malaya: equal citizenship would be given, it stated, to all people, irrespective of race or religion, who lived in Malaya and 'regarded Malaya as their true home and the object of their loyalty'. From this basis, it was hoped that a new, single 'Malayan' identity would eventually emerge out of the very diverse religions and races of Malaya.[13]

This same 'integrationalist' mood gradually affected the post-war United States, and had a profound impact on what was then called the 'negro question'. For all the fine words of the American Declaration of Independence, the United States had from its very inception been divided into three very distinct categories of Americans: indigenous Americans, immigrant Americans, and African Americans, the latter mostly the descendants of slaves, who did not 'emigrate' to America, but were imported as commodities. The confrontation between indigenous America and immigrant America was ultimately settled by what would now be called 'ethnic cleansing', and the herding of indigenous Americans into homelands.

The slavery issue haunted the politics and society of the United States for a century, and was only resolved by the American Civil War of 1861-1865. Emancipation from slavery, however, did not solve the issue of the relationship between white immigrant America and the now-liberated African-Americans. In effect, African-Americans became an underclass, separated from other Americans by a battery of local laws and conventions, and confined to their own schools, neighbourhoods, units in the armed forces, hotels and public facilities of all kinds. Their status was formally described as 'separate but equal'; in reality it was 'separate and unequal'.

In the 1950s and 1960s, African-American resistance to this state of affairs coincided with an increasingly powerful liberal consensus in the American mainstream. The Civil Rights movement headed by Martin Luther King forced the passage of Federal laws that eliminated the 'separate and unequal' status of African-Americans. The ideal of Martin Luther King and of the other Civil Rights leaders was that of the creation of a truly integrated, 'colour-blind' America where people would not be judged 'by the colour of their skin, but by the content of their character'.[14]

One of the major debates of the late twentieth-century United States has been the question of the success or failure of the Civil Rights legislation, and the accompanying welfare and education programmes designed to enable African-Americans to move out of their 'ghettos' and into the mainstream economy and society. There can be no question that a significant number of African-Americans, possibly up to 50 per cent, have moved into the mainstream, out of the inner-cities and into the middle-class suburbs. The fundamental problem for such people, however, has been that, while institutionalised racial discrimination had been removed by legislation, what might be called 'informal' or 'everyday' racial tension had not. For African-Americans, moving in white society there was – and is – the daily sense that a racially-based notion of their innate 'alienness' continued to make them outsiders. As a result, a huge gulf has developed between the integrated world of work, and the racially-separate world of everyday social interaction. The consequence is that, in the general relationship between immigrant America – still fundamentally white – and African-America, the economy is integrated, but American society has remained segregated.

This situation of informal racial segregation has, of course, been greatly affected by the more raw, overt racial tension between the white American mainstream and those African-American communities that have not integrated socially or economically, and remain trapped in the ghetto. In many of the big cities at least, these ghettos have created a kind of underclass or, to

use Marx's famous term, 'lumpenproletariat'. The alienation of this underclass from the rest of American society is virtually total, and made all the
more complete by the fact that, unlike the slaves of a previous era, even its
labour is not required by the modern economy.

It is this failure to achieve the ideals of the Civil Rights movement –
partial, in the case of middle-class African-Americans; complete, in the case
of the ghettos – that has led many African-Americans to question the feasi-
bility or even the desirability of integration. In his *Autobiography*, the militant
leader Malcolm X asserted that the innate racism of white America made the
gulf between it and African-America unbridgeable. This book (published in
1965) had a revolutionary impact, with its assertion that – within the same
space – two Americas lived in separate worlds, and its argument for what
amounted to a rethink of the whole strategy of 'integration'.[15] The problem,
however, for any attempt to redefine American identity, and evolve a new
relationship between white and African America that would be genuinely
'separate but equal', has been this: that, while African-Americans are, in
general, united in the sense of their enforced racial alienation from mainstream society, they are hugely differentiated in their relationship to the
mainstream economy. They may form a 'community' in the racial-cultural
sense, but not in the economic sense, since a large number of African-
Americans are fully integrated into the American economy.

'Multiculturalism' and national identity

Nevertheless, it was the African-American experience that opened the door
to a general questioning of the whole idea of integration, and a search for
positive alternative concepts of national identity which could accommodate
not just racial, but also cultural, difference. This search for a redefinition of
identity was also stimulated by the great increase of emigration from Asia,
Africa, the Caribbean and Latin America into North America, Western
Europe and Australasia after 1945. This resettlement of a whole new citizenry in the white world, alien in terms of culture and colour, not only put
huge strains on the overoptimistic 'integration' thesis, but also raised for the
new non-indigenous communities the question of how to reconcile two concepts of 'roots': roots in the land in which they actually lived; and roots in the
culture and society they had left.

It is out of this background that 'multiculturalism' was born. The attempt
to define multiculturalism and assess its real significance is, however, fraught

with difficulty. It should, in the first place, be noted that multiculturalism is primarily a phenomenon of the West, the English-speaking world in particular. In Asia and Africa, the heyday of 'multiculturalism' was the colonial era, when colonial powers presided over hugely diverse societies and cultures, and where different communities in a particular colony lived in their own separate worlds, united only in their subjection to overall colonial authority. The Palestine mandate area under British rule provides an excellent example of a colonial multicultural society (see the mandate terms outlined in document 2 of chapter 8). In post-colonial Asia and Africa, national integration and the creation of unified national identities is the prevailing objective.

'Multicultural' is itself a loose term, with many potential pitfalls. Clearly, the term means something more significant than 'multiracial', which is merely the description of a society that contains a number of different races. It is possible, for example, to envisage a society that is 'multiracial' but 'unicultural'; to an extent, indeed, this was the essence of the post-1945 'integrationalist' ideal. 'Culture', however, implies not just a distinct racial-ethnic identity, but a whole way of life and an agreed set of values – and, furthermore, the existence of a community where such a way of life can be sustained. But 'culture' is such a fluid, slippery term that the relationship between racial identity, ethnic-linguistic identity, cultural identity (defined in general as a 'way of life') and religious identity is almost impossible to delineate clearly.

These complexities are, unfortunately, grist to the mill of academic theory. Indeed, the whole problem of clarifying the meaning of 'multiculturalism' has been immensely complicated by the fact that the term has been appropriated by academics, literati and what might be called the 'media intelligentsia'. Such people – forever flitting between airports, conferences and television studios – tend to use the term 'multiculturalism' as a symbol of the new, exciting, mobile 'post-modern' world of optional values and identities in which they themselves thrive.

In fact, multiculturalism, far from being a 'celebration' of a new cosmopolitan era, is rather the opposite: a search for certainty and status in an alien and threatening world. Traditionally, immigrant groups have either dispersed into the mainstream of society or remained insulated from the rest of society within their own community. Multiculturalism is at the root an attempt to reconcile the maintenance of a sense of culture and community while at the same time engaging – as a community – with the wider society; an attempt to balance between separateness and participation.

The difference between the strategy of integration and that of multiculturalism is in the end a matter of nuance rather than a clear-cut distinction.

In the classic ideal of integration, there would be a right to equal citizenship for all who inhabit a state and owe it their primary political loyalty, and a single core national identity and culture would be emphasised in the schools, history-books, the media and other areas of public life. In such a system, diverse communities and cultures may flourish, but only in the private sphere, and it would probably be implicitly expected that there would be a gradual process of 'merging' through time into a cultural mainstream. In multicultur-alism, the idea of an equal and undifferentiated citizenship is, on the whole, accepted, but there is a questioning of the idea that a 'core' identity should be promoted; at the very least, it is suggested that this identity should be rede-fined to take into account the diversity of cultures within the society. Furthermore, it is asserted that the diversity of cultures should be given greater emphasis in the public spheres of education; the promotion of 'values', religious or civic; the interpretation of national history; the dissemination of culture and language; and access to the media.

It can be seen, therefore, that the difference between integrationalist and multicultural strategies centres on the issue of defining 'core' identity. While integrationalists would normally accept that the 'core' identity of a nation is not immutable, and that it may over time be influenced by minority cultures within the society, they would tend to differ with the 'multiculturalist' over the question of whether such a 'core' identity should evolve naturally, or should in a sense, be 'negotiated'.

The debate over multiculturalism and national identity echoes in a fasci-nating way the central themes of earlier debates in eighteenth and nine-teenth-century Europe. In the ideological conflict over the legitimate origins of government, traditionalists such as Burke or de Maistre had emphasised the importance of historical continuity in a state – the 'contract' between generations – as a source of political legitimacy, as against the French revolu-tionary view that sovereignty ultimately lay in the hands of living communities. The same kind of fundamental difference divides those who see national identity in essentially 'organic' terms, and those who take a more pragmatic and flexible view of the concept of the nation. Likewise, in the nineteenth century conflicts over racial identity – as we have seen in the case of anti-semitism – a central issue of contention was the relative importance of what might be called 'roots in the blood' compared to 'roots in the soil': roots, that is, in the land one inhabits. This is a major preoccupation in the debate on multiculturalism today.

To a very great extent, the long-term validity of multiculturalism for non-indigenous communities hinges on their ability to maintain cultural 'roots':

both in the communities concerned, and through contact with the cultural 'homeland'. It is true that the greater mobility of the modern world makes it easier to maintain these contacts. On the other hand, it is very likely that the attrition of time will weaken these contacts through the generations. A living identity – sustained by language, and by family and community contacts with the homeland – will probably gradually transform into a mere sentimentalised and ritualised replica of that identity. A threat to the continued cultural vitality – perhaps even the survival – of such communities is also posed by the very nature of modern economies, which demand above all things flexibility and mobility. It is possible that only the least economically successful elements of these communities will remain within what will increasingly become impoverished and isolated ghettos. In such circumstances, multiculturalism would gradually cease to be a form of creative engagement with the wider society; instead, ethnic or religious community leaders would tend to see the wider society as an ever-present 'threat' to the community concerned and its values.[16]

There is also a real danger that the assertion of the rights and voice of non-indigenous communities in the public sphere will lead to the 'politicisation' of identity, or the 'ethnicisation' of politics. Engagement in political and public life as a community in order to promote and defend that community's interests, and compete for public resources, can rapidly degenerate into the kind of ethnic politics or 'sectarianism' that we see in Northern Ireland, and that is increasingly affecting the politics of the United States.[17] In a society dominated by ethnic politics, democracy becomes demography. (In this context, it is noticeable that the British census has more and more become a subject of political and ethnic controversy.) Every area of public life is then permeated by the issue of ethnicity and identity, and the ideal of impartial citizenship is lost: as we have seen in recent jury trials in the United States, where there is an increasing tendency to assume that juries make decisions on the basis of racial affiliation rather than an impartial consideration of the evidence. Corruption in public life is another inevitable consequence. It need hardly be added that an environment dominated by ethnic politics, far from reducing, vastly increases racial tension.

There is a world of difference, however, between multiculturalism which attempts to politicise identity, and a concept of multiculturalism that asserts the right of different cultures to coexist in the private area of civil society, by-and-large outside the realm of politics and public policy. The latter definition of multiculturalism in fact differs very little from a liberal version of 'integration', since it broadly accepts the integrationalist objective in the arena of public policy, reserving multiculturalism for the huge private area of social life beyond politics and public affairs. Naturally, such a 'depoliticisation' of the issue of identity requires a general confidence in the will and ability of the state to treat its citizens equally and protect its non-indigenous minorities from racism.

It also, ideally, requires less political and public discussion of the issue of national identity. Partly because of the demands of the modern media for endless controversy, and partly because of the pressure on modern academics to generate debates that will yield publications, there is in the modern era – to use the words of Dr Johnson – 'a rage for saying something when there's nothing to be said'.[18] This ceaseless public controversy over the issue of identity – which invariably generates more heat than light – undoubtedly makes its own substantial contribution to increased racial tension.

It is in the end, in any case, doubtful whether national identity is a political issue that can be legislated for or bargained over. National identity is always in a state of continual evolution, and it will evolve in ways that are mostly unpredictable by any particular generation. In an open society, the survival, absorption or evaporation of non-indigenous cultures will ultimately depend on individual choices made in what might be called the 'marketplace' of society. Attempts to rush, manipulate or check this slow evolutionary process are as foolish as the attempts of previous generations in Europe to uproot the existing political and social order and create a 'brave new world' by fiat. The history of twentieth-century Europe teaches us the potentially dreadful consequences of such presumptuous endeavours.

NOTES ON CHAPTER 10

1   Britain and France exercised joint colonial rule over the New Hebrides islands in the Pacific until the independent state of Vanuatu was created. Andorra in the Pyrenees Mountains between France and Spain is under a complex form of joint Franco-Spanish sovereignty.

2   Immanuel Kant, *Perpetual Peace* (Los Angeles, United States Library Association Inc., 1932).

3   In fairness to Woodrow Wilson and his international plans, it should be noted that there have very rarely – if ever – been wars between anything resembling truly democratic states.

4   The Argentinean military Junta of 1982 – hitherto one of the most

hated in Argentina's chequered history – gained overnight popularity from all parts of the political spectrum when it invaded and occupied the Falkland Islands. When, a few months later, it was forced to withdraw from the Falklands, the Junta immediately collapsed. It had failed to achieve the one goal that might have given it legitimacy in the eyes of the Argentinean public.

5 A striking example of this is the Arab-Israeli War of 1973.

6 Other contentious or ambiguous cases are: India's occupation by force of the Portuguese colonial territory of Goa in December 1961; the Chinese takeover of Tibet – over which Chinese sovereignty had been asserted but not exercised for some considerable time – in 1950; the Indian occupation of parts of Kashmir in 1947; and the Moroccan and Mauretanian occupation of the former Spanish Sahara in 1976.

7 For a fascinating discussion of the ambiguities and contradictions in these high-minded statements adopted by the United Nations, however, see Gerard Chaliand's essay, 'Minority Peoples in the Age of Nation-States', in Gerard Chaliand (ed.), *Minority Peoples in the Age of Nation-States* (London, Pluto Press, 1989), pp 1-11.

8 By far the best and most lucid statement of the principles of communism is to be found in Karl Marx and Frederick Engels, *The Communist Manifesto*, published in 1848.

9 One Coca-Cola advertisement of about a decade ago showed children of all races clutching coke bottles and singing together in what appeared to be the United States' Congress building: a perfect image of the relationship between American-style free-enterprise democracy, a new multi-racial world of youth 'singing in perfect harmony' – and, of course, Coca-Cola. However depressing older generations may find this picture of the modern world, it is surely an improvement on the images of youth portrayed in the Europe of the 1930s and early 1940s.

10 Edward Said, *Orientalism* (London, Routledge and Kegan Paul, 1978).

11 Samuel Huntington, 'The Clash of Civilisations?' *Foreign Affairs*, No. 3 (Summer 1993), pp 22-49.

12 Jean-Paul Sartre, 'Portrait of an Antisemite', in Walter Kaufmann (ed.), *Existentialism from Dostoevsky to Sartre* (New York, The World Publishing Co., 1963), pp 270-287. Sartre's 'Portrait of an Antisemite' was originally published in English in *Partisan Review* (Spring 1946). Sartre's use of the term 'freedom of opinion' is characteristically ambiguous. There is all the difference in the world between the prohibition of the public expression of what are considered to be offensive opinions

that might disturb public order, and an attempt to eradicate such opinions by educational, psychological or other means.

13   See Colonial Office, *British Dependencies in the Far East 1945-1949* Cmd 7709 (London, HMSO, 1949), p 52. The Malays, as the (more or less) indigenous inhabitants of Malaya, deeply resented this plan, which they felt to be a threat to their political status, their culture and their identity. The British prudently withdrew the scheme.

14   See Stephen B. Oates, *Let the Trumpet Sound: A Life of Martin Luther King Jr* (New York, Harper Perennial, 1994), p 261.

15   See Malcolm X and Alex Haley, *The Autobiography of Malcolm X* (London, Penguin Books, 1968). The book was first published in 1965.

16   For discussions about the Jewish community in England in this context, see articles in *The Observer*, 2 February 1997; and 23 February 1997.

17   See Mark Falcoff, 'North of the Border', in *Times Literary Supplement* (17 May 1996), pp 14-15, for an analysis of Hispanic identity in the United States.

18   See James Boswell's *The Life of Samuel Johnson*, entry for the year 1758.

Select Bibliography

General

St Augustine, *City of God* (London, Oxford University Press, 1963)

St Thomas Aquinas, *Selected Political Writings*, edited by A.P. d'Entrèves (Oxford, Basil Blackwell, 1959), especially 'On the Government of the Jews', pp 84-95

Arberry, Arthur J. (trans.), *The Koran Interpreted* (London, Oxford University Press, 1986)

Aristotle, *Politics*, translated by Benjamin Jowett (Oxford, Clarendon Press, 1963)

Baldick, Julian, *Homer and the Indo-Europeans: Comparing Mythologies* (London, I.B. Tauris, 1994)

Bowra, C.M., *The Greek Experience* (London, Sphere Books, 1973), especially chapter 1, 'The Unity of the Greeks'

Burke, Edmund, *Reflections on the Revolution in France*, edited by Conor Cruise O'Brien (London, Penguin, 1986)

Cragg, Kenneth (ed. and trans.), *Readings in the Qur'an* (London, Harper Collins, 1993): a useful introduction to the basic tenets of Islam via the text of the Qur'an

Dante Alighieri, *De Monarchia*, edited by E. Moore (Oxford, Clarendon Press, 1916)

Dante Alighieri, *Monarchia*, translated and edited by Prue Shaw (Cambridge, Cambridge University Press, 1996)

Dante Alighieri, *Monarchy and Three Political Letters*, edited and translated by Donald Nicholl and Colin Hardie (London, Weidenfeld and Nicolson, 1954)

Darwin, Charles, *The Descent of Man, and Selection in Relation to Sex* (London, John Murray, 1913), especially chapter vii, 'On the Races of Man'

Darwin, Charles, *The Origin of Species, by Means of Natural Selection, or the Preservation of Favoured Races in the Struggle for Life* (Harmondsworth, Penguin, 1968)

Finley, M.I., *The World of Odysseus* (Harmondsworth, Penguin, 1962), especially chapter 4, 'Household, Kin and Community'

Georges, Pericles, *Barbarian Asia and the Greek Experience* (Baltimore, Johns Hopkins, 1994)

Guillaume, Alfred, *Islam* (Harmondsworth, Penguin, 1969): a useful introductory study

Herder, Johann Gottfried von, *Reflections on the Philosophy of the History of Mankind* (Chicago, Chicago University Press, 1968)

Homer, *The Iliad*, translated by Richmond Lattimore (Chicago, Chicago University Press, 1961)

Homer, *The Odyssey*, translated by Richmond Lattimore (New York, Harper and Row, 1967)

Kaufmann, Yehezkel, *The Religion of Israel: From its Beginnings to the Babylonian Exile* (Chicago, University of Chicago Press, 1960)

Kitto, H.D.F., *The Greeks* (Harmondsworth, Penguin, 1964)

Lewis, Bernard, *The Political Language of Islam* (Chicago, Chicago University Press, 1991)

McDermott, Kevin and Jeremy Agnew, *A History of International Communism from Lenin to Stalin* (London, MacMillan, 1996)

McLellan, David, *Marx* (London, Fontana Paperbacks, 1975)

McLellan, David, *The Thought of Karl Marx* (London, MacMillan, 1980)

Maistre, Joseph de, *On God and Society: essay on the generative principle of political constitutions and other human institutions*, originally published 1808-9, edited by Elisha Greifer (Chicago, Henry Regnery, 1959): the best short introduction to de Maistre's political ideas

Meek, Theophile James, *Hebrew Origins* (New York, Harper and Brothers, 1960)

Paine, Thomas, *Common Sense* (Harmondsworth, Penguin, 1976): contemporary justification of the American Revolution

Paine, Thomas, *Rights of Man* (Harmondsworth, Penguin, 1969): a reply to Edmund Burke's *Reflections on the Revolution in France*

Peters, F.E., *A Reader in Classical Islam* (Princeton, Princeton University Press, 1994)

Rousseau, Jean Jacques, *The Social Contract* (New York, Hafner Publishing, 1960), especially Book 2, 'On Sovereignty and the General Will'

Quint, David, *Epic and Empire: Politics and Generic Form from Virgil to Milton* (Princeton, Princeton University Press, 1993)

Rist, John M., *Augustine: Ancient Thought Baptized* (Cambridge, Cambridge University Press, 1994)

Tacitus, Publius Cornelius, *Germania*, with translation into German and commentary by Eugene Fehrle (Munich, J.F. Lehmanns, 1929): for those who can read German, an intriguing example of the way the *Germania* was interpreted in the inter-war era in Germany

Tacitus, Publius Cornelius, *On Britain and Germany*, translated by H. Mattingley (Harmondsworth, Penguin, 1948)

Ullmann, Walter (1965), *A History of Political Thought: The Middle Ages* (Harmondsworth, Penguin, 1965)

Virgil, *The Aeneid*, translated by Allen Mandelbaum (New York, Bantam Books, 1978)

Watt, W. Montgomery, *Islamic Political Thought: The Basic Concepts* (Edinburgh, Edinburgh University Press, 1968)

Nationalism

Acton, Lord John, 'Nationality', in *The History of Freedom and Other Essays* (London, MacMillan, 1907), pp 270-300: a classic defence of the multi-national state

Anderson, Benedict O'G, *Imagined Communities: Reflections on the Origin and Spread of Nationalism* (London, Verso, 1991)

Ardrey, Robert, *The Territorial Imperative: a Personal Enquiry into the Animal Origins of Property and Nations* (London, Fontana, 1970)

Burke, Victor Lee, *The Clash of Civilizations: War-Making and State-formation in Europe* (Oxford, Polity Press, 1996)

Canetti, Elias, *Crowds and Power* (Harmondsworth, Penguin, 1973), especially chapter entitled 'The Crowd in History'

Caplan, Richard and John Feffer (eds), *Europe's New Nationalism: States and Minorities in Conflict* (Oxford, Oxford University Press, 1997)

Clark, Donald and Robert Williamson (eds), *Self-Determination: International Perspectives* (London, MacMillan, 1996)

Clausewitz, Carl von, *On War*, edited by Anatol Rapoport (Harmondsworth, Penguin, 1968), especially section entitled 'War as an Instrument of State Policy', pp 401-410

Cobban, Alfred, *The Nation-State and National Self-Determination* (London, Collins, 1969)

Curcija-Prodanovic, Nada, *Heroes of Serbia* (London, Oxford University Press, 1963): an example of the myths that can sustain nationalism

Dann, Otto and John Dunwiddy (eds), *Nationalism in the Age of the French Revolution* (London, Hambledon, 1988)

d'Encausse, Helene Carrere, *The Great Challenge: Nationalities and the Bolshevik State, 1917-1930* (New York, Holmes and Meier, 1991)

Dunn, Seamus and T.G. Fraser (eds), *Europe and Ethnicity: The First World War and Contemporary Ethnic Conflict* (London, Routledge, 1996)

Fulbrook, Mary (ed.), *National Histories and European History* (London, UCL Press, 1993)

Gellner, E., *Nations and Nationalism* (Oxford, Blackwell, 1983)

Greenfeld, Liah, *Nationalism: Five Roads to Modernity* (Cambridge, Mass., Harvard University Press, 1992)

Gulbernau, Montserrat, *Nationalisms: The Nation-State and Nationalism in the Twentieth Century* (Oxford, Polity Press, 1995)

Haas, Ernst B., *Nationalism, Liberalism and Progress*, volume 1, *The Rise and Decline of Nationalism* (Ithaca, Yale University Press, 1997)

Heater, Derek, *National Self-Determination: Woodrow Wilson and his Legacy* (London, MacMillan, 1994)

Hinsley, F.H., *Nationalism and the International System* (London, Hodder and Stoughton, 1973)

Hobsbawm, Eric, *Nations and Nationalism Since 1789: Programme, Myth, Reality* (Cambridge, Cambridge University Press, 1992)

Hutchinson, John and Anthony D. Smith (eds), *Ethnicity* (Oxford, Oxford University Press, 1996)

Hutchinson, John, *Modern Nationalism* (London, Fontana, 1994)

Kamenka, Eugene, *Nationalism: The Nature and Evolution of an Idea* (London, Edward Arnold, 1976)

Kedourie, Elie, *Nationalism* (London, Hutchinson, 1974)

Kellas, James G., *The Politics of Nationalism and Ethnicity* (Basingstoke, MacMillan, 1991)

Kohn, Hans, *The Idea of Nationalism: A Study of its Origins and Background* (New York, MacMillan, 1946)

Kohn, Hans (ed.), *Nationalism: Its Meaning and History* (New York, D. van Nostrand, 1971)

Leopardi, Giacomo, *Leopardi's Canti*, translated by John Humphreys Whitfield (Naples, S. Scalabrini, 1962): an example of the link between poetry and romantic nationalism

Lewis, Saunders, *Presenting Saunders Lewis*, edited by Alun R. Jones and Gwyn Thomas (Cardiff, University of Wales Press, 1983)

MacDiarmid, Hugh, *Selected Poems* (Harmondsworth, Penguin, 1970), especially 'A Drunk Man Looks at the Thistle' (1926), a famous poetic assertion of Scottish national identity

Mazzini, Joseph, *The Duties of Man and Other Essays* (London, J.M. Dent, 1907)

Mill, John Stuart, *Three Essays: On Liberty, Representative Government, and The Subjection of Women* (London, Oxford University Press, 1975)

Morgenthau, Hans, *Politics Among Nations* (New York, Alfred A. Knopf, 1967): a classic study of international relations

Namier, Louis B., *Avenues of History* (London, Hamish Hamilton, 1952), especially 'Nationality and Liberty', pp 20-44

Namier, Louis B., *Conflicts: Studies in Contemporary History* (London, MacMillan, 1942)

Nimni, Ephraim, *Marxism and Nationalism* (London, Pluto, 1994)

Orwell, George, *The Decline of the English Murder and Other Essays* (Harmondsworth, Penguin, in association with Secker and Warburg, 1975): see essay entitled 'Notes on Nationalism', pp 155-172

Orwell, George, *The Lion and the Unicorn: Socialism and the English Genius*, with an introduction by Bernard Crick (Harmondsworth, Penguin, 1982)

Renan, Ernest, 'Qu'est-ce qu-une nation?', in *Discours et Conférences* (Paris, Calmann-Levy, 1928); an English translation of 'What is a Nation?' may be found in Alfred Zimmern (ed.), *Modern Political Doctrines* (London, Oxford University Press, 1939)

Schama, Simon, *Landscape and Memory* (London, Harper Collins, 1995)

Schopflin, George and Geoffrey Hosking (eds), *Myths and Nationhood* (London, Hurst, 1997)

Schulze, Hagen, *States, Nations and Nationalism: From the Middle Ages to the Present* (Oxford, Blackwell, 1996)

Sellers, Mortimer (ed.), *The New World Order: Sovereignty, Human Rights and the Self-Determination of Peoples* (Oxford, Berg, 1996)

Seton-Watson, Hugh, *Nations and States: An Enquiry into the Origins of Nations and the Politics of Nationalism* (London, Methuen, 1977)

Simpson, David, *Romanticism, Nationalism and the Revolt Against Theory* (Chicago, Chicago University Press, 1993)

Smith, Anthony D., *The Ethnic Revival* (Cambridge, Cambridge University Press, 1981)

Smith, Anthony D., *The Ethnic Origins of Nations* (Oxford, Blackwell, 1986)

Smith, Anthony D., *National Identity* (London, Penguin, 1991)

Smith, Anthony D., *Nations and Nationalism in a Global Era* (Oxford, Polity Press, 1995)

Stalin, Joseph, *Marxism and the National and Colonial Question* (London, Lawrence and Wishart, 1947): the official international communist 'line' on nationalism and nationalities for most of the Soviet era

Temperley, H.W.V. (ed.), *A History of the Peace Conference of Paris*, volume 5: *Economic Reconstruction and Protection of Minorities* (London, Henry Frowde, and Hodder and Stoughton, 1921)

Wallas, Graham, *Human Nature in Politics* (London, Constable, 1929), especially part II, chapter 4, 'Nationality and Humanity'

Wicker, Hans-Rudolf (ed.), *Rethinking Nationalism and Ethnicity: the Struggle for Meaning and Order in Europe* (New York, Berg, 1997)

Woolf, Stuart (ed.), *Nationalism in Europe: From 1815 to the Present* (London, Routledge, 1995)

Race and national identity

Appiah, K. Anthony and Amy Gutmann, *Color Consciousness: The Political Morality of Race* (Princeton, Princeton University Press, 1996)

Augstein, Hannah Franziska (ed.), *Race: The Origins of an Idea 1760-1850* (Bristol, Thoemmes, 1996)

Benedict, Ruth, *Race and Racism* (London, The Scientific Press, 1943): a classic on the subject, written at a crucial time

Chaliand, Gérard, *Minority Peoples in the Age of Nation-States* (London, Pluto Press, 1989)

Deburg, William L. van (ed.), *Modern Black Nationalism: From Marcus Garvey to Louis Farrakhan* (New York, New York University Press, 1996)

Du Bois, W.F.B., *The Souls of Black Folk* (London, MacMillan, 1997); originally published in 1903

Esman, Milton J., *Ethnic Politics* (Ithaca, NY, Cornell University Press, 1994)

Foster, Lawrence and Patricia Herzog (eds), *Defending Diversity: Contemporary Philosophical Perspectives on Pluralism and Multiculturalism* (Amherst, Massachusetts University Press, 1994)

Garnsey, Peter, *Ideas of Slavery from Aristotle to Augustine* (Cambridge, Cambridge University Press, 1996)

Glazer, Nathan, *We are All Multiculturalists Now* (Cambridge, Mass., Harvard University Press, 1997)

Horton, James Oliver and Lois E. Horton (eds), *A History of the African-American People: The History, Traditions and Culture of African-Americans* (Detroit, Wayne State University Press, 1997)

Kymlicka, Will, *Multicultural Citizenship: A Liberal Theory of Minority Rights* (Oxford, Clarendon, 1995)

MacDougall, Hugh A., *Racial Myth in English History* (Montreal, Harvest House, 1892)

Malcolm X, *The Autobiography of Malcolm X*, written with the assistance of Alex Haley (London, Penguin, 1968)

Modood, Tariq, Sharon Belshon and Satnam Virdee, *Changing Ethnic Identities* (London, Policy Studies Institute, 1994)

Oates, Stephen B., *Let the Trumpet Sound: A Life of Martin Luther King Jnr* (New York, Harper Collins, 1994)

Parekh, Bhikhu C., *Rethinking Multiculturism* (Basingstoke, Macmillan, forthcoming 1998)

Rand Corporation, *America and Europe: A Partnership for a New Era* (Cambridge, Cambridge University Press, 1997): a Western perspective on contemporary international relations

Ratcliffe, Peter (ed.), *'Race', Ethnicity and Nation: International Perspectives on Social Conflict* (London, UCL, 1994)

Rex, John, *Ethnic Minorities in the Modern Nation-State: Working Papers in the Theory of Multiculturalism and Political Integration* (London, MacMillan, 1996)

Robinson, Cedric J., *Black Movements in America* (London, Routledge, 1997)

Spencer, Ian R.G., *British Immigration Policy Since 1939: The Making of Multi-Racial Britain* (London, Routledge, 1997)

Stavenhagen, Rodolfo, *Ethnic Conflicts and the Nation-State* (London, MacMillan, 1996)

Wilson, Fiona and Bodil Folke Frederiksen, *Ethnicity, Gender and the Subversion of Nationalism* (London, Cass, 1995)

Ireland

Beaslai, Piaras, *Michael Collins and the Making of a New Ireland* (Dublin, Phoenix Press, 1926)

Beattie, Geoffrey, *We are the People: Journeys Through the Heart of Protestant Ulster* (London, Heinemann, 1992)

Bell, J. Bowyer, *The Secret Army: The IRA* (New Brunswick, Transaction Publishers, Rutgers University, 1996)

Bew, Paul and Gordon Gillespie, *Northern Ireland: A Chronology of the Troubles, 1968-1993* (Dublin, Gill and MacMillan, 1993)

Boyce, D.G., *The Irish Question and British Politics 1868-1996* (Basingstoke, MacMillan, 1996)

Boyce, D.G. and Alan O'Day (eds), *The Making of Modern Irish History: Revisionism and the Revisionist Controversy* (London, Routledge, 1996)

Boyce, D.G. (1995), *Nationalism in Ireland* (London, Routledge, 1995)

Bowman, John, *De Valera and the Ulster Question 1917-1973* (Oxford, Clarendon, 1982)

Boyle, Kevin and Tom Hadden, *Ireland: A Positive Proposal* (Harmondsworth, Penguin, 1985)

Brown, Terence, *Ireland: A Social and Cultural History 1922-1979* (London, Fontana, 1981)

Bromage, Mary C., *De Valera and the March of a Nation* (London, Hutchinson, 1956)

Bruce, Steve, *The Edge of the Union: The Ulster Loyalist Political Vision* (Oxford, Oxford University Press, 1994)

Bruce, Steve, *The Red Hand: Protestant Paramilitaries in Northern Ireland* (Oxford, Oxford University Press, 1992)

Carson, William A., *Ulster and the Irish Republic* (Belfast, William W. Cleland, nd)

Catterall, Peter and Sean McDougall (eds), *The Northern Ireland Question in British Politics* (London, MacMillan, 1996)

Cochrane, Feargal, *Unionist Politics and the Politics of Unionism Since the Anglo-Irish Agreement* (Cork, Cork University Press, 1997)

Connolly, Cyril, 'Comment' in Irish number of *Horizon*, volume V, no. 25 (January 1942): an interesting comment on Ireland during the Second World War period

Connolly, James, *Erin's Hope: The End and the Means* (Rutherglen, P. Walsh, 1910)

Connolly, James, *Ireland Upon the Dissecting Table: Connolly on Ulster and Partition* (Cork, Cork Workers' Club, 1972)

Connolly, James, *Labour, Nationality and Religion* (Dublin, New Books, 1954); first published in 1910

Connolly, James, *Selected Political Writings* (London, Cape, 1973)

Deane, Seamus, *Strange Country: Modernity and the Nation – Irish Writing Since 1790* (Oxford, Clarendon, 1997)

De Valera, Eamon, *The Testament of the Republic* (Dublin, Irish National Committee, 1922)

Edwards, Ruth Dudley, *Patrick Pearse: The Triumph of Failure* (London, Gollancz, 1977)

English, Richard and Graham Walker (eds), *Unionism in Northern Ireland: New Perspectives on Politics and Culture* (London, MacMillan, 1996)

Fall, Cyril, *The Birth of Ulster* (London, Constable, 1996); first published in 1936

Kee, Robert, *The Green Flag: A History of Irish Nationalism* (London, Weidenfeld and Nicolson, 1972)

Kee, Robert, *The Laurel and the Ivy: The Story of Charles Stuart Parnell and Irish Nationalism* (London, Hamish Hamilton, 1993)

Kiberd, Declan, *Inventing Ireland* (London, Jonathan Cape, 1995)

Kinahan, Timothy, *Where Do We Go From Here? Protestants and the Future of Northern Ireland* (Blackrock, Columba Press, 1995)

Neil, Frank, *Black '47: Britain and the Irish Famine* (London, MacMillan, 1997)

O'Brien, Conor Cruise, *Ancestral Voices: Religion and Nationalism in Ireland* (Dublin, Poolbeg, 1994)

O'Brien, Conor Cruise, *States of Ireland* (London, Hutchinson, 1972)

O'Brien, Maire and Conor Cruise, *A Concise History of Ireland* (London, Thames and Hudson, 1972)

O'Connor, Ulick, *A Terrible Beauty is Born: The Irish Troubles 1921-1922* (London, Granada, 1981)

O'Day, Alan, *Irish Nationalism 1798-1922* (London, Routledge, 1997)

O'Faolain, Sean, *De Valera* (Harmondsworth, Penguin, 1939)

O'Faolain, Sean, *The Irish* (Harmondsworth, Penguin, 1947)

Paisley, Ian R.K., *Ulster: The Facts* (Belfast, Crown Publications, 1982)

Pakenham, Frank (Earl of Longford), *Eamon de Valera* (London, Hutchinson, 1970)

Pakenham, Frank (Earl of Longford), *Peace by Ordeal* (London, New English Library, 1962)

Pearse, Padraic Henry, *Collected Works: Political Writings and Speeches* (Dublin, Maunsel and Roberts, 1922)

Tillyard, Stella, *Citizen Lord: Edward Fitzgerald 1763-1798* (London, Chatto and Windus, 1997): recent biography of a participant in the 1798 Irish Rising

Whyte, John, *Interpreting Northern Ireland* (Oxford, Clarendon, 1990)

Antisemitism

Abramsky, C., Maciej Jachimczyk and Antony Polonsky (eds), *The Jews in Poland* (Oxford, Blackwell, 1986)

Almog, Shmuel, *Nationalism and Antisemitism in Modern Europe 1815-1945* (Oxford, Pergamon Press, 1990)

Aronson, I. Michael, *Troubled Waters: The Origins of the 1881 Anti-Jewish Pogroms in Russia* (Pittsburgh, University of Pittsburgh Press, 1991)

Bentwich, Norman, *The Jews in our Time* (Harmondsworth, Penguin Books, 1960)

Lazare, Bernard, *Antisemitism: Its History and Causes* (Lincoln, Nebraska University Press, 1995); first published in 1894

Bullock, Alan, *Hitler: A Study in Tyranny* (Harmondsworth, Penguin Books, 1962)

Burrin, Philippe, *Hitler and the Jews: The Genesis of the Holocaust* (London, Edwin Arnold, 1994)

Cesarini, David (ed.), *Genocide and Rescue: The Holocaust in Hungary 1944* (New York, Berg, 1997)

Cohn, Norman, *Warrant for Genocide: The Myth of the Jewish World-Conspiracy and the Protocols of the Elders of Zion* (Harmondsworth, Penguin, 1970)

Crowe, David M., *A History of the Gypsies of Eastern Europe and Russia* (London, I.B. Tauris, 1995)

Dawidowicz, Lucy S., *The War against the Jews 1933-1945* (Ardmore, PA, Seth Press, 1986)

Denman, Hugh, 'The Vicissitudes of Yiddish', in *TLS*, 3 May 1985, p 503

Dostoevsky, Fyodor Mikhailovich, *Devils*, translated by Michael R. Katz (Oxford, Oxford University Press, 1992)

Dostoevsky, Fyodor Mikhailovich, *The Diary of a Writer*, translated and annotated by Boris Brasol (New York, George Braziller, 1954)

Epstein, Isidore, *Judaism* (Harmondsworth, Penguin, 1970)

Fishman, William J., *Jewish Radical: From Czarist Stetl to London Ghetto* (New York, Pantheon, 1974)

Fromm, Erich, *The Fear of Freedom* (London, Routledge and Kegan Paul, 1960): a classic study of the psychological foundations of Nazism

Gilbert, Martin, *The Holocaust: The Jewish Tragedy* (London, Collins, 1986)

Gilbert, Martin, *The Routledge Atlas of the Holocaust* (London, Routledge, 1993)

Gilbert, Martin, *The Routledge Atlas of Jewish History: From 2000 BC to the Present Day* (London, Routledge, 1993)

Golding, Louis, *The Jewish Problem* (Harmondsworth, Penguin, 1938)

Goldsmith, Emanuel, *Modern Yiddish Culture: The Story of the Yiddish Language Movement* (Fordham University Press, 1997)

Hamsun, Knut, *Hunger* (London, Pan, 1976): first published in 1890, the significance of this book is noted in footnote 7 of chapter 7

Hindus, Milton, *Céline: the Crippled Giant* (New Brunswick, Transaction Publishers, 1997)

Hitler, Adolf, *Mein Kampf* (*My Struggle*) (London, Hurst and Blackett, 1938)

Jäckel, Eberhard, *Hitler's World View: A Blueprint for Power* (Cambridge, Mass., Harvard University Press, 1981)

Kadish, Sharman, *Bolsheviks and British Jews: The Anglo-Jewish Community, Britain and the Russian Revolution* (London, Cass, 1992)

Levi, Primo, *The Drowned and the Saved* (Harmondsworth, Penguin, 1989)

Levi, Primo, *If This is a Man* (London, The Bodley Head, 1960): this book and the above describe and reflect on personal experiences of the Holocaust

Lewis, Bernard, *Semites and Anti-Semites: An Inquiry into Conflict and Prejudice* (London, Weidenfeld and Nicolson, 1986)

McClelland, J.S. (ed.), *The French Right: From de Maistre to Maurras* (London, Jonathan Cape, 1970)

Oxaal, I. et al, (eds), *Jews, Antisemitism and Culture in Vienna* (London, Routledge Kegan Paul, 1987)

Parkes, James, *An Enemy of the People: Antisemitism* (Harmondsworth, Penguin, 1945)

Poliakov, Leon, *The History of Anti-Semitism* (London, Elek, 1960)

Rauschning, Hermann, *Germany's Revolution of Destruction* (London, William Heinemann, 1939)

Rezzori, Gregor von, *Memoirs of an Anti-Semite: A Novel in Five Stories* (London, Pan, 1981): a fascinating picture of the early-twentieth-century milieu of antisemitism and revolutionary change in the province of Bukovina

Sartre, Jean-Paul, 'Portrait of the Antisemite' in Walter Kaufmann (ed.), *Existentialism from Dostoevsky to Sartre* (Cleveland, The World Publishing Company, 1963)

Segal, Binjamin W., *A Lie and a Libel: The History of the Protocols of the Elders of Zion*, translated and edited by Richard S. Levy (Lincoln, University of Nebraska Press, 1995)

Sholom Aleichem, *Inside Kasrilevke* (London, Robson Books, 1973)

Singer, Isaac Bashevis, *The Spinoza of Market Street* (Harmondsworth, Penguin, 1981): fictional representation of life in the Pale of Settlement

Steiner, George, 'On the Edge of Hunger', in *TLS*, 31 January 1997, p 3: on Hitler's youth in Vienna, and the cultural and political milieu

Wistrich, Robert S., *Anti-Semitism: The Longest Hatred* (London, Mandarin Paperbacks, 1992)

Wistrich, Robert S., *Hitler's Apocalypse: Jews and the Nazi Legacy* (London, Weidenfeld and Nicolson, 1985)

Wistrich, Robert S., *The Jews Of Vienna in the Age of Franz Joseph* (Oxford, Oxford University Press, 1990)

Zangwill, Israel, *Dreamers of the Ghetto* (London, William Heinemann, 1908)

Zangwill, Israel, *Children of the Ghetto* (London, J.M. Dent, 1909).

Zionism

Avineri, Shlomo, *The Making of Modern Zionism: The Intellectual Origins of the Jewish State* (London, Weidenfeld and Nicolson, 1981)

Crossman, Richard, *Palestine Mission: A Personal Record* (New York, Harper and Brothers, 1947)

Fromkin, David, *A Peace to End all Peace: Creating the Modern Middle East 1914-1922* (London, Penguin, 1996)

Herzl, Theodor, *The Jewish State* (New York, Dover Publications Inc., 1988)

Hertzberg, Arthur, *The Zionist Idea: A Historical Analysis and Reader* (New York, Harper and Row, 1959)

Koestler, Arthur, *Promise and Fulfillment: Palestine 1917-1949* (London, MacMillan, 1983)

Kornberg, Jacques, *Theodor Herzl: from assimilation to Zionism* (Bloomington, Indiana University Press, 1994)

Lacqueur, Walter and Barry Rubin (eds), *The Israel-Arab Reader: A Documentary History of the Middle East Conflict* (London, Penguin, 1984)

Minczeles, Henri, *Histoire Génerale du Bund: Un Mouvement Révolutionnaire Juif* (Paris, Austral, 1996)

O'Brien, Conor Cruise, *The Siege: The Saga of Israel and Zionism* (London, Collins, 1986)

Palestine Royal Commission, Report, Cmd 5479 (London, HMSO, 1937)

Palestine Partition Commission, Report, Cmd 5854 (London, HMSO, 1938)

Vital, David, *The Origins of Zionism* (Oxford, Clarendon, 1975)

Vital, David, *Zionism: The Crucial Phase* (Oxford, Clarendon, 1987)

Vital, David, *Zionism: The Formative Years* (Oxford, Clarendon, 1988)

Wasserstein, Bernard, *The British in Palestine: The Mandatory Government and the Arab-Jewish Conflict* (Oxford, Blackwell, 1991)

Wheatcroft, Geoffrey, *The Controversy of Zion: How Zionism tried to resolve the Jewish Question* (London, Sinclair-Stevenson)

Zipperstein, Steven J., *Elusive Prophet: Ahad Ha'am and the origins of Zionism* (Berkeley, California University Press, 1993)

Zweig, Ronald W., *Britain and Palestine During the Second World War* (Woodbridge, Boydell and Brewer, 1986)

Arab Nationalism

Antonius, George, *The Arab Awakening: The Story of the Arab National Movement* (New York, Capricorn Books, 1965); first published in 1938

Chomsky, Noam, *Peace in the Middle East? Reflections on Justice and Nationhood* (New York, Pantheon Books, 1974)

Dekmejian, R. Hrair, *Egypt under Nasir: A Study in Political Dynamics* (London, University of London Press, 1972)

Devlin, John F., *The Ba'ath Party: A History from its Origins to 1966* (Stanford, Hoover Institution Press, 1976)

Donohue, John J. and John L. Esposito (eds), *Islam in Transition: Muslim Perspectives* (New York, Oxford University Press, 1982)

Elpeleg, Zvi, *The Grand Mufti: Haj Amin al-Hussaini, Founder of the Palestinian National Movement* (London, Cass, 1993)

Friedman, Isaiah, *The Question of Palestine: British-Jewish-Arab Relations* (New Brunswick, Transaction Publishers, 1993)

Gilbert, Martin, *The Routledge Atlas of the Arab-Israeli Conflict* (London, Routledge, 1993)

Haim, Sylvia (ed.) (1962), *Arab Nationalism: An Anthology* (Berkeley, University of California Press, 1962)

Hanna, S.A. and G.H. Gardner, *Arab Socialism: A Documentary Survey* (Leiden, Brill, 1969)

Hitti, Philip K., *History of the Arabs* (London, MacMillan, 1960)

Hourani, Albert, *Arabic Thought in the Liberal Age 1798-1939* (London, Oxford University Press, 1970), especially chapter XI, 'Arab Nationalism'

Hourani, Albert, *A History of the Arab Peoples* (Cambridge, Mass., The Belknap Press of Harvard University Press, 1991)

Kent, Marian (ed.), *The Great Powers and the End of the Ottoman Empire* (London, George Allen and Unwin, 1984)

Kurdi, A.-A., *The Islamic State: A Study Based on the Islamic Holy Constitution* (London, Mansell Publishing Co., 1984)

Lacouture, Jean, *Nasser* (Paris, Editions du Seuil, 1971)

Laroui, Abdallah, *The Crisis of the Arab Intellectual: Traditionalism or Historicism* (Berkeley, University of California Press, 1976)

Lewis, Bernard, *Race and Color in Islam* (New York, Octagon Books, 1979)

Masalha, Nur, *Expulsion of the Palestinians: the Concept of 'Transfer' in Zionist Political Thought 1882-1948* (Washington DC, Institute for Palestine Studies, 1993)

Masalha, Nur, *A Land Without a People: Israel, Transfer and the Palestinians, 1949-1996* (London, Faber, 1996)

Muhammad Muslih, *The Origins of Palestinian Nationalism* (Washington DC, Institute for Palestine Studies, 1988)

Nasser, Gamal Abdel, *Egypt's Liberation: The Philosophy of the Revolution* (Washington DC, Public Affairs Press, 1955)

Porath, Yehoshua, *The Emergence of the Palestinian-Arab National Movement 1918-1929* (London, Cass, 1974)

Porath, Yehoshua, *The Palestinian-Arab National Movement: From Riots to Rebellion, 1929-1939* (London, Cass, 1977)

Rejwan, Nissim, *Nasserist Ideology: Its Exponents and Critics* (New York, Wiley, 1974)

Said, Edward, *The Politics of Dispossession: Struggle for Palestinian Self-Determination* (London, Chatto and Windus, 1994)

Said, Edward, *The Question of Palestine* (London, Routledge Kegan Paul, 1980)

Schulze, Kirsten et al (eds), *Nationalism, Minorities and Diasporas: Identities and Rights in the Middle East* (London, I.B. Tauris, 1996)

Smith, Charles D. (1996), *Palestine and the Arab-Israeli Conflict* (London, MacMillan, 1996)

Stephens, Robert, *Nasser: A Political Biography* (London, Allen Lane, 1971)

Vatikiotis, Panayiotis, *Nasser and His Generation* (London, Croom Helm, 1978)

Index

Aasen, Ivar 70-1
Académie Française 69
Achaemenian Empire 39
Acropolis 45
Act of Union (1800), 100
Actium 6
Adam 27
Addresses to the German Nation (Fichte) 63
Aden 197, 199
Aeneas 6
Aeneid (Kotlarevsky) 70
Aeneid (Virgil) 6
Aflaq, Michel 201
Africa 18, 91-2, 208, 229, 232
    nation-states 223, 225
    nationalism 83, 88
    see also North Africa; South Africa
African-Americans 230-2
Afrikaner nationalism 71
The Age of Revolution (Hobsbawm) 71
Aglauros 45
Albania 97, 222
Algeria 103, 197, 201
Alliance Israélite 134, 136
Alsace-Lorraine 90
America 39, 48, 99, 141, 221
    see also Latin America; North America;
    South America; United States of America
American Civil War 231
American Revolution 11, 12, 48, 226
Anderson, Benedict 68-72
Andorra 236
Anglo-Irish Agreement (1985) 104
Anglo-Irish Treaty (1921) 102
Anglo-Saxon 43
Antisemitic Alliance 137
antisemitism 121-37, 139-62, 166, 169,
    172, 178-9, 229, 230
Arab Empire 133
Arab-Israeli war, 1973 202, 237
Arabia 171, 196, 197, 199
Arabic language 122, 195, 196

Arabs
    nationalism 195-217
    race 39, 42, 56, 133
    and Zionism 171, 172, 173, 187, 188,
    214-15, 222
    see also Palestine
Aramaic 133
Argentina 220
Aristotle 5, 9, 13, 15, 16
Armenia 88
Arndt, Ernst Moritz 64
Aryans 121, 132-3, 134
Asia 83, 87, 88, 91, 223, 225, 229, 232
    see also individual countries
Ataturk, Kemal 84
Athens 39, 42, 45
Augustine of Hippo, Saint 8, 9
Augustus, Emperor 6, 19
Australia 225, 232
Austrian Empire 75, 77, 136
    collapse 76, 79, 80, 81, 84, 85, 143, 171
    racial minorities 78, 80, 90, 167
Austrian Social Democratic Party 150
Auto-Emancipation (Pinsker) 176-83
Azherbaijan 88

Babylonia 39
Bagatelles pour un Massacre (Céline) 146-9
Baghdad 171, 209
Balfour, Arthur 171, 173
Balfour Declaration 171, 172, 184-91, 194,
    199, 209-10, 212
Balkans 70, 78, 90
Bangladesh 223, 225
Bartók, Béla 71
Ba'th (resurrection) movement 201, 202
Bavarians 64
Beirut, American College 71
Belarus 87
Belgium 80, 88, 89-90, 219
Belorussia 142
Beni-Israel *see* Israelites
Berlin 66, 143
Bessarabia 81

Bessenyei, György 69
Bible 7, 15
    see also Torah
Boers 71
Bohemia 64, 69
Bolshevism 79, 80, 143, 144, 157, 158, 167
    see also Communism
Bosnia 79, 81, 86, 87, 105, 222
Brest-Litovsk, Treaty of 81
Britain 42, 43, 48, 55, 56, 77, 233
    and Arabs 197-201
    see also Palestine
    and Ireland 78, 98-106, 109, 220
    and Jews 188
    and Palestine 83, 184-6, 188, 214
    and World War I 79, 80, 82
    and Zionism 170-4
British Empire 88, 171, 220, 223, 230
Budapest 70, 143
Bukovina 81, 97
Bulgaria 70, 78
Bullock, Alan 150-5
Bund, Jewish 167
bureaucracy 71-2
Burgundians 40, 43
Burke, Edmund 12, 14, 234
Burma 83, 224
Byzantine Empire 8

Cairo 209
Canada 102
Capet, House of 40
capitalism 227
Caribbean 232
Carlovingian Empire 39
Catholics
    Northern Ireland 56, 98, 99, 101,
        104, 105
    and Orthodox church 9
Caucasus 82, 87, 88, 205
Celan, Paul 145
Céline, Louis-Ferdinand 146-9
Celts 42, 98, 101, 133
Charles the Great (Charlemagne) 9
China 39, 237
Christian Social Party 126, 151

Christianity 7-9, 10-11, 13, 40, 78, 133, 226
    Arab Christians 172, 195, 212
    and Islam 229
    and Jews 135, 145
    and race 122
City of God (Augustine) 8
Civil Rights movement 231-2
class 3, 33, 58, 59, 121, 143
Cleopatra 6
climate 5, 13, 18, 27
Cold War 202, 222
colonialism 28, 99, 202, 207-8, 224, 229
    and Arab nationalism 195-217, 210-11
    and Zionism 168-9
colour 122, 153
communications 228
Communism 58, 59, 79, 80, 143, 150,
    200, 227
    see also Bolshevism
The Communist Manifesto (Marx) 140
Constantine I, Emperor 8
Copts 71
corruption 235
Croatia 51, 81, 86, 87, 222
Crusades 205
culture 12, 37, 45, 122, 228, 232-6
Cyprus 223
Cyrillic alphabet 69
Czechoslovakia 76, 81, 82, 84, 85, 87, 219,
    222
Czechs 69, 78

Dáil Eireann 102
Damascus 171, 199, 209
Dante Alighieri 9, 13, 15-19, 220
Darwin, Charles 37, 168
de Valera, Eamon 104, 113-17
Deane, Seamus 117
Declaration of Independence (USA) 32, 35,
    48-50, 230
Declaration of the Rights of Man and of
    the Citizen (France) 12, 20-1
decolonisation 223-5
democracy 33-6, 50-2, 57, 77, 198, 221-2,
    235
    see also sovereignty

demography 235
Denmark 43, 70
The Descent of Man (Darwin) 37
Diary of a Writer (Dostoevsky) 127-9
diaspora 123, 169, 177
diversity 22-30
Divine Comedy (Dante) 19
Dobrovsky, Josef 69, 71
Dostoevsky, Feodor 127-9, 132
Dreyfus affair 142, 166
Dreyfus, Captain Alfred 142
Drumont, Edouard 132
Dublin 99, 101, 102
Dutch East Indies 223, 224
    see also Indonesia
Dutch Empire 88
Dvořák, Antonin 71
dynastic states 32, 33, 40-1, 54, 55, 77

East Timor 223
Easter Rising, 1916 101, 107, 115
economy 46, 57-9, 84, 143, 227
education 57, 66-7
Egypt 39, 195, 201, 204-11
    and British rule 197, 198
    independence 83, 199
    Six Day War 201, 202
*Egypt's Liberation: The Philosophy of the
    Revolution* (Nasser) 204-11
Eire 114
    see also Ireland; Irish Free State; Irish
        Republic
Emancipation Act, 1829 100
Emmet, Robert 100
End of a Berlin Diary (Shirer) 161-2
England 10, 11, 39, 40, 42, 44, 55, 218
    see also Britain
English language 62, 228
Enlightenment 11, 12, 33-4, 127, 145,
    221, 226
Eritrea 223, 225
Estonia 81, 82, 84, 87
Ethiopia 223, 225
ethnic cleansing 87, 175, 230
    see also genocide
ethnicity 38, 56, 86, 122, 235

    and nationalism 76, 85, 139, 143, 166,
        226
ethnography 6, 39, 41, 42
Etruscans 42
Europe 3-31, 216, 222
    and colonialism 168, 202, 207-8, 225
    nation-states 143
    racism 132, 228-30
    self-determination 75-92, 171, 221
European Union (EU) 218, 219, 229

Falkland Islands 220
fascism 84
federation 52
Fichte, J.G. 60-7
Finland 70, 81, 82, 84
folklore 70, 71
Fourteen Points (Wilson) 80, 82, 84, 89-90
France
    colonialism 88, 171, 197, 199, 207
    dynastic state 10-11, 39, 40, 41, 77
    ethnography 42, 43, 121
    and Jews 134, 136, 142, 171
    language 44, 62, 65
    and Sardinia 78
    World War I and aftermath 79, 80, 81, 90
    mandated territories 82, 83, 199, 200
La France Juive (Drumont) 132
Franks 40, 43
French Revolution 11, 12, 34-5, 41, 55, 64,
    66, 226
    influence on Ireland 100
Front de Libération Nationale (FLN) 201

Gaddafi *see* al-Qadhafi, Muammar
Gaelic language and culture 98, 99, 100,
    101, 104, 117
Gaelic League 101, 115
Garamantes 18
Gauls 42, 43
Gaza 175, 202, 212, 215
Geneva 84
genocide 97, 125, 144, 145
    see also ethnic cleansing
geography 5, 13, 18, 46, 47, 50, 56
George III, King 11

Georgia 88
Germania (Tacitus) 6, 22-6
Germany
  education 67
  Empire 78, 82, 83, 91-2, 171
  ethnography 4, 6, 13, 36, 40-4, 122
  and German foreign nationals 51, 76
  and Jews 4, 124, 134, 136, 181
  antisemitism 142, 143, 144
  language 11, 39, 60-3, 64-5, 68, 69, 70
  nation-state 77
  World War I and aftermath 79, 80, 85,
    86, 87, 90, 171
  World War II 157-60, 173
Geschichte der bömischen Sprache und ältern
  Literatur (Dobrovsky) 69
Gibraltar 220
Goa 237
Gobineau, J.A., Comte de 121
Golan Heights 202, 212
Goths 40
government 12, 18, 20, 34-5, 49, 50
Greece 5, 42, 77, 78, 133, 222
  nationalism 68-71
Greek classics 69
Grieg, Edvard 71
Gypsies 228

Ha'am, Ahad 169
Hadiths 196
Hebrew 122, 123, 133, 167, 170, 196
Herder, Johan Gottlieb von 13, 14, 26 30,
  61, 62, 65
Herzl, Theodor 169, 170, 176
Hess, Moses 126
history 50
  and identity 37
  and language 68-72
Hitler: A Study in Tyranny (Bullock) 150-5
Hitler, Adolf 157-60, 228, 229
  antisemitism 143-5, 150-6, 161-2, 228,
    229
  and Eastern Europe 81, 86, 87, 122
Hobsbawm, Eric 68, 71
Holland 40-1
  see also Netherlands

Hollywood 228
Holocaust 145, 174
  see also Jews
Holy Places 190
Holy Roman Empire 9, 10
Home Rule Bill, 1912 101
Homer 5
Hourani, Albert 212-17
human rights 11-12, 13, 20-1, 34, 35, 226,
  227
Hungary 51, 81, 84, 85, 87, 181
  nationalism 68-71

Iberic race 42
Ibo people 224
identity 3-4, 5, 10-13, 37
  and language 60
  see also national identity
Ignotus 69
Iliad (Homer) 5
Imagined Communities: Reflections on the
  Origin and Spread of Nationalism
  (Anderson) 68-72
imperialism *see* colonialism
India 83, 222, 223, 224
Indo-European language group 122
  see also Aryan
Indochina 223
Indonesia 223, 224
industrialisation 57, 58
integration (multiculturalism) 230, 231,
  232-6
international relations 77
international system 220-5
  see also League of Nations; United Nations
IRA *see* Provisional Irish Republican Army
Iran 133, 219, 229
Iraq 201, 202, 223, 224
  and British mandate 83, 171, 199
  and Kurds 219
  see also Mesopotamia
Ireland 40, 78, 84, 98-117, 218
  constitution 1937 103, 104
  general election results 1918 112-3
  see also Northern Ireland; Ulster
Irish Citizen Army 110

Irish Free State 102, 113
  see also Eire; Ireland
Irish Parliamentary Party 100, 101, 107
Irish Republic 101, 102, 107, 110
  see also Eire; Ireland
Irish Republican Brotherhood 100, 110
Irish Volunteers 110
irredentism 64, 85, 98
Islam 198, 209, 226, 229
  Arab identity 195, 196, 197, 200, 202
  unity 9, 10, 13, 203, 208
  see also Muslims; Ottoman Empire
Islamic Reform movement 198
Israel
  ancient Jewish homeland 7, 18, 123, 189
  modern state 226, 229
    creation 141, 174, 175, 189, 200, 201
    relations with Arabs 202, 215, 216,
    217, 222
  see also Palestine
Israelites 39, 42
Italy 82, 88, 90, 158
  national identity 11, 36, 42
  unification 40, 77, 78

Jabotinsky, Vladimir 168
Janáček, Leoš 71
Japan 158
Jerusalem 136, 173, 202
Jesuit College of St Joseph 71
Jesus Christ 7
Jewish National Fund 213
Jews 4, 7, 39, 65, 188
  conspiracy theory 132-8, 140-1, 146,
    147-9, 154, 155
  cosmopolitanism 4, 122, 123-7, 139-40,
    143, 144, 177, 179-80
  emancipation 125, 142, 180
  migration from Europe 141, 142
  nationalism 85, 145, 165, 176-83, 184-5,
    190
  persecution 3, 124, 132, 178-80
  settlement in Palestine 173, 175, 187,
    199, 212, 213
  see also antisemitism; pogroms; Zionism
Johnson, Samuel 48, 236

joint sovereignty 220
Jordan 83, 171, 199, 201, 202, 215, 216
Joseph II, Emperor 70
Judaeo-Bolshevism 229
Judaeophobia see antisemitism
Judaism 9, 10, 123, 125, 165, 169, 226
Der Judenstaat (Herzl) 176

Kant, Immanuel 220-1
Karens 224
Kashmir 224, 237
Kazinczy, Ferenc 70, 71
Keating, Geoffrey 108
Kedourie, Elie 60-7
Kenya 103
Kharkov 70
Kiev 70
King, Martin Luther 231
Koraes, Adamantios 69
Korea 222, 223
Kotlarevsky, Ivan 70
Kufa 209
Kurds 193, 219-20, 224

language 54, 99, 115-16, 228
  and national identity 4, 11, 33, 37, 43-5,
    47, 50, 55, 56-7, 60-3, 64-5, 68-72, 235
  and race 39, 65, 122
Lao people 223
Latin 61, 70
Latin America 232
  see also South America; Spanish America
Latvia 82, 84, 87
law 18, 20-1, 90
Law of Return, 1950 175
League of Nations
  international system 79, 84, 87, 90, 222
  and Jewish homeland 188, 190
  mandates 82-3, 91-2, 171, 184, 199
Lebanon 83, 171, 187, 199, 215, 216
Lenin, V.I. 80-1, 227
Libya 197, 199, 201
Lithuania 81, 82, 84, 87, 134
Lombards 40
Loyalism, Ulster 101
Lueger, Karl 126, 151

Macedonia 86, 87, 222
Magyars 51, 70
Maistre, Joseph de 12, 14, 234
Malaya 223, 230
Malaysia 223
Malcolm X 232
Mamelukes 205-6
mandates 82-3, 91-2, 171, 199, 200
  British 172, 212, 232
Manx language 117
Mark Anthony 6
Maronites 71
Marx, Karl 140, 227, 232
Marxism 58, 59, 150, 155, 156, 158
Mauretania 237
Maurras, Charles 65
Mecca 171, 196, 209
Medina 196
Mediterranean 3-31
Mein Kampf (Hitler) 150-6
Memorandum on the threat facing Germany in 1936 (Hitler) 157-60
Mesopotamia (Iraq) 133, 171
Middle East 173
  see also individual countries
migration 232
Mill, John Stuart 35, 50-2
Moldova 87
Monarchy (Dante) 9, 15-19, 220
Mongols 205, 207
Moniteur de l'Empire 66
Montagu Declaration 83
Montenegro 78, 86, 90
morality 4, 5, 7, 25-6
Morocco 237
Moses 18
Muhammad, Prophet 9-10, 13, 196
multi-national states 50-2
multiculturalism 230, 231, 232-6
Munich 143
music 27, 29
Muslims 82, 122, 170, 172, 196, 212
  see also Islam
mythology 28

Napoleon 66, 75
Napoleonic wars 100
Nasser, Gamal Abdul (Jamal 'Abd al-Nasir) 201, 202, 204-11
nation-states 55, 75-6, 80, 87, 218-20
  Africa 223, 225
  Asia 223, 225
  Europe 83-8, 143
  and international system 220-2
  and Islam 226
  and race 228
national consciousness 56-7, 60-3, 176-8, 180-1, 209-10
national identity 41, 47-8, 54, 56, 60, 218, 234, 235
  Arab 196-203, 205-6, 208, 209
  and economic interest 46
  evolution 236
  and geography 46
  Indonesia 224
  Irish 113-17
  Jews 182
  and language 43-5, 68-72
  and multiculturalism 232-6
  and race 41-4
  and religion 45-6
National Socialist German Workers' Party (DSDAP) *see* Nazis
nationalism 4, 56, 57-9, 221-2, 224, 226-8
  Africa 88
  Arab 198, 199, 200-4, 210-11
  Asia 88
  dynastic states 32, 79, 83-8
  Germany 60-7, 77-8
  Greece 68-71
  Hungary 68-71
  Ireland 98-117
  and Islam 10, 198
  Jewish 165
  and race 50-2, 64, 76, 121-3, 166
  Romania 68-71
  Turkish 198
  see also national consciousness; national identity
Nationalism (Kedourie) 60-7
Nazis 4, 15, 65, 87, 122, 143, 144, 145, 172

Netherlands 40-1, 122, 197
  see also Holland
New Hebrides 236
'New Order' (Hitler) 87
New Testament 7, 15
New Zealand 225, 232
Nigeria 224
Normans 40, 43
North Africa 197, 198
North America 225, 232
  see also Canada; United States
North American Free Trade Area (NAFTA)
  218
Northern Ireland 56, 102, 104, 105, 218,
  219, 220, 235
  see also Ulster
Norway 70, 71

O'Connell, Daniel 109
O'Daly, Angus Mac Daighre 109
Odyssey (Homer) 5
O'Gnive, Fearflatha 109
Old Testament 15
Orange, House of 41
Orange Order 117
Orientalism (Said) 229
The Origin of Species (Darwin) 37
Orthodox church 8-9, 78
Ottoman Empire 75-80, 82-3, 90-2, 170-1,
  197-9, 212-13

Pacific Rim 229
Paine, Thomas 21
Pakistan 222, 223, 225
Pale of Settlement 141, 142, 144, 145, 167,
  169, 170
Palestine
  and Arab unity 200-2, 209-10, 212-17
  British mandate 83, 172-4, 184-6, 188,
    199, 214, 233
  partition 173-5, 186-91, 216, 217, 223
  West Bank 175, 202, 212, 215
  and Zionism 168-73, 181, 200, 212-3
Pan-Slav movement 78, 122
Papacy 8, 9, 10
Parnell, Charles Stuart 100

Parsees 39
Patrick, Saint 115
Patriotism and its Opposite (Fichte) 63, 67
Paul, Saint 19
Pearse, Padraic 101, 107-9
Peel Commission (1937), 173, 186
Pelasgians 42
Persian Empire 228
Phaiakia 5
Pinsker, Leo 176-83
Plato 5
pogroms 126, 141, 142, 166
Poland 76, 78, 81, 82, 84, 85, 87, 90, 122
  and Jews 124, 144, 167, 172
political legitimacy 11
Political Testament (Hitler) 161
politics 7, 8, 36, 58, 61, 235
Politics (Aristotle) 5
Polyphemos 5
Pontius Pilate 7-8
Portugal 197
Portuguese Empire 88
The Proclamation of the Irish Republic,
  24 April 1916 110-11
Protestants 10, 56, 98, 101, 105
Protocols of the Elders of Zion 141, 146-9
Provisional Irish Republican Army (IRA)
  103, 105
Prussia 44, 63, 64, 66, 77-8, 90
Punjab 224

al-Qadhafi, Muammar (Gaddafi) 201
Qur'an 10, 13, 196

race 4, 36, 38, 228, 230
  discrimination 5, 121-3, 126, 132, 144-5,
    153, 228
  German 6, 22, 23
  and language 65
  and national identity 41-4, 47, 56, 230-1
rationalism 34
Reflections on the Philosophy of the History of
  Mankind (Herder) 26-30
Reformation 10
religion 11, 21, 47
  and identity 3, 4-5, 45-6

persecution 124
and the state 7-10, 12, 33, 50, 54
Renan, Joseph Ernest 39-48, 56
Rights of Man (Paine) 21
Roman Empire 6, 9, 13, 22, 39, 40, 133, 228
and Christianity 7, 8, 42
and Jews 123
Romania 68-71, 76, 78, 81, 85, 87, 90,
136, 181
Romanians in Hungary 51
Rothschild family 140
Russia 229, 230
Communist state 82, 86-7, 227
international organisations 229, 230
and Jews 124, 125, 127-9, 136, 141-2,
166, 181
Tsarist Empire 75, 76, 77, 78, 79, 141
World War I 80, 81, 85, 89, 171
see also Soviet Union; Ukraine
Russian Academy 69
Russian language 44, 70

Sadat, Anwar 202
Said, Edward 229
Sardinia 78
Sartre, Jean-Paul 230
Schlegel, August Wilhelm von 62
Schleiermacher, Friedrich Ernst Daniel 60
Scotland 40, 55, 56, 218, 219
Scythians 18, 43
self-determination 57, 60-7, 76, 81-4, 105,
171, 200, 221
and colonialism 224
and education 66-7
and Fourteen Points 84
and human rights 227
Semites *see* Jews
Semitic languages 122, 196
separatist movements 224
Serbia 78, 79, 80, 81, 90
Serbo-Croat 70
Serbs 51, 78, 86, 222
Seton-Watson, Robert William 70
Shevchenko, Taras 70
Shirer, William R. 161-2
Siam 223

Sikhs 224
Silesians 64
Sinai Desert 202, 212
Sinn Féin 101, 102, 103
Six Day War, 1967 201, 202, 212
slavery 5, 28, 231
Slavonic language 69
Slavs 39, 42, 43, 122, 127-9, 133
South 78, 81, 86
Slovakia 86, 87
Slovaks 51, 78
Slovene 70
Slovenes 81, 86
Slovenia 87
Smetana, Bedřich 71
Social Darwinianism 168
social democracy 156
Social Democratic and Labour Party
(SDLP) (Northern Ireland) 104
Social Democratic Party (Austria) 152, 155
socialism 77, 144, 198, 200, 202
society 3, 11, 12, 22-30, 57-9, 204-5
Solzhenitsyn, Alexander 129
South Africa 122
South America 225
South Pacific Islands 92
sovereignty 33, 34, 39, 56, 219-20
see also democracy
Soviet Union 82, 83, 85, 144, 158, 202, 218
break-up 75, 219, 222
communist ideology 84, 87, 145
and Jews 143, 174
and Russian Revolution 79
Spain 10, 11, 44, 219, 220
Spanish America 44, 232
see also Latin America; South America
Sparta 39, 42
Sri Lanka 224
Stalin, Joseph 167
Stormont parliament 102
Sudan 197, 198, 224, 225
Sudetenland 82
Suez Canal 171, 199, 201, 207
Swedish language 70
Switzerland 39, 41, 44

Syria 187, 201, 206
  Christian nationals 195
  French mandate 83, 171, 199
  and Jews 202, 212, 216
  and Kurds 219
  and Palestininian Arabs 215

Tacitus, Cornelius 6, 13, 22-6
Tamils 224
Tibet 237
Tone, Wolfe 100
Torah 7, 123
Transjordan 186, 189, 190, 215
  see also Jordan
Transylvania 81
Trnava 70
Trojan War 5
Trotsky, Leon 140
Tunisia 197
Turkey 84, 90, 219, 222, 229
Turks 56, 170, 171, 197, 198

Ukraine 81, 82, 87, 142, 222
Ukrainian language 70
Ulster 98, 99, 100, 101, 102, 103
  see also Northern Ireland
Ulster Defence Association (UDA) 105
Ulster Unionist Party 104
Ulster Volunteer Force (UVF) 105
Union of Soviet Socialist Republics (USSR)
  see Soviet Union
United Kingdom of Great Britain and
  Northern Ireland *see* Britain; Northern
  Ireland
United Nations 174, 201, 222, 225, 226-7
United States of America 41, 44, 56, 80,
  228, 229
  Declaration of Independence 32, 35, 48-50
  global role 222, 229-30
  and Jews 142, 174
  language 44, 56
  race 56, 122, 230, 231, 235
  unity 15-21, 203, 204, 212-17
Universal Declaration of Human Rights 226
Universal Jewish Alliance 137
USSR *see* Soviet Union

Vanuatu 236
Vatican State 75, 218
Verdun, Treaty of 40, 42
Vienna 126, 151, 152
Vietnam 223
Vilna 134
Virgil 3, 6, 13, 15
Visigoths 8
Volunteers (Irish Republican) 115

Wales 55, 56, 218, 219
West Papuans 224
Western Europe 10, 232
What is a Nation? (Renan) 39-48
Wilkes, John 48
Wilson, President Woodrow 80, 82, 84, 86,
  89-90, 221
World War I 76, 79-83, 85, 101, 200
  Arab nationalism 199
  and Zionism 170-2
World War II 86, 144, 173, 174-5
World Zionist Organisation 169-70, 172

Yemen 199, 201
Yiddish 124, 167
Young Irelanders 115
Yugoslavia 81, 84, 85, 86, 87, 219, 222

Zimbabwe 103
Zionism 165-91, 194, 200, 213-15, 226
  see also Jews; Judaism